Introduction

Two subjects that always interested me as a child were history and government especially in relation to how they interact. From early civilization up until the late eighteenth century, government and therefore history has been predominantly controlled by a select few whose family had come to power through superior strength or favorable fortune. These rulers maintained their power through the prowess of their military or the more intelligent through the creation of a state religion usually with them at the center as the "son of god" in regard to ancient Egypt, "representative of god" in France with King Louis XIV, or even god himself in the case of King Herod Agrippa from the Roman Empire. As time progressed revolutions did hardly anything to help the common people. It was often only a changing of a king or a dynasty which could be either more or less favorable than the last. Ultimately these changes were not governed by the will of the people and as a result, the general population often suffered.

One of the few exceptions during this era was the Greek city-state of Athens. The Athenian democracy created by Cleisthenes lasted only a couple centuries but has left a major impact on the world. The influence of this Greek democracy can be seen through the many references to it in the Federalist Papers, a series of newspaper articles written by three American patriots: First Supreme Court Chief Justice, John Jay; first Secretary of the Treasury under the Washington administration, Alexander Hamilton; and the fourth President of the United States James Madison. In this Greek democracy there were three sections. The Ekklesia is often considered the most important and was responsible not only for the creation of laws but also for foreign policy with neighboring countries and city-states. This differs from the more modern American model because foreign policy is now thought of as an executive function and lawmaking a legislative one. In addition to this Athens had the Boule which was a council of men representing the ten tribes of the city-state. The third piece to this ancient masterpiece was the court system called the Dikasteria which created a forum to prosecute criminals by a randomly selected jury of their peers.

As governments evolved and time moved closer to the political marvel which is the creation of the United States of America, people slowly began to take control of their governments. In 1215 Archbishop Stephen Langton with the help of English barons forced King John to sign the Magna Carta which set history on the course to greater political freedom and reinstated the important concept of separation of powers. This document also created a more powerful and influential parliament. Although the document only empowered men of high status and not commoners, the clauses dealing with seizure of property and imprisonment could be extrapolated for all classes in society. This artificial extension of the Magna Carta is aided further by its use of "free man" which in that age dealt only with aristocracy but now includes people of all genders, races, and national origins. How did government evolve from the Magna Carta to the United States Constitution? Who and what were the propelling forces behind this? Another great English example of political innovation is found in the 1689 English Bill of Rights. Over four-hundred and fifty years after the signing of the Magna Carta, the English people finally had a significant document that protected some very important individual freedoms. Although it did not guarantee pure freedom of speech it did state that "the freedom of speech, and debates or proceedings in parliament, ought not to be impeached or questioned in any court or place out of parliament." In addition to this it disallowed standing armies in time of peace without the consent of parliament. These two revolutionary documents contested the often conventional wisdom that the king is to be the sole executive, legislator, and judiciary.

These events ushered in and accompanied the Age of Enlightenment which was marked by greats such as Charles de Montesquieu, Jean Jacques Rousseau, and François-Marie Arouet (Voltaire). Although each of these revolutionary scholars brought something different to the table, their names are often placed with those such as Socrates for their incessant and unconditional questioning of the very structure of European society. This includes not only politics but also religion in the case of Voltaire and Denis Diderot, the creator of the most famous early Encyclopedia. Montesquieu introduced the concept of separation of power while also questioning the possibility of a non-communal republic, which was an argument of the anti-federalists that the authors of the Federalist Papers had to address. From Switzerland, an intellectual outcast, Rousseau, began his work on tackling the question of whether liberty can coexist with government which had been posed by Thomas Hobbes. The work of these men and that of their predecessors such as John Locke fueled both the French and American revolutions which in part has shaped the world for the better. New countries forming in South America and more recently Africa and eastern Europe have followed the example put forth by these men. Although these philosophers provided a good foundation, there is often trouble with the application of even the most perfect political principles. Through the years we have corrected some of the more noticeable mistakes but have often left many unresolved problems or have oversimplified the issue at hand and have therefore created an erroneous solution.This leads us to the issues of today that taint the grand experiment which is the United States of America.

Growing up, my family was extremely right-winged and for a while I championed the conservative cause. Then I realized, the problem was not that "blue" was winning over "red" but that those were our only two options. I began to interact with people who held beliefs that were in stark contrast to my own. This caused me to begin a search for a system of reconciliation that would allow for coexistence between differing groups. I also came into contact with different ideological groups which had formed into tiny, insignificant parties and wondered how they were to attain their true goals. The Libertarian party which is generally considered right-wing has no chance of rising to importance without splitting the Republican party and therefore handing elections to the Democrats. Likewise, the Green party, a more liberal organization, has no chance of a rise to power without indirectly helping the party which they more deeply oppose. The idea that a gradual and steady rise of both third party options simultaneously is valiant but almost impossible to execute. Who is to decide which right-wing party and which left-wing party should be able to rise to this position? Who is to say that this will satisfy the original goal? While four parties to choose from is better, over time people would run into the same problem and again the orchestration of a similar event would be even further complicated. In addition to this who is to say that you may only classify parties by right or left winged? What about a middle-ground party? While thinking of such a day with more options is pleasant, using conventional methods will never work. The screams and cries of people pleading "Vote third-party" are as disorganized as they are pathetic. If any real change is to be expected the people of the United States must execute and embrace a concise plan. A plan that will be detailed in the following pages.

As I aged I began to discover more disturbing things about the party system. Not only did it silence the voices of true progressives that were outside of the bounds of the party, but it also silenced those who tried to enter. By saying that they silenced them I am not referring to political "mudslinging" or dismissive terms such as "radical." Rather, I am referring to the very infrastructure of the two major parties in the United States. This concept became increasingly apparent in the race for the Democratic Party's nominee. A slogan from the Democratic National Convention stating: "Let's keep fighting for progress," is a poor example of what the party actually stands for. The Democratic party allows present and former leaders and elected officials to become "superdelegates" which often stand in the way of true reform. The argument might be made that the "superdelegates" provide a certain amount of stability to the party and that certain checks and balances must be provided. Although this is true to a point, the attitude of the American people will always favor consistency unless the need arises for real political change. People in office often become distant to the true problems facing the country and even if aware of a problem they often need coercing by both the people and different media outlets. This process also is found in the Grand Old Party(GOP) although former leaders and elected officials are not involved. There is less conversation about "superdelegates" among the ranks of this party and the subject is hardly ever brought up. True change is especially rare in both parties even when the people desire it.

Although the Democratic Party is often shamed and attacked in the media for their use of "superdelegates," in the 2016 Republican primaries a more elusive and destructive force was at work. Although it is most apparent in the Republican ranks, the principle can be applied to all republics and democracies around the world. Long-standing frontrunner and ultimate victor Donald Trump, a charismatic and controversial "outsider," was faced up against a large field of career politicians with the exceptions of Ben Carson and Carly Fiorina. Although the more conventional and more experienced candidates together had enough percentage of the vote to gain victory, their cause was paralyzed and ultimately defeated by its many divisions. These divisions lasted until the end when four candidates congressman Ted Cruz, governor John Kasich, congressman Marco Rubio, and businessman Donald Trump were the only ones left standing. Although together the supporters of the former three would have been able to defeat Donald Trump, many of these candidates delayed their campaign cancellation. In addition to this Ted Cruz and Marco Rubio, who I would consider monozygotic twins concerning ideology and political plans, ruthlessly attacked each other and threw around the term "flip-flopper" while Donald Trump, who used to be a liberal until he "flip-flopped" on every major political issue, stood by and watched with an appropriately arrogant smirk on his face.

A more simple example of this concept would be the issue of marijuana legalization which will be discussed more directly later. For this analogy, there will be three groups each one is represented by a candidate and each group has thirty-three percent of the vote. For simplification each candidate is running on this single issue. There are the people with adamant opposition to all marijuana, the people who want to lessen the punishment for offenders, and those who want unconditional legalization. In this situation if this issue is voted upon each candidate will receive approximately the same number of votes even though that does reflect popular consensus. Realistically the amount of people who agree with the second party is closer to sixty-six percent. Even if you do not agree with the legalization of marijuana, the principle that a democratic or republican form of government should reflect the will of the people still stands. This is a classic example of one sheep being able to tell two wolves whether they should be smoking weed.

In addition to this, many common elements of modern government prove that we have not fully moved past our humble beginnings. In a few cases, the United States resembles the primitive medieval governments which now are considered loathsome. Throughout American history family dynasties have crept into government. The Kennedys, the Clintons, and the Bushes are all names that come to mind. This had become increasingly apparent in the 2016 presidential race. Although ultimately defeated after being chewed up and spit out by long-standing frontrunner Donald Trump, Jeb Bush showed promise in the beginning of the election cycle. In addition to this Hillary Clinton rose to become the Democratic nominee despite various scandals that surrounded her and popular discontent with her attitude which was perceived by many to be pretentious and arrogant. It is possible to trace their run for the White House back to previous offices that they had held (Jeb bush was governor of Florida and Hillary Clinton was Secretary of State under the Obama Administration), but these previous offices can be easily connected to their family roots. This point was further exemplified when, although very cautiously, both candidates brought their prestigious family members on the campaign trail. Jeb received help from both his brother, former president George W. Bush, and father, former president George H.W. Bush, after previously trying to distance himself from the family name by omitting it from his campaign slogan "JEB!" Hillary eventually allowed her husband Bill Clinton to speak after feeling pressure from rival Bernie Sanders, a lively and charismatic senator from Vermont.

In addition to America's inclination to perpetuate dynasties, which often causes politics to resemble a reality television show, there also seems to be a natural infatuation with the idea of a single leader. Although a few eras have been marked by great Congressmen such as Daniel Webster and Henry Clay more often than not we tend to separate American eras by presidents. The Jacksonian era and the Reagan years are just two examples. This categorization of history often oversimplifies modern politics and causes illogical and unconstitutional shifts of power towards the executive. While the usurpation of power through "executive orders" is apparent, there is no one willing to combat it. It transcends party lines and has not only been seen with Barack Obama and George W. Bush but has also tainted administrations decades prior. When the executive gained the power to legislate and the legislative branch was composed of men and women too cowardice to fight, the degradation of this country began. Our intricate and once strong system of governance is now crushed by a power hungry individual with no knowledge of the centuries of fighting which brought about this beloved form of government. This is when we are beginning to revert back to more primitive forms of government like that of China or Nicaragua. Although these "representatives" of the people are initially or indirectly elected, restraints on their power while in office are nonexistent and there is no guarantee of the fulfillment of campaign promises. The United States must stand by the principles its government was based upon while taking logical and constitutional steps to solving modern problems. When this occurs, these changes can not be reversed by a single politician picking up a pen but by a more accurate representation of the general will.

In the following chapters an account of the most influential, controversial, and sometimes strange revolutions will be given. These revolutions will be categorized into the following sections: Ancient, recent, modern and postmodern. An ancient revolution constitutes anything before the fall of Western Rome. This includes the unification of Egypt and various events in Grecian history. Recent revolutions advance from this point up to but not including the French Revolution. This is where modern revolutions begin, going through the American Revolution and up to the present. The lesser known events in Africa and eastern Europe will also be detailed in this section. Postmodern revolutions are not yet part of history and encompass all potential changes in government around the world. In this section, future revolutions that either need to or will happen will be discussed, whether it be to local, state, federal, or global government. After the foundation of history is laid, we can proceed to more ideological endeavors. Although more radical changes are possible, smaller and more digestible advances must precede these. In this second section of the book, current faults with this country's government will be brought to light, discussed, and potentially solved. After those occur a more comprehensive plan can be executed. This final plan will include four levels of government: local, state, federal, and global. Each level will be discussed individually and all the proposed powers and responsibilities will also be stated.

Section 1: Revolutions of History

Revolution through physical conflict has been a useful mechanism of change for the past few millenniums. Although many dismiss this process as primitive or barbaric, it has given rise to the more civilized means of change which shapes society today. For most of human history people were controlled by a select few rulers. These rulers came to power through intellect and military strength but the approval of a significant amount of the populous was also required for any change in government. After raised to that position of power, there was no longer a need to please and therefore through fear and intimidation, a ruler could control both those who aided and those who opposed his rise. Intelligent minds recognized the fact that checks need to be placed on leaders, which gave rise not only to representative councils and legislative bodies but also to the idea that people are discerning enough for self-government. Although monarchies and dictatorships still persisted, the example from a few nations showed that if people did not blow out the light of liberty in their hearts, they could, through a collaborative effort, bring about lasting change. Although this is true, many people have never had the chance to experience representative government and therefore have no desire for it. These are the places with the need for the greatest amount of change. Middle eastern countries such as the Kingdom of Saudi Arabia and the African Kingdom of Swaziland are a disgrace on this very modern era. The true governments of the world which are based upon the general will should use their economic interactions to discourage dictators, which are no more than modern day barbarians. Their family lines are no more than chains that hold back the people from true freedom. No help should go to a man who thinks it is morally sound to have hundreds of thousands of square miles of land wasted on a pompous ruler who gained power by heredity and not by the will of the people.

In addition to this, we should promote change in places with a crude or destructive form of "democracy." The "People's" Republic of China is a poor excuse for anything resembling representative government. One party, the Communist Party of China, has overwhelming control of both the military and media. This party disallows negative speech directed towards the government which cements their power. In addition to these horrific examples comes a few more benign inconveniences. The monarchs of Europe, although politically worthless, serve no purpose and should be degraded to the level of the "commoners" which their families once oppressed. The progressive liberals of America, in accordance with their insistence of an apology in regards to white oppression of various minorities, should also demand the same from the fortunate prodigy of tyrants. In the United States, few citizens commemorate previous oppression committed by their ancestors, while people from around the world praise the remnants of monarchy in Europe. They act as if these families are anything more than regular people dressed in over glorified costumes. The former example of China shows that a change in people's heart must precede a revolution, while the latter example of European monarchies is meant to show that people's emotional connection and fascination with overlords is not easily severed. Even though much of this seems anti-European, it is not meant this way. I admit that the United States had it easier in the fact that it never had a direct monarchy of its own and its political ties to Great Britain were never as strong as those native to the British Isles. In addition to this, a severe distaste for monarchy grew due to the fact that free spirited men from the colonial America resented being controlled by a country thousands of miles away. This distaste grew as appeals for representation were repeatedly denied. Western Europe can also be proud of the fact that while many great political minds came from the North American continent, the true pioneers of the field hailed from the "Old World." Many of these greats had to suffer however due to the fact that their proposed systems had not yet been implemented, and therefore certain monarchs expressed displeasure of these critiques in a very assertive manner. This provides an adequate introduction and we will now enter into the often gruesome world of governmental change, starting with ancient times and progressing into the theoretical future.

Chapter 1: Ancient Revolutions

Even though the unification of upper and lower Egypt has no known leader, its effect on the world has been unimaginable. Under the demand of Ptolemy II Philadelphus, a scribe and priest named Manetho used the knowledge available at the time to create a history of Egypt which started with Menes and went to the fourth century

B.C. This Egyptian priest gave credit to Menes in regard to the unification of Egypt although this widely regarded as false by the historical community today. Famous Egyptologist James Henry Breasted considered the work of Manetho nothing more than a "compilation of puerile folklore" which was "hardly worthy of the name history." Although little is known about this unifying revolution, it created one of the most influential civilizations of that era.

In a different but not completely separate area of the globe, a ruler named Luganda came to power through the priesthood in the Middle Eastern city-state of Lagash which is situated close to the Tigris and Euphrates rivers. This oppressive king was ousted from power by Urukagina. While in power Urukagina instituted many changes including decreasing the power of the priesthood in government. Although a great reformer, he failed as a military leader and Lagash was ultimately sacked by its mortal enemy, the city-state of Umma. This example shows the importance of maintaining a certain degree of stability while change is taking place.

Farther away, the Compatriots Rebellion in China forced King Li of the Zhou dynasty into exile. In addition to raising taxes, this ruler created a law which allowed him to execute anyone who spoke out against him. Although his actions were horrible, they partially resemble the current administration of that region. Whatever the case may be, this caused some of his own soldiers with the help of many commoners to revolt. They crowned Gong Bo He as regent, but after fourteen years King Li died in exile and his son King Xuan took the throne. This is a great example of how dynasties were extremely hard to destroy throughout early history.

In Egypt, King Apries was a military man. After taking the Phoenician port of Sidon, he decided to attack Cyrene. This decision backfired and the battle was lost. In addition to this, the soldiers mutinied and devoted themselves to Amasis as a new king. Civil war ensued and Amasis finally was victorious. King Apries was either imprisoned or killed in battle but was given a proper burial. After his victory, Amasis implemented certain reforms. Although strictly overseen by himself, he opened up trade with the Grecian city-states. He extracted tribute money from Cyprus and ruled over an extremely wealthy time in Egyptian history.

One of the most influential ancient revolutions was the establishment of the Roman Republic after the fall of the Roman Kingdom. Although the history of Rome is muddled with mythology, certain information has been generally agreed upon. The Romans had seven kings and the last of these was a cruel tyrant. Popular distaste for this ruler led to the beginning of the revolution. Now Porsenna who was an Etruscan king tried to take power but was thwarted. The Romans then elected two consuls to power which began their republic. Although a crude example of popular government originally, it grew in strength and began giving more power to different classes of citizens. The patricians or higher class dominated the government in the beginning but the plebeians or lower class slowly gained advantages. A plebeian revolt took place due to the extreme debt of the lower class. Plebeians in the army made a pact that they would not fight for the patricians and set up their own city. It was apparent to the patricians that Rome would not survive without their help so they proposed certain reforms. This included the termination of debt and the liberation of plebeians from debtors prison. In addition to this, the plebeians were allowed to elect two officers who held the power to veto unjust laws. Although it moved closer to modern government, the Republic also weakened. Eventually, the Roman Republic collapsed due to the economic effects of slavery and civil wars caused by social tensions.

On a nearby peninsula, the Athenian Revolution occurred which was a counter movement to the takeover of the city by Isagoras and his Spartan allies. Isagoras was attempting an overturn of the government while Cleisthenes, an Athenian reformer, was exiled as part of the 700 families known as "The Accursed." The citizens trapped Isagoras and his allies at the Acropolis and forced a surrender. The Spartans left while the men with Isagoras were executed. Although they took back the city, Isagoras had escaped their clutches. Cleisthenes was nominated to create a government for Athens called "demos", an early version of democracy.

After overthrowing their tyrant, the city-state of Athens tried to help its Grecian neighbors to the east free themselves from their foreign Persian rulers. The Persian kings were not concerned with the art and education of these city-states and made them pay tribute. Cyrus was the king who conquered the territory of Ionia. When the conquest was finished, Artaphernes (the ruler of Sardis, the western capital of Persia) met with leaders of the various city-states to form a treaty which was meant as a deterrence to fighting. Artaphernes knew not only of the Grecian city-states tendency for fighting but also of their extreme intolerance for Persian rule. In 499 BC, Aristagoras, the leader of the city-state of Mellitus, violated the treaty and tried to take possession of its neighbor Naxos. After this failed attempt, he feared retaliation from both Darius (the new emperor) and Artaphernes. Aristagoras determined that the only way out of this predicament was to dig himself a deeper hole. He incited a rebellion and called for every Ionian city-state to throw off the chains of their foreign tyrants. Knowing the strength of the Persian Empire, Aristagoras traveled to Sparta to appeal for help before King Cleomenes. The Spartans rejected his request and so he went to their less militaristic counterpart, Athens. They agreed due to the fact that Athenians believed that war with Persia was already pending. Aristagoras and his men with the help of the Athenians then began to jointly fight Persia. Ionians set fire to the capital of Sardis, while Persian troops destroyed the Grecian ranks in Ephesus. Persia slowly advanced through Asia Minor, crushing all the rebellions. Eventually, Aristagoras fled the Mellitus and left Pythagoras in charge of the city. The Persians in 494 BC reclaimed it and the rebellion died out due to lack of unifying leadership. In addition to this, the Athenian support of the rebellion gave Persia the motive it needed to attack the Grecian peninsula. Although usually not referred to as a revolution, these events did change this region even if it did not enhance the government. The rebellions cemented Persian rule while ending the age of enlightenment for this area. This revolution also emphasizes the need for local rule by the people.

While rebellions against foreign rule are important, they can also instigate internal change. One example of this, the slave revolt, is extremely challenging to execute because of the difficulty of unification and often close monitoring by masters. This becomes increasingly apparent while studying the Spartan helot rebellions. Helots were state owned slaves which were assigned to Spartan citizens. They are thought to be descendants of both the original inhabitants of Laconia, which was the territory of the city-state on Peloponnesus, and Messinia. Although treated relatively kindly in relation to African slaves in early America, the helots yearned for freedom. The Spartans trusted these state-owned slaves to hold certain positions such as boat rowers and lower level troops but they lived in constant fear of rebellion. One of these rebellions occurred directly after an earthquake in Laconia which triggered a revolt in Messina. This grew to the point that Sparta asked Athens for help although their relations were often tense. Cimon, an Athenian aristocrat, eventually convinced the council to send hoplites. Despite the urgency of the situation, Sparta rescinded their appeal due to their apprehension that the democratic Athenians would sympathize with the Helots which were fellow Greeks kept in bondage. The Athenians were extremely offended by this decision. Much later the Persians, in an attempt to perpetuate division amongst Greek city-states, supported the rise of Epaminondas from Thebes. This military superpower defeated Spartan forces with half the amount of men. In addition to this, he attacked Peloponnesus and freed the helots from Messina in 370 BC. The slaves in Laconia were not freed for over a century and a half after the emancipation in Messina.

Before Roman control of Egypt, the Persians came to power in this region. Through the battle of Pelusium, Cambyses II from Persia established Egypt as a satrapy. Cambyses was looked upon in a negative light not only by Egyptians but also by ancient historians. He took income from the temple which fueled hate from his subjects. Aryandes was appointed as the ruler of this region and had to pay 700 talents of silver which was double that of Phoenicia, Cyprus, and Palestine. Eventually, this ruler was put to death by Darius for striking coins and his presumably arrogant attitude. "Aryandes had been made governor of Egypt by Cambyses, later he was executed by Darius for making himself equal to the king. When he learned that Darius intended to leave a memorial surpassing anything other kings had left, Aryandes did likewise and was punished for it," said Herodotus, a Greek historian. Although still Persian, King Darius was looked upon more favorably. He returned items which had been taken from the temple and decreased the amount of tribute required. In addition to this, he provided funds to repair the temples in Karnak, Fayum, and Memphis. King Darius also focused on the importance of irrigation and completed a canal which had been started by Necho. Although much of this kept him busy, he still took time to compile Egyptian law to improve order in this satrapy. After Darius died a less favorable king took his place.

A new king named Xerxes was wary of the Egyptians and did not appoint them to positions in government over the territory. Instead, he appointed his brother Achaemenes to rule and increased the servitude of the Egyptians. A rebellion then broke out which was relatively easy to crush. Although this is true, this event emphasizes the natural desire for a people to be free and self-governed. Xerxes was assassinated and another revolt occurred with Inaros from Libya as the leader. Although the Egyptians were fighting the powerful Persian army, the Athenians had decided to help this oppressed people. The decision from Athens was not made because of ideological reasons but rather was due to the fact that Persians had historically been their enemies. Charatimides, a Greek commander, diverted troops from Cyprus and attempted to relieve the Egyptian forces. The Athenians won a naval battle and laid siege to the Persians in Memphis. More men from Persia helped break the siege and trapped the rebels on the island of Prosopitis. The Persians eventually came to terms with Athens and the leader of the attempted revolution, Inaros, was executed after hiding in the marshes.

After this, rebellion broke out in a different section of the globe. The end of the Qin dynasty was the beginning of a golden age in Chinese history. The last unifying ruler of this era was Qin Shi Huang. Although a strong country, this Chinese dynasty would not have lasted without his leadership. This man therefore looked for a source of immortality, originally with sorcerers and magicians. Ironically, his search for life ended in death. He died by drinking a poisonous potion in 210 BC and this triggered a major change in Chinese government. The king's eunuchs Li Si and Zhao Gao initially kept the death a secret due to the precarious situation in which it placed China. The oldest son of the king, Fusu, was killed while fighting so Huhai, the younger son, was crowned. His new regal name was Qin Er Huang. Although he was the official leader, Zhao Gao controlled the empire. This eunuch had Li Si and his family killed to cement his power in the government. Although originally an adequate leader, the unofficial commander ultimately failed and the fourteen year dynasty crumbled despite Qin Shi

Huang's prediction that this dynasty would last ten thousand generations. Qin Er Huang tried to blame Zhao Gao but the new emperor had not yet gained the trust of the army. Eventually Zhao Gao forced the emperor to commit suicide. The once independent states of Han and Chu started a civil war and attempted secession. Although secession is often considered negatively due to the American Civil War, it has served a positive purpose in history. Eventually Ziying, the new ruler, succeeded in killing Zhao Gao but the revolution had grown to strong. Although only a rebellious state, soldiers from Chu assassinated the new ruler. Emperor Gaozu was the first ruler of the Han Dynasty which lasted for over four hundred years. This marked the beginning of a good time in Chinese history.

Both Boudicca's Revolt and the Celtiberian Revolt attempted to diminish Roman control over western Europe. Although separate revolts, their ultimate goal was the same: freedom from Roman control. The backstory of Boudicca's Revolt shows truly how barbaric, the Roman "civilization" could be. Foreseeing Roman control of Britain, the King of Iceni gave half of his wealth to the Romans attempting to ensure friendly relations. Eventually this King died and the Romans came back demanding more money. When it did not come immediately, they hung the Queen, Boudicca, by her wrist and flogged her publicly and raped the deceased king's two daughters. The Romans did not know what they had coming. With the help of the Druids and her Celts, she attacked Colchester and ultimately defeated the Romans. They slaughtered everyone in this fort and did not wince at their massacre. After this Legio IX was ambushed by the resistance outside of Longthorpe. Eventually after several other defeats, the governor of Britannia, Suetonius Paulinus, subdued the army and Boudicca ingested poison to maintain her dignity. The Druids were followed by Paulinus and massacred. This attempted revolution ultimately ended in failure. In addition to the Celts, Spanish subjects also were determined to throw off Roman rule. The Celtiberian War was a long struggle due to the Celtic guerilla tactics but the rebellion was finally subdued because of their lack of military experience. These two examples did not bring down the Romans, but a different kingdom would soon fall.

When Alexander the Great died, his vast territory was divided among his generals. Antigonus obtained Greece while

Seleucus and Ptolemy battled in the east. The Seleucid Empire, which had been created by Seleucus, eventually won after Antiochus III took Egypt and Palestine for himself. He originally left the Jewish people alone but attempted to begin a system of Hellenism in this region. The Jews strongly opposed this due to their monotheistic beliefs and his plan was delayed. Although he ultimately failed, Antiochus IV, his son, continued the original plans of his father. He held absolutely no respect for Jewish tradition which he made obvious through his mistreatment of their holy items. He set up an altar to Zeus and allowed pigs to be sacrificed in the temple. Deuteronomy 14:7-8 says, "Nevertheless, you are not to eat of these among those which chew the cud, or among those that divide the hoof in two: the camel and the rabbit and the shaphan, for though they chew the cud, they do not divide the hoof; they are unclean for you. The pig, because it divides the hoof but does not chew the cud, it is unclean for you. You shall not eat any of their flesh nor touch their carcasses." In addition to these offenses, this ruler banned certain staples of Judaism such as circumcision and the Sabbath.

Eventually their oppressors pulled the last straw and a revolution occurred. A government official tried to make Matthias offer a sacrifice to a Greek god. The official was killed and Matthias with his five sons garnered support from their fellow Jews who had not completely converted to the ways of Hellenism and foreign rule. These leaders were from the Hasmonean family but were also commonly called the Maccabees. After his father's death Judah Maccabee led the fight against the Seleucids. He began by conquering a force of Syrians being led by Apollonius. He continued to succeed by defeating Seron in the battle at Beth-Horon. Lysias, then appointed by Antiochus IV, decided troop movements but was defeated by Judah at Beth-Zur. After this Judah marched into Jerusalem and consecrated the defiled temple. In addition to this, he set up the famous eight-day celebration of Hanukkah. Religious freedom for the Jews was restored but fighting resumed. Nicanor from Syria tried to take Jerusalem but was unsuccessful. He died while his army was defeated. Judah Maccabee eventually died in a battle near Elasa at the hands of the Syrian commander Bacchides' forces. Simon Maccabee was the only brother to survive these conflicts and he began the eighty year period of rule for the

Maccabean family in the region. Although not Levites, this family acted not only as the political rulers but also the priests. Eventually internal conflict destroyed this state and the Romans took control from the locals.

Although also marked by various periods of peace and prosperity, the Han dynasty had its share of rebellions and an eventual revolution. As previously mentioned the Han dynasty itself spawned through rebellion. Liu Bang took out the last Qin ruler and eventually took power. Although eighteen separate kingdoms had declared their independence, the Han and Chu kingdoms were the two main groups and the various other states had allied with one of them. The Han ruler ultimately conquered the Chu and gained power over China. In the Han dynasty, the emperor gave land grants to family members, hoping that they would be loyal. This turned out to be an incorrect hypothesis and the Rebellion of the Seven Kingdoms occurred.

The Han dynasty was temporarily paused by Wang Mang. He was originally a regent due to the fact that the emperor was too young but he took power for himself and started the Xin Dynasty. Although many of his reforms would be considered just by today's standards, they were too radical for China at the time. These changes included banning slavery and changing the currency. The Chimei, a peasant army, stormed the capital at Chang'an and killed Wang Mang. Liu Xiu from the original Han family defeated the Chimei and set up a new capital in Luoyang. This emperor took back Korea and Vietnam while the emperors that followed ushered in a golden age. After this age, the emperor's eunuchs and generals fought for power and influence. The Yellow Turban Rebellion and the Five Pecks of Rice Rebellion began which shifted power to the military and the generals. A general named He Jin plotted to kill all the eunuchs but they found out and in response killed him. This angered He Jin's soldiers and in return they killed all the eunuchs. Dong Zhou, another general, marched into the city and set up Xian as an emperor to rule through. Dong Zhou in turn was killed and Cao Cao took his place ruling through Xian. Cao Cao was defeated in certain battles and eventually died. Xian stepped down from power and placed Cao Cao's son, Cao Pi. He proved to be an ineffective unifier and his weak position caused China to split into three kingdoms.

This shows the necessity of a strong constitution which sets up a separation of powers when a territory is as vast as that of China. Although true in many circumstances, the point is magnified in this case due to the fact that in this period of Chinese history, China controlled both Vietnam and Korea.

Slavery always breeds revolt and revolution due to the inherent injustice which it is founded upon. Although important to note, good treatment by masters often does not quench the desire to fight for freedom, even if risking life is required. Rome is no exception to this rule and had three notable slave revolts before the Common Era. The First, Second, and Third Servile Wars involved not only plantation and household slaves, but also gladiator fighters in the last war.

The First Servile War occurred in Sicily, the island south of the Apennine Peninsula, and was caused by the shift of power from the Carthaginians to the Romans. Due to this change which happened after the Second Punic War, much of the conquered land was bought by distant estate owners. This caused the plantations to be mismanaged and the slaves became underfed and malnourished. The leader of this first war, Eunus, was thought to have magical powers which his owner, previous to the revolt, took full advantage of. As part of his comedy act, this slave described a world where the landowners in the audience were subjugated by him and how he would become their king. To gain money he would say that he would have mercy on those who tipped him. Although his vision was never fully brought into reality, the men in the crowd would not be laughing about what was to come. After he started a rebellion, he appointed a commander named Cleon from Cilicia who was eventually killed by the Romans. Eunus was captured but died before punishment.

The Second Servile War happened in the same location and had the same outcome as well. This war was brought about by the demands of Italians which predated an alliance between them and the Romans. The Italians wanted slaves of their ethnicity to be released from their Roman masters on the island of Sicily. Although strong, Rome agreed because of their desire for the alliance. Slaves of non-Italian ethnicities were confused by this agreement and were left thinking that they too had been freed. The governor called them back to their masters, but having inhaled the pure air of freedom, many of the slaves did not back down. Salvius, a former slave, who was later called Tryphon led this revolt. With the help of a Cilician named Athenion, about twenty thousand infantrymen, and two thousand cavalrymen, Tryphon created a punishing force. Although this is true, Aquilius quelled this unsuccessful revolt that had the potential to become a revolution.

The Third Servile War is often considered the most famous of the three. This is possibly due to the fact that the rebel leader, Spartacus, had an estimated 70,000 troops at one time. Spartacus was an escaped gladiator who lived with a group of bandits up in the mountains. Although a strict commander, many slaves from the Italian mainland were encouraged enough to join his ranks. After raiding the towns and army groups for food and arms, Spartacus planned on retreating over the Alps and going to freedom. Many of his men objected to this idea because they desired to stay. Crassus from Rome attacked the rebellious forces and ultimately the Romans annihilated them with their leader Spartacus. Although none of these revolts ended in victory, these events emphasize the importance of liberty for all people regardless of ethnicity. Slave revolts are often unsuccessful because of the difficulty to find significant amounts of arms and ammunition. In addition to this, unification is challenging with supervision from masters. Although this is true, these revolts and the later examples in America can be used to open people's eyes to injustice when they are too ignorant to see or when they turn their faces away because they have too much invested in the negative situation. People try to argue about the evil of these slaves sometimes murdering their masters but until these landowning families lost something, it was unlikely that they would have noticed what they had stolen from their slaves. This unjust system had taken away all three unalienable rights that are stated at the beginning of the Declaration of Independence: Life, liberty, and the pursuit of happiness.

Although the leader of the next rebellion lost his war with Rome and was later humiliated by being dragged behind Julius Caesar's carriage, he was eventually honored by the French through a statue in the city of Alesia. This Celtic hero named Vercingetorix was born in the Gallic kingdom of Arverni and succeeded in becoming the only ruler of a united Gaul which is similar geographically to modern day France. His father, Celtillus, was the ruler of the tribe and after his death, Vercingetorix replaced him. Celtillus' death came after his attempt to defeat surrounding tribes and unite Gaul under his family. After the threat from Julius Caesar, these tribes were finally convinced to join forces. Conquering the Veneti in the north of Gaul, Caesar had gained the land he needed for a later successful invasion of the British Isles. Germanic tribes had been the enemy of the Celts for a long time and for awhile Rome helped the Celts defend their land. The Romans eventually started attacking the Celts and conquered much land. Carnutes in the north, rebelled against the Romans and killed several government officials. The news of this event spread like wildfire down to Arverni and Vercingetorix wished to take an army to help the Gallic neighbors. Although he held power, the elders disagreed with his idea and he was exiled from the capital. Vercingetorix then went around Gaul and united more than ten separate tribes. He began launching an attack and Caesar who was heading back to Rome, quickly turned around after hearing the news. With troops and weaponry, he crossed the Alps during the winter. Valaunodunum, Cenabum, and Noviodunum were all defeated by the Romans under the command of Caesar. Although these setbacks sent the Celtics staggering, they began to regroup and gained an alliance from the powerful tribe of Aedui. Then Vercingetorix implemented a scorched earth military strategy on his own land; nothing was left for the advancing Roman army. After some time they came to the city of Avaricum and decided to defend instead of burn the fort. The Romans laid siege to the city and eventually defeated the Celtics there in battle.

Although they had just suffered a harsh defeat, Vercingetorix's army soon recovered in time to defend the capital of Arverni in Gergovia. The Roman forces were repelled and started heading towards Lutetia which is modern day Paris. The modern day city can trace its name to the tribe in which Lutetia was found, Parisii. Vercingetorix encountered the Roman cavalry and retreated to Alesia. Plutarch, the historian, recounted these events and estimated that there were one hundred and seventy thousands Celts in the fort and three hundred thousand outside waiting for battle. The men outside eventually left the battle while the men inside starved.

The fort surrendered and Vercingetorix was sent to Rome and humiliated. Although this leader was defeated, his unification of Gaul set the modern boundaries of France and strengthened the power of the Rome. This empire was a republic but that was about to change.

The last revolution before the Common Era which will be detailed in this book. After conquering the Gauls and gaining much land in the British Isles, Julius Caesar was ordered back to Rome by Pompey who had been elected Consul. Before his expeditions in the west, Caesar, Pompey, and Crassus had created what historians call the First Triumvirate. After Crassus was killed in battle, Pompey rose to power and began to implement reforms which helped the patrician class at the expense of the plebeians. Caesar favored reforms which were popular and less aristocratic. Before leaving for Gaul, Caesar had been consul and had committed offenses for which the Roman government wanted punishment. If Caesar followed the orders of Pompey and arrived in Rome without his army then he would be promptly arrested. Due to this fact, he crossed the Rubicon River with his legions and Pompey fled to Egypt. Although the Egyptians had been welcoming to him on a previous trip, they killed him because of their belief that the gods were with Julius Caesar. Although Pompey had been a rival, Caesar was mad at the Egyptians for their actions and ousted their ruler, Ptolemy XIII, from power. This is when Caesar had an affair with Cleopatra who he eventually brought back to Rome but never married.

As ruler, Caesar continued to rule until members of the senate, which included his friend Brutus, killed him on the senate floor. They believed that Caesar had usurped too much power and was threatening the republic. Although certain rulers before him had committed actions outside of the constitution, none had taken it as far as Caesar. He did not follow the pure example of Cincinnatus, who after being set up as dictator, gave his power back after the threat was gone. George Washington was inspired by him when he set the precedent of the two-year term. This precedent lasted for over a century and a half without the need for law before Franklin Roosevelt violated the non-verbal agreement and was elected for four terms. This was one of his various negatives which included trying to increase the number of Supreme Court Justices so that he could manipulate the interpretation of the Constitution to his standard. Whatever the case may be, the Roman Republic ended.

The new Roman Empire, which had gone back to a more primitive government than their already corrupt republic, encountered some hard times at first. Their extreme desire for land and influence caused them to make new enemies with every campaign. In addition to this, the vast amount of land which they had amassed was sometimes challenging to govern. The Great Illyrian Revolt came after the conquering of this group of individual tribes by the Romans. This happened in a series of wars which were sparked by the fact that Illyrian pirates were disrupting commerce across the Mediterranean and the various other seas surrounding the Apennine Peninsula. These eastern neighbors although not unified and often ethnically different, were known for their barbary.

Over two hundred years after these people were subjugated, Bato the Daesitiate was supposed to join Roman forces to aid in the destruction of a Germanic tribe. Instead, Bato started to fight the Roman forces and defeated them. Bato of the Breuci joined the action and became another leader of the revolt. At Moesia and Sirmium, these rebels weakened Roman forces through inflicting a great number of casualties. Emperor Augustus and his officials in Rome were concerned due to the fact that the rebellious territory lay close to the Apennine Peninsula and therefore could attempt an assault on the empire's capital. Caring deeply about the safety of the empire, Tiberius was ordered to abandon efforts in Germany and focus on the revolt. Being discovered that he did not have the strength necessary for victory, Germanicus was also sent. In addition to this Rhoemetalces, King of Thracia, who was a Roman ally brought troops. Although a large force already, many slaves were given freedom in return for fighting. It is ironic how Rome used an enslaved people to ensure peaceful subjugation of the conquered.

Despite the effort of those involved, finally the revolt was quelled in 9 AD, but it was soon replaced by one in Germany and a group of Roman soldiers who mutinied. This Germanic war was led by Arminius who eventually stunted the Roman advances and kept Germany independent. The battle in Teutoburg forest was an extreme failure by Rome and many of their men were captured. Although some were eventually ransomed and returned to Rome, many fell victim to sacrifice or slavery. This man is now hailed as a national hero for the Germans. Although the Romans subjugated several different groups, this practice was also common in the continent of Asia.

As mentioned earlier, Vietnam had been defeated by the Chinese. Two unexpected heroes came from the shadows and for a short time created a state independent of Chinese subjugation. Trung Trac and Trung Nhi, also known as the Trung Sisters, gathered eighty thousand people to resist the Chinese government. The former was married to a lord named Thi Sach while both came from a royal family. In 40 AD they succeeded in driving their enemy out of the country. Trung Trac was nominated as ruler and created a few reforms in the short period of time she had. Although these sisters had expelled their enemy, this event did not bring peace. The Chinese incessantly attacked Vietnam in an attempt to regain lost territory. In 43 AD they succeeded and country of Vietnam disappeared for a time. The sisters are said to have ingested poison or drown themselves as a way to die nobly. With this, the short revolution had lost all of the advances previously made.

Certain revolutions have a just cause which can be diluted by the unjust actions of radical leaders who execute them. This thought is paralleled by the statement that egregious acts should not be avenged through atrocities. In saying this, The Great Jewish Revolt was a humiliating event which weakened the cause for Jewish independence from their Roman overlords. Following Roman control over Israel in 63 BC, the empire committed several sacrilegious acts. The supposedly mentally retarded emperor, Caligula, infuriated the Jews by attempting and failing to force them to put up a statue of himself in their temple as a god. Although this rebellious act put the Jews in a precarious situation, they were saved by the assassination of Caligula. Hatred for Caligula was bound to be festered due to his detestable actions and attitude.

This emperor was in the same family line as Julius Caesar. Even though this is true, the line had fallen previously from power when Augustus nominated his stepson Tiberius as his successor. To quiet the predicted outburst, Augustus suggested that Tiberius adopt Germanicus, Caligula's father, as his son to continue the original family line. After Augustus' death, Germanicus suspiciously died after being called to the east by Tiberius. Germanicus' wife propagated the conspiracy that Tiberius was involved. In turn, the new emperor sent her to prison where she died. In addition to this, he jailed two of her sons who also died. Although this is true, Tiberius spared the life of the youngest son, Caligula. This can now be seen as a mistake. While in his teenage years, the future emperor Caligula is said to of had incestuous relations with his sister. The young man also struggled with anger. Tiberius sent Caligula to the island of Capri where he tried to teach him respect.

Later, the unpopular Tiberius eventually died although it is unknown whether he died of his illness or suffocation by Caligula. This young and angry child took power after Tiberius' death. At first, he instituted popular reforms such as reduction of taxes and creation of sporting arenas but after some time he became severely sick. Although he recovered, he was never the same. He was haunted by painful headaches and therefore participated in peculiar practices. In his spare time, he forced mothers to watch the execution of their children and he roamed the palace dressed as a woman. The people finally had enough and a guard killed him. His uncle Claudius succeeded him as emperor. Although Caligula was dead, the atrocities continued. Certain scrolls of scripture were burned and Roman soldiers stripped in the Jewish sanctuary. As usually the case is, acts of such unnecessary disrespect often cause more moderate and nonviolent sections of the population to be radicalized. The head tax collector stole silver from the temple which served as the last straw. The Jews revolted and destroyed a Syrian force. Although originally successful, the Zealots, as they called themselves, suffered some crippling losses. After these events, the radical Zealots began killing more moderate Jews in Jerusalem. Romans sieged the city and watched as civil war broke out inside the gates. Radicals burned large amounts of food to expedite the need for a fight with the Romans. After the Jews were done killing themselves, the Romans joined in and easily defeated the disunified group of rebels. The second temple was destroyed at the end of the fighting. This example of revolt shows that fighting often had a religious backing.

Like Caligula's reign, the start of Nero's rule as emperor went smoothly, but after some time he began to act crazed. These types of actions set the scene for rebellion and revolution. A senator named Vindex decided to start fighting Nero and nominated Galba as the new emperor. Although he had heart, Vindex did not publicize his revolt effectively. The commander, Rufus, easily conquered Vindex's army to avoid a war in Gaul which he was expecting. After this confusion, the Senate recognized Galba as the new emperor. Nero, in turn, committed suicide. The soldiers who brought this rebellion were disrespected and the commander was replaced by Flaccus. Also, the Batavian soldiers who were trusted with the protection of Galba were let go from that position. Galba was lynched after an army in southern Germany proclaimed that Vitellius was the true emperor. Otho, who had assassinated Galba, began to fight this unofficial nomination for power. Being the better commander, Vitellius defeated Otho's army and Otho killed himself. Vespasian also attempted to rise up against this powerful commander but after only one year, his reign ended.

While the fighting was still occurring between Vespasian and Vitellius, the latter requested men from Flaccus. Although less powerful, Flaccus denied this request due to the fact that he sensed an upcoming revolt. A sort of draft was implemented and the Batavians, who had already been highly recruited, were asked for more soldiers. This ill-advised move by Vitellius caused corruption which in turn breathed rebellion to life. Corrupt recruiters required bribes from the elderly to escape the draft of soldiers. Due to this infringement on common decency and a few other examples, a man named Julius Civilis, whose brother had been killed by the Romans on apparently asinine allegations, called a meeting to discuss Roman control of Batavia.

After he gained the support of men through his speeches and began to formulate a plan, this new rebel commander asked the Cananefates and their leader Brinno in the north for help. Civilis called on these tribal neighbors to revolt and they served as a distraction from the Batavians. After this surprise, Civilis began searching for other people groups that desired freedom from Rome. In addition to the Batavians, Friesians, and Cananefates, he also gained alliances from tribes in Germany and Gaul. Although Tacitus, the Roman historian, often minimizes the efforts of Flaccus, the aforementioned Roman commander, so that this historical event better aligns with his narrative of the world. In all reality, Flaccus was competent. He not only was placed in an unfortunate situation, but he also handled it relatively well. Even though Tacitus belligerently berates Flaccus for his supposed inaction, it can now be seen that the commander sent for reinforcements before the fighting began. This action does not agree with the account of Tacitus which paints him as inept, but rather shows a keen military sense. Small fights soon began and both sides won a few. In addition to sending for Aquilus, the other commander, Flaccus also began to obtain more equipped fighters. In the small fights, the Romans were combatting auxiliaries which were lighter troops that were easier to defeat. Due to this fact, Flaccus obtained two legions for an upcoming battle. Some Batavian men were being led by a man named Claudius Labeo.

Although it is unclear why, Julius Civilis was one of his enemies. Some historians suggest that some of the tension between the two men could be explained by their generational differences. Batavia had allied with Rome and the government of Rome accepted them as citizens. Part of Civilis' argument for freedom from this connection was the feeling that Rome was treating them more as subjects than as allies. Part of the custom as Roman citizens in Batavia was to be partially named after the emperor. The first name of a Batavian was a Roman emperor and the last was a family name. The aforementioned generation gap can be clearly seen through the first name of the two men. While Julius Caesar is often considered the first emperor of Rome, Labeo's first name is that of Caligula's uncle who took over for him after his death. Although this does not fully explain the hatred, it is the beginning of an understanding. In addition to the generational difference, Labeo had opposed the aristocracy which previously had governed Batavia. When the fighting on the Batavian island began the Romans lost their Batavian cavalry and a couple auxiliaries which were scared off. In the end, the Batavians were victorious. Rebellious tribes of "barbarians" had succeeded in defeating two Roman legions.

Despite Labeo's importance to the battle, he was exiled by Civilis to Friesland. The Batavians celebrated this win and rightfully so. The Romans would likely stop the fighting and offer a treaty. Although this is true, the tides took a turn for the worse after Civilis communicated with Vespasian who was coming from Judea and still wanted the throne. Vespasian would grant Batavian independence if Rome's emperor. Due to this fact, Civilis went to the fort at Xanten and asked the commanders there whether or not they sided with Vespasian. These commanders called Civilis a traitor and stayed faithful to the current emperor Vitellius. The historian Tacitus continues his verbal war with Flaccus by saying that he should have attacked the Batavian army on their way back home. Although this may have been a successful plan, it would have jeopardized land that was more precious and valuable to the Romans.

In addition to continuing with his narrative of the inept commander in Flaccus, this historian also attempted to continue his story of contrast between Roman civilization and the barbarism which supposedly comes from the edge of the world. Although he tried, this point was difficult to convey when the "civilized" Romans are embroiled in civil war and the "barbarians" have created a unified army. Due to the forts loyalty to Vitellius, Civilis began a siege. At first, he tried attacking but eventually decided to starve the inhabitants out. While this was occurring, sections of the army were raiding particular villages and tribes which had decided to become loyal to Rome. Flaccus set up guards to keep the Germans from entering the battle and prepared for a fight. Sending messengers, he also requested the help of Roman soldiers in Spain, Britain, and Gaul. Advancing towards Civilis came to a halt because of the invasion of the Apennine Peninsula by Vespasian. Though Vitellius fought to preserve his power, he ultimately failed and Flaccus with Vocula, another Roman commander in around the same area of the empire, swore an oath to the new leader.

Although Vespasian's victory should have ended the fighting, Civilis seemed to want more. He attacked the armies of Flaccus and Vocula in the dead of night . Tacitus the historian still hated Flaccus for some reason and acted as if he were caught off guard and saved by luck. Quite the opposite is actually true. Civilis was successful near the beginning of the battle. While the Romans knew an attack was coming, they did not know which night would be chosen. After grouping together they began fighting better and soldiers which Flaccus had ordered from Basque, a northern region of Spain, arrived to help the Romans. While casualties were high on both sides, Civilis lost some of his best troops. His army that was still at Xanten was now vulnerable to attack. The Roman plans to attack the Batavians at this fort and lift the siege was interrupted by news that a different group of barbarians was attempting to take Mainz, an even more important fort when compared to Xanten. These rebellious forces were eventually driven off.

Although this is true Civilis was aided by the Roman soldiers who killed their commander Flaccus at a festival. Vocula's men also attempted an assassination but it their efforts proved inadequate. Another revolt further confused Rome, and Civilis tried to take advantage of the situation. Vocula relieved Mainz from the Batavians and headed towards Xanten. Recently, Julius Civilis had contacted Julius Classicus about the possibility of Classicus revolting against the Romans as well. Due to his pride and his desire to continue his family's royal tradition, he consented and his cavalry deserted Vocula. Julius Sabinus and Julius Tutor joined Classicus whose revolt is historically considered separate from that of the Bavarians. These three men fought for what they called the Gallic Empire and they quickly named Sabinus emperor. The new emperor faked his own death which disheartened the Gallic Empire's band of followers. Although the Gauls called upon these men to stop fighting, they joined the ranks of Civilis. Although the Gallic Empire began to be victorious in battle, they did not lose their barbaric customs. Civilis' Germanic allies, after defeating an enemy, burned the whole town down with everyone inside. In addition to this Civilis is said to have handed over prisoners to his children to use as target practice. Continuing victoriously, Civilis took Cologne and made it his capital. Although this gave him reason to celebrate, Claudius Labeo had come back on the scene. Escaping his exile from Friesland, Labeo began to attack the Batavians at home. Civilis gladly took advantage of the opportunity to fight Labeo and he eventually convinced Labeo's men to join his side. Although Labeo escaped his clutches, this was a major morale booster for the Batavians. While Civilis was off fighting at home, a new Roman commander entered the scene. Quintus Petillius Cerialis was a relative of Vespasian and an experienced fighter. Certain rebel armies retreated as the Romans advanced which encouraged the campaigning leader. The rebels attempted a night attack which ultimately failed and Civilis arrived too late. His capital of Cologne had already been taken and the forces left there had been dismantled. The revolt never recovered and Julius Civilis eventually surrendered to the Romans. His life is presumed have been spared but little is known about his death. Thus ended a very confusing rebellion that was to be followed by many more.

The Kitos War was a group of loosely connected revolts that plagued the Roman empire starting in 115 AD. This war was carried out by the Jews who in certain regions committed atrocious acts upon not only their enemies but also on non-combatant civilians. "They would cook their flesh, make belts for themselves of their entrails, anoint themselves with their blood, and wear their skins for clothing. Many they sawed in two, from the head downwards. Others they would give to wild beasts and force still others to fight as gladiators," said Dio Cassius, a Roman historian. Sympathies of modern people can never be materialized for the unnecessary and abusive decisions of the Romans when the oppressed act in such a manner. Although gruesome, knowledge of this revolt can prove beneficial in certain ways.

In the region of Cyrenaica, a ruler named Lukuas became powerful among the Jews and wrought destruction. He destroyed various Roman temples despite the fact that Jews had expected Romans to respect their holy sites. The idea that religious and historical sites should be respected has been contested in modernity. Conquering a sizable section of the middle east recently, the Islamic State of Iraq and Syria has disregarded this ideology and has ruthlessly torn down landmarks that had dominated the landscape for centuries or even millennia before their existence. Religion does not need to be discussed but the problem should be addressed.

With the rise of the Jewish army, many of the inhabitants of Cyrenaica were killed. Often this happened to such an extreme degree that settlers had to be imported from other sections of the empire to compensate for loss and to replenish the farmers who cultivated the fields. Lukuas did not contain his destruction to only one region as he moved into Alexandria, Egypt. More religious sites were destroyed and the city was burned. Although known for his aggravating yet strategically useless decisions, he stepped down to a new personal low. This rebellious leader's actions eclipsed those of the "barbarians" in the lands of Britain, Germany, Gaul, and Batavia.

He violated the nonverbal pact of humanity which establishes respect for those who have passed on. During his time around Alexandria, Lukuas destroyed the grave of Pompey, a member of the First Triumvirate. After his time spent in Egypt, Lukuas moved on to Judea. There Lukuas' two brothers Julian and Pappus were executed by the Romans. Lukuas' revolt was eventually brought to rest although his final fate is undetermined. Although these three revolts were unified by a common leader, Artemion began a separate resistance on the island of Cyprus. These actual barbarians killed two hundred and forty thousand Greek inhabitants before the Romans crushed the rebellion. A ban on Jews entering the island was set in place to discourage similar events. After these revolts, the Romans continued to antagonize the Jews and this caused of the third of this group of wars between the Jews and the Romans. Problems were continually surfacing.

Emperor Hadrian began his reign by treating the Jews with respect and they responded by being peaceful. This did not last however and plans to reconstruct the temple were canceled. In addition to this, he relocated Jews from their homeland and into north African sections of the empire. Not acting on impulse, the Jews instead of initially rebelling contented themselves with preparations. Forts were created in caves to stash needed items and through their cunning, the Jews obtained Roman weaponry. An ingenious plan was formulated in which Roman weapons that the Jews created for the empire were purposely built with mistakes so that they would be returned. Attacks by Jews prompted strict rule which further infuriated them. The emperor installed a strict regional king named Rufus who executed the ban on circumcision and raped Jewish women. Both severely violated their religion and the former was an ancient practice that began at the beginning of the Jewish nation. Genesis 17:10-11 states: "This is my covenant with you and your descendants after you, the covenant you are to keep: Every male among you shall be circumcised. You are to undergo circumcision, and it will be the sign of the covenant between me and you." This was all very disrespectful but the last offense was the greatest.

Although he had a regional ruler, Emperor Hadrian still made certain specific laws for this region. He began to establish a city within Jerusalem called Aelia Capitolina after himself and the Roman god Jupiter. The Jews eventually rebelled and conquered both Rufus and Marcellus, the governor of Syria. This revolt became known as Bar-Kokhba named after its leader. Although able to easily defeat these smaller forces, Hadrian sent in the aforementioned Julius Severus with the governor of Rome's German territory, Hadrianus Quintus Lollius Urbicus. Casualties were high on both sides and fighting was moved to the Jewish headquarters at Bethar. Waiting destruction, it finally came to the Jews and all in the city were killed. This was the unofficial end to the revolt and ushered in a period of Jewish suffering. In addition to the usual religious intolerances such as bans on circumcision and studying of the Torah, the Romans also sold Jews into slavery and killed off nonviolent leaders of the region. Jews also had to submissively watch their capital become paganized and their country renamed from Judea to Syria Palestina.

After this, fighting returned to the Asian continent. The end of the Three Kingdoms Period in China has a more confusing backstory. As mentioned earlier Xian, the last ruler of the Han dynasty, was used as a puppet by Cao Cao. Due to this fact, he was made the duke of Wei. He later passed this title on to his son Cao Pi who attempted to take all of China. Emperor Xian had no backbone and Cao Pi would have succeeded if two leaders in southern China had not fought for power. Liu Bei took over the area called Shu while San Quan controlled Wu. The ruler of the kingdom of Wei and his successor Cao Rui fought various battles with Shu although there was almost no net gain of land on either side. Although they fought valiantly, they were no match when compared to the power of this division of China. However the Cao family would not hold power forever, and a new line eventually took over. Following Cao Rui was Cao Fang, whose power was taken by a regent named Sima Yi who controlled the kingdom through the spineless leader. Sima Shi, Sima Yi's son, took over and replaced Cao Fang with Cao Mao. Sima Shi died and his brother Sima Zhao took over and had Cao Mao killed for attempting to regain power in the kingdom. After Cao Mao died, he was replaced by Cao Huan who succeeded in defeating Shu which ended the Three Kingdoms Period. Sima Yan, Sima Zhao's son, had Cao Huan step down so that he could be the ruler of this new period called the Jin Dynasty. However, China did not remain at peace for long.

Although legend has seeped into the story of Triệu Thị Trinh or Lady Trieu, there are still certain historical points that are important to note. The legend of her riding into battle wearing gold armor with four foot long breasts while riding an elephant is most likely fictional, but her heroic deeds in battle are not. The quite abnormal description of her above was due to the social situation in Vietnam at the time. Being under Chinese rule for a long time now, these subjugated people were expected to follow the teachings of Confucius which at the time were being encouraged by the government for the social order that they were intended to inspire. For women, there were four virtues that they were told to follow: Behavior, speech, appearance, and labor. These were instructed in addition to the three submissions of Confucianism which were obedience to father, husband, and son. Although this is true, the former matriarchal culture of the Vietnamese often still showed through in times of chaos and war. According to some accounts, her parents died and she was forced to live with her brother. Her sister-in-law was apparently cruel to her so Lady Trieu killed her. She began a rebellion in the mountains and her brother went after her. Apparently not as angry about his wife's death as one might expect, he was convinced to join in the fighting. Although this revolution was not as successful as the Trung sisters', it still is glorified by the Vietnamese today. Her army was eventually confronted by a large Chinese force and this female heroine killed herself.

These stories of failed rebellions and disunification among the ranks of these potential revolutionaries are becoming disheartening. The next rebellion follows the same narrative and is relatively quickly crushed by the Roman army. The Crisis of the Third Century was a chaotic period of time in Spain and Gaul during their rule by the Romans. Although led by Amandus and Aelianus who were landowners retaliating for high taxes, this rebellion was composed of army deserters, runaway slaves, and overly worked peasants from this region. Together they were known as the Bagaudae fighters. Following the usual perspective of Roman writers, Claudius Mamertinus, a Roman official and author, described these rebellious people as two-shaped monsters. Although this belief system was tolerated then, it can now be seen that the desire for freedom is not barbaric but universal among all populations. The rebellion lasted from 284-285 and was dismantled by Caesar Maximian. Although he crushed this rebellion, "barbaric" tribes would persistently resist until the Roman Empire had disintegrated.

The War of the Eight Princes in China and similar rebellions ushered in a period of disunity which lasted longer than the existence of the United States. As mentioned before the Sima family had taken power from those belonging to the Cao Wei Dynasty. The Jin dynasty was later created, but this government did not establish peace. The courts were constantly under attack. In a war started by Empress Jia-Hou, Xianbei conspired with a guard named Wang Jun to defeat other princes. A Hun named Liu Yuan was released to counter this dual but quickly began fighting the Jin dynasty. He succeeded in conquering the Jin capitals of Luoyang and Xi'an and set up what he called the Hunic Han Dynasty. While already begun in the north, this ushered in the Sixteen Nations Period for all of China. This would define the land of China for over one hundred years.

Although it changed the course of history, the decision of Constantine the Great to favor Christianity has been omitted. This edict does not fall into the definition of revolution or revolt due to the fact that its goal was not to overthrow the existing government. Although this is true, certain effects of the change will be discussed. Constantius II continued the favoritism of Christians to a more harsh degree. Leaders in Christianity misused their power and persecuted the Jews by burning down synagogues. Isaac of Diocaesarea led a revolt which was eventually put down by a regional king named Constantius Gallus. The rebellion began by seizing power in Isaac's hometown but had little time to expand after that. The Jewish rebels tainted the otherwise acceptable goals of the attempted revolution by needlessly killing Greeks and Christians. The city was destroyed by the Roman forces and even Jewish children's lives were not spared. In this short revolt, multiple injustices were shown on each side.

The implementation of Christianity as the new state religion had some other serious effects on Rome. Although it aided the poor in Rome who followed this religion, it weakened the empire. It led to a decreased status of the emperor from god to hereditary ruler. This was not the only cause by any means but served mostly as a reality check for the Roman people. Decreeing in 330 AD, Constantine divided the empire into two different sections. The western half was ruled out of Rome and the East received the new capital of Constantinople. Differences became apparent between the two. Although Latin had been spoken for centuries in the whole empire, the East decided to accept Greek as its official language. In addition to this, the Roman Catholic religion was practiced in the West while Greek Orthodox was widely accepted in the East. The great army of the West was also severely injured by inept leadership and the profusely common practice of hiring mercenaries. The east became stronger economically which widened the already deep chasm between them. Inflation caused more problems while a trade deficit was created with the East. Higher prices of agricultural products caused by decreased supply and attacks from pirates and other attackers further weakened the West.

The mercenaries described earlier were of a Germanic background, as they often are throughout history, and were placed in the position of fighting people from the same ethnicity. The lack of loyalty led to a victory for the invaders and a sack of Rome. This type of activity became extremely common and eventually different Germanic tribes began taking sections of the once great empire for themselves. The Franks congregated in France while the Saxons and Angles settled in Britain. The attack which marks the official end of Rome for certain historians was led by Odoacer, who was a Germanic tribe leader. Romulus Augustus, the current emperor, was no match and the civilized city of Rome was ruled by people that they considered barbaric. This is the end of what is categorized as the ancient period of revolutions. Throughout all of this power had changed hands many times. In this section, we have seen the rise of the Persian and Roman Empires with their participation in the subjugation of native inhabitants. The Vietnamese rebellions against their strong oppressor, China, has been detailed. This resistance in eastern Asia will continue. Although power has been passed back and forth, the general will has never been represented adequately. Exceptions can be found in Athens and the Roman Republic although both represent primitive versions of popular government especially in the case of Rome. Looking closer at the government, representation for the lower classes was often inadequate while the aristocratic and wealthy families took the power. In this era before certain great, political revolutionaries from the Age of Enlightenment, people had not yet realized their true power. Passing power from one despot to another was not an eternal cycle which entrapped all of civilization. Although despotism continued, the fall of western Rome brought a new surge of regional government which better suited the people. The following chapter will describe a new age in political theory and the application of government.

Chapter 2: Recent Revolutions

Recent revolutions encompass the fall of Rome until the American Revolution. This time period includes the dark ages of Europe and the increase in Muslim power in northern Africa, the Middle East, and even Spain. Trade routes were discovered to Asia and the Americas were colonized by Europeans. Although this new section of the globe under the Caucasians committed atrocities not only on the native population but also Africans, who were shipped like cargo to the European colonies, it also formed the experimental ground needed for the creation of modern government. The hypocrisy of subjugation while preaching freedom was clearly seen, and some of the problems were dealt with rather quickly. This period launched the world into new understanding through great thinkers and discovery. The precursor to the modern age, while flawed, propelled society forward. Here the real story begins.

Before the Islamic Period, the religion of Zoroastrianism dominated the region of Persia, later known as Iran. Although its followers are often considered open-minded and accepting of other religions, they did not hesitate in crushing sects within Zoroastrianism, which they believed violated and polluted their beliefs. One religious rebel was Mazdak.

The main theme of this Persian religion was the invisible fight between good and evil which manifests itself in society. Good is seen as the ultimate victor over evil, and their conflict is often shown through the contrast of light and darkness respectively. Mazdak introduced the idea that evil came through anger, greed, and jealousy in addition to more radical social reforms. Mazdak's ideas included equal distribution of land and wealth which he considered the natural order. Although kings are usually the repellants of revolutionary ideas, the seated ruler in Persia brought Mazdakian teaching to a high standing in the country. However, this did not last long because of actions were taken by the king's son and successor named Prince Noshirvan. He consulted his advisors and decided to suppress the radical ideas and bring ideological peace to the nation. Through extreme violence, the prince finally accomplished his goals. He invited Mazdak and many of his followers who were unaware of his opposition to a feast and massacred them. With no leadership or guidance, this sect was contained to the history books. The Book of Mazdak was destroyed and a complete collection of his teachings does not exist. After this, a very odd rebellion occurred in Western Rome.

Four separate horse racing teams attempted to flex their political influence in Constantinople. The major teams green and blue with the minor teams white and red instigated the revolt. These members of the Nika Riot were formerly violent rivals both on and off the racing track. They had formed mobs for protection and after some members of the blue and green teams were executed, the emperor Justinian attempted to capture instigators who had fled. The leaders of the revolt nominated a royal leader, Hypatius, the nephew of a former emperor. Justinian proceeded to lock himself in the palace while much of the city was burned down. Considering flight, the emperor was convinced otherwise by his wife and ordered his generals Mundas and Belisarius to quell the rebels. Many of the members of the different teams were then cornered into the Hippodrome, a horse racing arena. Hypatius was executed and important supporters were exiled from the kingdom. After the defeat of the rebels, the damage was surveyed and nearly half of the city was negatively impacted with thirty thousand dead.

Fighting also continued in the eastern side of the globe. The Huns were pushed out of China and began marauding around eastern and central Europe. Despite this alleviation, the Chinese still had problems of their own to deal with. To cement his power, Yang Jian executed all the imperial princes to create the new Sui Dynasty. The Chen from the south did not resist his advances and China was quickly reunified after centuries of divisions. After this, the new emperor broke up the power of aristocratic families and the religious leaders who retained loyalty to nonexistent dynasties. General Yang Su aided him in this goal. As is often the case, new reforms were implemented by this new ruler. A canal was constructed and a currency was created that was uniform throughout the new empire. In addition to this, the military which had previously been restricted to those of the Xianbei ethnicity was expanded to include other Chinese citizens.

After the emperor's death, Yang Guang succeeded him as emperor. Although he ruled peacefully for some time, his brother Yang Liang tried to seize power but was suppressed. Unreasonable taxes, which often precede rebellion, had been placed on the lower class to fund the construction of Jiangdu, dikes, and forts around the kingdom. A rebellion from a man named Yang Jian resulted in mass hysteria and the massacre of thousands of civilians. After the draining of the treasury, a domino effect was started. A drought which affected much of the country further ignited the anger and discontentment of the people. The kingdom of Goguryeo in Korea was attacked by China, but the offensive move was unsuccessful. The cost of war burdened the common people. In Shandong, Liu Badao and Wang Pu began their rebellion. Meanwhile in Hebei, Dou Jiande, and Sun Anzu started a rebellion of their own. From the developed south came the rebel army of Du Fuwei and Fu Gongshi. In Wagang, Di Rang came with the largest army of them all. Many peasants joined the movements of these armies, but they were mostly lead by wealthy families. Members of the royal family also decided to join the fighting. Yang Xuangan and Li Yuan were two members who fought the established government. The latter dethroned Emperor Yang, who had killed upwards of thirty thousand of his subjects, and installed Yang You. In addition to this, Yang Hao and Yang Tong were both supported as emperor. Yuwen Huaji killed the former and declared that he was emperor of Xu. Li Mi fought against Wang Shicong for control of the capital and lost. Liu Yuan retained the kingdom and founded the Tang dynasty while General Shicong became emperor of the region of Zheng. This marked the beginning of a new era for China with the destruction of the Sui dynasty and the founding of the Tang.

The Jewish people's ambitious and independent spirit which caused many different revolts and revolutions should be a source of pride. While this is true, they must also be aware of the many atrocities committed by their people close to the turn of the century. The Byzantine Empire, which had been created out of eastern Rome after western Rome fell, struggled to hold on to certain territories in the present day Middle East. In 611 AD the Kingdom of Persia attempted to conquer Syria and Judea, both of which were held by the government in Constantinople. With the help of the Jews which had been subjugated by the Byzantine Empire, the Persians were victorious and the champions rode triumphantly into Jerusalem. The religious revolution which converted Constantine had irritated the Jews and they retaliated. After her conversion, the mother of Constantine, Helena, sought to commemorate the life and death of Jesus. This desire led her to order the building of a shrine near Golgotha and the tomb of Joseph of Arimathea. With disregard for the common courtesy which usually dictates a certain respect for religious sites, this chapel was destroyed. The site which had been reconstructed after this was again dismantled by Muslim invaders.

Heraclius, the Byzantine emperor, eventually won back this land but both countries involved had used up a substantial section of their treasury. As a punishment for their participation, Heraclius ordered the massacre of Jews in Judea. In yet another act of disreverence, the emperor ordered the demolition of synagogues and forced the Jews within his kingdom to convert to Christianity. After these orders, he commanded the king of the Franks in modern day France to continue the massacre, but he refused. Rebellion and civil war are still commonplace in this section of the globe.

A very strange revolution occurred somewhere in the region between modern-day Poland and the coast of the Adriatic Sea. A Frankish merchant named Samo participated in campaigns against the Pannonian Avars on behalf of a Slavic union that he had created. Presumably, this was caused by financial interests which were being disrupted originally by the Avars. After the failed siege of Constantinople by various tribes including the Avars, the Slavic tribes, primarily the Wends, rebelled against their masters. With the help of Samo, they were victorious and set up a new kingdom. They pushed back their rivals and took their homeland for themselves.

Although this victory brought a sense of security, various wars were soon begun with the Franks. Originally these were based on religion. The polytheistic culture of Samo's Slavs did not sit well with the Franks. Peace eventually came from a treaty with the Frankish king, Dagobert I. This did not last however with the news that certain Slavs had committed crimes against the Franks. Samo's response that he would first have to investigate was not satisfactory and war was resumed. Although a newly formed union, the Slavs obtained a major victory at the Battle of Wogastisburg. Continuing victoriously, the Slavs protected their borders well for the remainder of Samo's life. After Samo's death, however, the union crumbled and the Avars continued their subjugation. This was caused by the fact that the Slavs government was not strictly hereditary. No fit commander was found within Samo's large family so the great country which he had built dissolved.

In the Middle East, the death of Muhammad severely affected the Muslim world in much of the same way. Certain groups of people believed that his cousin and son-in-law Ali was the rightful heir to the territory he had gained. These people later became Shiites while the Sunnis that opposed them created the Umayyad Caliphate. Although these form the two major groups today, the Kharijites used to be a formidable force. These were originally followers of Ali but due to their strict piety, denounced his control after he began to making deals with the Umayyad. While his opposition's leaders acted like the ordinary people, Mu'awiyya of the Umayyad dressed more elegantly and in many ways mimicked the culture of the Byzantine Empire. He and his son, Yazid, accepted their monetary systems and even employed the help of Christians. Ali's son, Husayn, was killed by Yazid which caused the breakout of war. Although the beginning of his siege of Mecca was successful, Yazid died and his son Mu'awiyya II was too young to rule. Marwan ibn al-Hakam and Ibn al-Zubayr fought for power.

A rebel named al-Mukhtar was defeated by Ibn al-Zubayr but he in turn was defeated by Marwan ibn al-Hakam's son, 'Abd al-Malik. The conqueror restored Umayyad control over the region. After his campaign however Mecca and the Kaaba were in disarray. The Kaaba is a stone building which houses the sacred black stone. This relic, according to Muslim tradition, was from the time of

Adam and Eve and guided them to a place where God wished for them to build an altar and sacrifice. His son, al-Walid I, succeeded him as ruler and brought conquest and art. During this time the Muslims advanced into Spain across the strait of Gibraltar and conquered this region. If it had not been for Charles "The Hammer" Martel at the Battle of Tours, advancements could have been made across Europe. While the Muslim invaders did have an impressive culture, tribes were already tired of foreign subjugation. After this ruler, the Umayyad had many weak kings and eventually fell prey to the Abbasids. Abdallah ibn Ali took hold of the region and killed many of the Umayyads.

   While Muslim rule in the Iberian Peninsula had already been enacted, nobody had cemented it yet. When the Abbasids took over the much of the Middle East, Abd-ar-rahman and his brother Yahya were forced to flee to northern Africa. While Abd-ar-rahman eventually made it there, his brother was killed by the ruthless regime. Remaining cautious, Abd-ar-rahman decided to continue from Africa and into Spain. Ethnic tensions were on the rise with the Berbers hating these foreign invaders. Although this is true, a weak ruler named Yusef retained some power over the region. Abd-ar-rahman began communicating with Yusef and the king offered him a land grant and one of his daughters. While this was by no means what Abd-ar-rahman wanted, he most likely would have accepted the terms of the agreement. This was true until Obeidullah, a companion of Abd-ar-rahman, was offended by the king's messenger. Although trying not upset his commander, Obeidullah drew his sword because the messenger mocked him for not being able to write Arabic. A war was started and Yusefs troops were defeated by the small group of bandits led by Abd-ar-rahman in the valley of the Guadalquivir River. After his victory, he rose to be the ruler of said peninsula and tried to restore peace between the Arabs and Berbers. Although this proved to be quite a task, the Abbasid was not yet finished with him either. They attempted to storm the capital but Abd-ar-rahman defeated them and severed the heads of their leaders. These he promptly sent to the Abbasid rulers in the Middle East as a warning to not cause trouble. Overcoming many obstacles, Abd-ar-rahman succeeded in setting up a government that lasted over two and a half centuries.

Counted as one of the bloodiest civil wars in history, the An Lushan Rebellion devastated China over the reign of three Tang emperors. Fighting began in 755 AD and was instigated by General An Lushan. This man was extremely cunning and deceived Emperor Xuanzong into giving him more power. In addition to a free house and land grants, the emperor gave him command of over one hundred and sixty thousand men. To rid himself of distrust within the high position, he succeeded in convincing one of the emperor's concubines to adopt him. Eventually, he rose to a strong enough position, and he decided that his army was prepared enough to start fighting. Although their main goal was the capital in Chang'an, An Lushan first captured the major city of Luoyang in which he began his own capital. Slowly marching forward, the rebel leader was successful in conquering the Emperor Xuanyang's capital. The emperor fled with his son and court over the mountains. Although severely weakened, the emperor's son Li Heng took over and began ruling in Lingwu. Now known as Emperor Suzong, he fought to regain the lost territory. Dissension began among the ranks of the rebels when An Qingxu killed his father, An Lushan, and took power. This power change however was not fully recognized with the revolt and Shi Shiming assassinated the new leader due to the fact that his father had been a friend since childhood. Emperor Suzong and his son took advantage of this situation and took back Chang'an and Luoyang. With this, the rebels did not have any major land holdings, and it slowly died.

The often hyper-tolerant culture of the modern Western world would be appalled by the practices which were relatively commonplace in Europe for much of the Middle Ages. Charlemagne, the Frankish king, who is known today for his devotion to the pursuit of education, sought to expand his kingdom. This occurred before he was crowned the Emperor of the Holy Roman Empire by Pope Leo III. The northwestern part of modern-day Germany was inhabited by the Saxons. While they had been benign during the reign of Charlemagne's father, Pepin, now they grew restless and burned down a Frankish church. Equating the four sections of Saxony: Westphalia, Eastphalia, Nordalbingi, and Engria, the king of the Franks sought revenge against all parties. To accomplish his goal, after seizing a fort, he burned down a tree trunk which the Saxons considered sacred. This sacrilegious act invigorated an already war-loving people, and they looked for an opportunity to retaliate. Despite this fact, Charlemagne continued to be victorious and eventually struck a deal with the rulers of the area.

With this war presumably put on hold, the king of the Franks turned his attention towards the Lombards. Although a competent military commander, Charlemagne did not anticipate the rise of Widukind, the new leader of a revolt in the lower class. With this new nuisance created, the Franks returned for a second fight and defeated all the sections of Saxony with the exception of Nordalbingi. There rulers were forced to become converts and Charlemagne left once again. A third campaign began, and forced baptism took place. Although the Franks had further cemented their subjugation, Widukind escaped with his life. Strong measures were instituted and participants in pagan practices were often executed. This led to increased Saxon anger and a desire to rebel. Another revolt took place and a Frankish army was destroyed. Charlemagne, not one for forgiveness, killed four thousand and five hundred Saxons. In addition to this the leader of the rebellion, Widukind was forced to disown his native paganism and swear allegiance to Charlemagne. After this the resistance to Frankish rule was severely impaired. The last major revolt was resulted in the deportation of ten thousand Saxons from Nordalbingi. Although this was the last major Saxon rebellion, some continued to fight for years after Charlemagne was crowned Emperor of the Holy Roman Empire in 800 AD. Despite the fact that these people had an extreme love of freedom and a devotion to their religion, they eventually had to succumb to the severity of reality. Now, fighting returned to China.

Despite sometimes oppressive rule by their Chinese rulers, the Vietnamese spirit never died. In 791 a man named Phung Hung began to fight against China. Although considered beloved by his own people and often called the "parent king," he was ultimately unsuccessful in his campaigns. Sadly his son had the same fortune. Their defeat, however, did not end the Vietnamese resistance which had begun centuries before.

Every so often, it is necessary to take a break from the cruel and sacrilegious practices of less developed societies and focus on the deeds of a tolerant and considerate foe. Already known for its toleration of different religions, Zoroastrianism was aided by the reputation of one of its last great leaders. Babak Khorramdin was known for hospitable treatment of the prisoners of war, women, and children. This sharply contrasted with the actions of his Arabian enemies.

Although young, Babak left a sizeable impression on a traveling man named Javidan Shahrak through his manners and speech. After becoming his mentor, Javidan taught Babak more about the Zoroastrianism that he would later fight and give his life for. From Babak's perspective, he was not only fighting against the Islamic government, but also for more traditional Persian culture and customs.

This newly created warrior found a partner in Afshin Kheydar and began combat in Iran. Although accounts vary about the size of his fighting force, several historians place it from one hundred to three hundred thousand soldiers. Many of these rebels had previously taken a pact to pacifism, but Babak convinced them that the task at hand was of great importance. Although their desire to take back the region for the somewhat suppressed group of Zoroastrians can be seen as noble, their plan to return the ruling class family of Sassanids to power shows that government for much of the world was still at a primitive stage. With his great leadership skills, Babak was able to recruit people from across the region and even allowed some former Muslims in his ranks. The Arab leaders saw the threat that Babak posed, and sent a succession of generals and military leaders after the rebel. First, Yahya ibn Mu'adh went but was defeated. This event reoccurred twice with the attacking armies of both Isa ibn Muhammad ibn Abi Khalid and general Ahmad ibn al Junayd. Finally in 827 AD the caliphate sent the army of Muhammad ibn Humayd Tusi who although unable to capture Babak was the first to defeat him in battle. Babak did not stay down for long and crushed an Arab army while killing its leader, Muhammad ibn Humayd Tusi at Hashtadsar. Defeat after humiliating defeat began to demoralize the Arabs. Due to this, arguably their best military leader, Haydar bin Kavus Afshin was sent to combat the rebel. The organized army was well prepared to fight the rebels and took stronghold of Badhdh. Increased pressure led to Babak fleeing to Armenia whose king did not wish to fight the

Arabs and therefore turned Babak over to his enemies. In addition to this, he was rewarded with gifts for the capture. As mentioned earlier, the Arabs did not share the belief of gentle treatment of their prisoners with Babak and sought to torture him. Instead of killing him quickly, they first cut off his legs and hands. After this they watched the rebel leader bleed to death. Although his captors had the upper hand then, he is now memorialized every year at his castle in modern day Azerbaijan. His words from a response to an armistice deal sent by the Arabs live on. "Better to live for just a single day as a ruler than to live for forty years as an abject slave." The idea that a citizenry could rule themselves while choosing their leaders was still in the early stages of development.

The Byzantine Empire and specifically its capital of Constantinople was a shining jewel which many people tried to conquer. Arabs, in particular, participated in a plethora of different attempts, the last of which occurred in 717 AD under the leadership of Sulaiman from the Umayyad Caliphate. Although this is true, it is said that Arab leaders in the Middle East supported Thomas the Slav in his rebellion against the Byzantine Empire. This empire was Orthodox, but its culture largely mimicked that of ancient Greece. The practice of iconoclasm had grown increasingly common in the church although many believed it was a sinful practice. These people ascribed to the strict interpretation of Exodus 20:4 which states: "You shall not make for yourself an image in the form of anything in heaven above or on the earth beneath or in the waters below." As seen today by the modern church, their efforts were ineffective and ultimately failed. His opposition to iconoclasm led Thomas the Slav and his followers to attempt a siege of Constantinople. Oppression by the practicers of iconoclasm also angered various ethnic and religious groups under the control of this vast empire. The siege began in 821, but only lasted a year due to the attack by Emperor Michael's allies and civil tensions between the different ethnic groups that composed Thomas' ranks. Thomas was thereafter trapped in the fort of Arcadiopolis and was eventually handed over to the emperor for execution. Despite the fact that their leader had just died, the rebels continued fighting for a couple more years until they were completely drained. After this, problems in the Middle East began again.

Through the help of Ya'qub bin Laith as-Saffar, the founder of the Saffarid dynasty, Muslim conquest continued. This dynasty lasted for a couple hundred years until its dissolution. Although its size was severely diminished after its first leader. At its peak, it covered parts of Iran, Afghanistan, and Pakistan. Ya'qub, its founder, gained a majority of that land in the first stage of that dynasty and was eventually recognized by the Abbasid rulers. To begin Ya'qub chose the capital of Zaranj. After this, he began conquering the region of Hindu Kush by overthrowing the dynasty of Persian Tahirid. Although much of the conquered territory had previously been ruled by local Buddhist leaders, Ya'qub forced conversion and led a strictly Islamic dynasty. His rule was seen as harsh and many of the tribes which he had conquered soon proclaimed independence. The power of the Saffarid dynasty was further diminished after the death of Ya'quib. Under the control of his brother, Amr bin Laith, the Samanids defeated them and took away most of their territory. Despite this misfortune, the dynasty continued in the small region of Sisten. Due to its small size, it was prone to attack and in 1002 AD Mahmud of Ghazni arrived, bringing this dynasty to an end.

Participation in the enslavement of Africans started long before the continent of North America was even colonized by European powers. Not including the institution of slavery by local African tribes, the Arab community was one of the first large-scale offenders. As mentioned before, slavery in ancient Greece and Rome was mostly regional. Although racial differences and racism are not main subjects in the Koran, the founder of Islam, Mohammed, did participate in the practice. This led to an acceptance of the practice in the early Muslim world. Much like the antebellum south in the United States, Africans were thought of as less than human due to their differences in appearance and customs. In both circumstances, these beliefs were widespread because the guilty party often sought a defense to justify their cruel and immoral actions. In America, these opinions were eventually seen as scientifically and ideologically absurd and led to the institution's dissolution. However, the more primitive state of all society in the ninth century led to the growth of slavery in the Arabian world.

On the banks of the Tigris and Euphrates rivers, major flooding had occurred which created marshes and swamps. To deal with this problem the land was given by the government to inhabitants with the agreement that they would fix the destroyed area. African slaves were imported to help with this work and were often treated badly. In response to injustices, the Africans formed an army and began the Zanj Rebellion. In the length of existence and size of forces, this rebellion eclipsed the war started by Spartacus and any armed conflict of slave insurrection in the United States before the Civil War. The massive conflict lasted for fifteen years and was composed of over five hundred thousand fighters. Although it began as only a group of slaves arming themselves with household items and not having any real ammunition, that quickly changed. A navy was created and chariots were obtained in addition to common weaponry. Originally led by an African named Sharih Habash, Ali Razi, a wealthy Persian quickly took over the position. The new commander invited all different types of people into his army. The homogenous group was infiltrated with tribal Arabs and Razi's fellow Persians. This was extremely useful for increasing the number of soldiers but near the end, a Persian soldier fighting with the slave revolt became a traitor. Ya'ghub, although a Persian nationalist who hated Arab rule, was repelled by the thought of equality for Africans. His treachery was extremely harmful to the rebellion and aided the cementation of Arab rule in this region.

Before this, closer to the beginning of the rebellion, a plan was formulated for the acquirement of land. The slaves were to simultaneously kill their Arab masters and take the land that they owned. The plan was extremely successful, especially when compared to Denmark Vesey's attempted slave rebellion in 1822. Unlike the African slaves of the Arabs, a significant portion of slaves in the United States's south had grown fond of their masters. This fact does not to discount the complete depravity of the system in general or the extreme cases of abuse. Rather it highlights a key difference which led to a different outcome. In Vesey's case, which will be discussed in more detail in the following chapter, a fellow slave informed authorities about the plot and all involved were executed. However, this did not happen in the Middle Eastern example. After land was acquired many of the slaves preferred a more communal economy and society. They adopted many of the reforms of Mazdak, who was mentioned earlier as the Persian social reformer. Although Razi's fight was obviously more successful than that of Vesey, it too eventually fell apart. After surrounding the slave capital of Mokhtarieh for two years, Razi fought his way through their lines. One last major battle occurred, but Razi was captured. In accordance with the typically gruesome methods seen before, the Arabs took his head and paraded it around the land to convince the slaves that their cause was also dead. Despite this event, groups of slaves continued fighting against their oppressors. Disunity and missed opportunities were two of the factors which led to the end of this lengthy revolutions.

Around the same time, another lengthy rebellion went on for a decade in China. Although ultimately defeated due to the betrayal of a family member, the effects of this were strong enough to bring down the Tang dynasty after the rebellion was over. The rebellion was led Huang Chao but it grew due to civil unrest which was caused by a number of factors. A succession of famines had ravished the land and the people had been overly taxed. While this is true, defeat of the better equipped and trained government troops came not only because of Chao's military skills but also because of the folly of the former. A period of peace in the Tang dynasty had caused many of the soldiers and commanders to become lax in their training. The newer generation having no real experience in war was also a problem. In addition to this, high-ranking military officials were not chosen based on skill and became squeamish at the sound of battle.

At the beginning of the conflict Huang Chao was not in the picture. Forces were led Wang Xianzhi but remained a minimal threat. At this small and insignificant level, Huang Chao entered as a common combatant. He quickly rose through the ranks of the rebellion until he encountered a problem. Wang Xianzi and he were not in accord with regard to military strategy. Due to this difficulty, the two split into separate sections and each created an army. Chao easily bested Xianzhi as a leader and quickly began to attack Emperor Xizong victoriously. In addition to this, he invited other marauders as members of his army. An alliance was created with Sang Rang while the fighting continued. Despite the success of many campaigns, Chao attempted to negotiate with the enemy on several occasions. The leader's primary concern seemed to be himself and the social recognition which he desired. He communicated with the emperor and said that he would cede his position as rebel commander if the government would make him military ruler of Tianping. Declining this offer, the emperor offered him the position of General of the Imperial Guard. Although this was not a powerless position, Chao was prone to anger and after this, he took control of several important cities. Luoyang was taken although Chao's ultimate goal was the capital in Chang'an. This goal was then fulfilled and the city was destroyed. The gem which had served as the capital of several previous dynasties was shattered, never to be used as the seat of the Chinese government again.

Although once strong, disease, which was a scary and unseen enemy, ravaged the camp. The decline was further aided by staggering military defeats. At the end of all of this misfortune, Chao's nephew, Lin Yan, killed his whole family. Without a strong leader for support the rebellion ceased but the dynasty which had fought against Chao would also begin to weaken. The fall of the Tang Dynasty ushered in the Five Dynasties Period. This era lasted for half a century until China would be united under the Song Dynasty.

While the Holy Roman Empire was still relatively young, in 987 AD the Byzantine empire was dealing with more rebellion. When Basil II was still a teenager John I died leaving power with the former. This is unusual because of the fact that Basil had an older brother named Constantine. During his reign, John had killed Nikephoros II Phokas which obviously angered the man's family. Although probably prepared to deal with this, nobody in the empire foresaw that Bardas Skleros, a personal friend of John, would turn traitorous and form an alliance with the the Phokas family. The servant Basil Lekapenos was given command of the kingdom due to the emperor's young age and he drove Skleros into exile. Thinking that he was wise enough to command, Basil II peacefully acquired the responsibilities of his servant. At around the same time, chaos challenged his courage. In Bulgaria, a relatively new territory to the Byzantine Empire which had been conquered by John, a revolt led by a man named Samuel occurred. Although having little experience, Basil II attempted to regain tracts of land which Samuel had taken.

Consequently, other rebel leaders returned. Both Skleros and the Phokas family returned to fighting simultaneously for revenge and power. Not having a sufficient number of soldiers, Basil II looked for potential allies. He found the help he needed in Prince Vladimir of Kiev, who was from modern day Ukraine. Having to participate in the practices of the Christian religion, the Byzantine emperor's sister was given to Vladimir on the stipulation that the pagan ruler would convert and join the Orthodox church. In return for this marriage, Basil II would receive six thousand troops to quell the rebellions. While able to deal with the domestic threat of Skleros and the Phokas family, the foreigners fighting for their freedom were still left standing. This resistance movement would last for over three decades until peace was restored. In addition to gaining back the land that was lost originally, Basil II also conquered territory which had not been possessed by the Byzantine Empire for over three hundred years. Bulgaria was now cemented by a strong Byzantine ruler and Samuel could not resist the powerful empire. This land and others would be added to the empire due to Basil II's leadership. Although suppressed for now Bulgaria eventually gained its independence.

Another rebellion against the Byzantine Empire occurred relatively soon after the last but had better results. The vassal state of Doclea was ruled by Stefan Vojislav, who had become tired of Byzantine rule. Due to this fact, he rebelled and defeated the well-established empire on various occasions. After the major defeat at Tudjemili, the small state was recognized by Emperor Constantine IX Monomachus. Today this is considered the first state of Montenegro, which is located on the Adriatic Sea. The independent state was passed on to Stefan's son Mihailo who continued to increase its prominence. Not adhering to his father's strict policy of hatred towards the Byzantine Empire, Mihailo married the niece of Constantine IX Monomachus. In addition to this, he increased the ruling status of this new kingdom in the church while expanding its borders as well. The lands of Raska and Bosnia were added to the kingdom. When Mihailo died, a fight broke out for the throne. Quickly one of Mihailo's sons, Bodin established his dominance. To punish his family for questioning his rule, Bodin exiled both a cousin and his brother. He proved himself worthy of the high position and continued the beneficial policies of the previous rulers. After his death the kingdom became embroiled in civil war and much of the gained territories were lost. Although this is true Montenegro became an independent state once again when it broke away from Serbia in modern history.

Although the account of Sayyidna Hasan bin Sabbah largely describes a religious movement, the story also involves cases of military conquest. Little is known about his ancestry although it was alleged that he came from a group of rulers out of Yemen. When he was still relatively young for the position, Hasan was appointed to the court of a ruler named Malik Shah. While he was qualified for the position, this action bred jealousy with fellow members of the royal service. Nizamul Mulk, who had been appointed as Wizarat, feared for his position. After Mulk sabotaged one of his projects, Shah called for Hasan to be arrested. Hasan learned of these happenings and escaped. His next home was where he developed his faith.

The Ismaili faith, a sect of Shiite Islam, was accepted by Hasan and he began to discuss religion with the locals. Healthy relations were maintained and he was asked to go to Egypt. After some time there he was imprisoned for his support of Hazrat Imam Nizar. Miraculously a wall of the jail collapsed and Hasan fled. This brought him to the fort called the Alamut. Although it is still unknown how, Hasan was able to peacefully acquire the fort. Two separate accounts differ. One says that he offered to pay for the fort while the other describes a sly plan. In the latter it is said that he asked the ruler of the fort for a tract of land the size of a stretched cowhide. This was consented to and Hasan spread pieces of the cowhide all over the Alamut. Although the first is more likely, both stories lead to the same conclusion. This was a huge success for Hasan, but his former enemies would not leave him alone. Mulk sent an army against him which was defeated. These disturbances were ended when the wife of Malik Shah persuaded her husband to execute Mulk. Although he had served for quite some time, Mulk did not support Shah's son as successor which disturbed Shah's wife. In addition to this Mulk had become hateful of the Ismaili faith which was starting to slowly be accepted by Shah. The death of Shah led to conflict within the royal family because his sons fought for a decade over the position of their deceased father. When one would gain an advantage over the others, they would attack Hasan. Although this is true, their focus on the throne led to more free time for Hasan and he capitalized on the opportunity by capturing seven important forts. Finally, a truce was made by the king's ultimate successor Saljuq Sultan Sanjar and fighting ended between the two groups. With less emphasis on war, he focused on the spread of the Ismaili faith. Even though he eventually succumbed to a deadly disease, during his life he had founded a protected homeland for people of his faith.

William I, also known as "The Conqueror," was a commander with rule extending from England to Normandy in modern day France. While still in power, he and his favorite son William II, fought against the king's eldest son, Robert Curthose, who tried to take parts of the kingdom. Although Robert rebelled against his father's rule, he was still rewarded in the will. William II, his father's presumed favorite, was given all of England while Curthose was given the territory of Normandy. This division of territory was not satisfactory to Robert Curthose nor his wealthy and powerful uncles Robert and Odo. With their help, Curthose took the forts of Tonbridge, Pevensey, and Rochester. The loyal subjects of William II fought back to regain the lost strongholds. After they accomplished this, William went on the offensive and began to take hold of large sections of Normandy. Due to these embarrassing losses Curthose and his allies consented to end the rebellion and reign peacefully.

Although he made peace with his family, his reign was marked by another war. The leader of this war against England was Malcolm III, also called Canmore, from Scotland. The early life of Malcolm was tainted with the traumatic experience of the violent death of his father, Duncan I. Before his story intersects with that of William II, Malcolm also became involved in a successful rebellion. Macbeth was the man who had killed Duncan and Malcolm looked for revenge. He found his opportunity in battle where he personally killed the family rival. The step-son of Macbeth who had replaced him as king was promptly assassinated and Malcolm set up a long lineage of rulers. This family line lasted for two hundred and fifty years and became important by ridding Scotland of Norse influence.

Although often considered barbarous by the royal governments of English history, the Scottish allowed the immigration of Anglo-Saxons after their defeat at the pivotal Battle of Hastings. Malcolm was known for adoption of certain aspects of the Anglo-Saxon culture and his second wife was even from that group. Although not immensely powerful, the Scottish king implemented raids on counties that bordered his kingdom. After this, these two men met on unpleasant terms. William II, defending his lands, with the help of his army forced the signing of the Treaty of Abernethy. This allowed Malcolm to continue rule of Scotland but included an article which forced him to swear allegiance to the English crown. If history has taught anything, it is the fact that the Scottish are not usually welcoming to foreign rule or degradation. Due to this fact, Malcolm continued to immerse himself in conflict with the country which he had recently sworn allegiance to. Ultimately this led to his death. While fighting at the Battle of Alnwick his life ended, but his kingdom would last for centuries.

Although many revolutions such as the American Revolution have created constructive and firmly established governments, other times rebellions are not based on the sound principle of the people's will and are doomed to failure. An example of each can be found in the following paragraph. First came the revolution of the Almohads which is an example of the latter. This, like many of the Islamic revolution, had a largely religious backing which developed into a military conflict. A man named Muhammad ibn Abdallah ibn Tumart failed to gain support in major cities but eventually formed a revolution that conquered territory on both sides of the strait of Gibraltar.

Looking for a people who would be sympathetic, he went back to his roots in the Atlas Mountains. There he formed his sect of Islam called the Almohads which would contest the Almoravids for power. Although the Almoravids were slightly repressive, they were nothing compared to the policy changes that the Almohads implemented. Christian and Jewish men were demoted from positions of power that they had risen to during the previous administration. Worse yet, religious tolerance became extinct and conversion became mandatory if a person wished to live. The first ruler claimed that he was a chosen by Allah but the leader that he chose for the position after his death established a traditional hereditary system.

Although extremely fascist in certain aspects of his governance, Tumart, while alive, implemented both a council of ten followers and eventually a tribal assembly. These changes to the Almohad government showed some traces of good government but these two institutions held very little power. To gain territory the cities of Marrakech and Sus in Morocco were targeted. After gaining these and other lands south of Gibraltar, attempts were made to attack parts of Spain. This was accomplished and southern Spain around the city of Cordova was captured. Now long after the death of the patriarch, Tumart, the government began to ease restrictions on non-Muslims and practice a greater degree of religious tolerance. The Maliki school of thought became accepted and reforms were made. Despite this fact, the people that they had conquered still yearned for freedom. Due to this yearning, a revolution of the former type began. For over a half century the Zenata Berbers fought for control of Morocco. They slowly moved across the area taking Almohad fortresses as they went. Although the Almohads attempted to defend their last fort of Marrakech, it fell as did their kingdom in the area.

The next rebellion began in the kingdom of Japan. The Hogen rebellion as it is called allowed for a long lasting period of Samurai power. At the beginning, two former emperors, Sutoku and Toba, stepped down from the throne and were succeeded by Konoe. They still retained power though, and each desired one of their sons to rule after Konoe. When Go-Shirakawa became emperor and Toba died, Sutoku began an insurrection. He started to gather allies for the upcoming conflict and gained the support of Minamoto no Tameyoshi and Fujiwara no Yorinaga. Despite his great number of men, Sutoku's palace was attacked by the men of Go-Shirakawa. It was decided to set the property ablaze, rendering it untenable, and Go-Shirakawa was victorious. The fighting lasted only a couple hours but its effects on Japanese history were extreme. The rebel forces of Sutoku scattered and according to the historical accounts of the time, the three major commanders eventually died. The Emperor Go-Shirakawa exiled Sutoku on a desolate island for questioning his power. After a Japanese court failed to sympathize with his situation, the rebel leader died of insanity. Fujiwara no Yorinaga was pierced by an arrow during the attack and sought medical treatment by arriving at his father's home. Rejected possibly due to criminal status or disgrace of the family, Fujiwara no Yorinaga severed his tongue and slowly died of blood loss. Minamoto no Tametomo was also banished to an island but unlike his leader, Sutoku, he did not become mad. Instead, he committed seppuku, honorable suicide in Japanese culture done through the cutting of the stomach, after he sank an incoming ship from the imperial navy. In this way the rebels were dealt with but Japan would face another short conflict only a few years later.

The Heiji Disturbance as it sometimes called was led by Fujiwara Nobuyori who was allied with a member of the Minamoto clan, Minamoto Yoshitomo. Although they originally were successful in their attempt to capture the palace, they were then defeated by Taira Kiyomori. This man became important to the former emperor Go-Shirakawa. The Minamoto clan proved the common maxim of "third time's a charm" when the son of Minamoto Yoshitomo, Minamoto Yoritomo, was successful in the Genpei Wars. After this major victory, the relatives of Taira Kiyomori were either executed or exiled to cement his power. Yoritomo established a government that would remain in authority for almost a century and a half.

Although a generic revolt due to the fact that its main cause was a hike in taxes by the emperor, this next rebellion is unique because it involves a very relatable aspect of modern Western culture; the outrageous cost of weddings. This did not pose a problem to the common people of the time, but the ruling family knew how to spend money. Attempting to raise money for the wedding celebration of the Hungarian king's daughter, the Byzantine Emperor, Isaac II, made the common people bear the load. This had become common practice during the reign of absolute rulers but as the gun was the great equalizer in the American West so the vote has been the equalizer in government and politics. An argument could be made however that in pure republics and democracies with a large percentage of poor people, those who have worked hard and become successful pay more than their "fair share." How much of their success is based on individual aptitude as compared to their situation at birth? These predicaments and balancing acts will be further addressed in the political section of the book. Now back to the historical.

When dividing the needed money between regions of his empire, Emperor Isaac seemed to harshly target an area in the Haemus Mountains on the Balkan Peninsula. Due to this fact, the area composed of both Vlach and Bulgarian people sent two representatives named Asen and Peter. They met Emperor Isaac at Kypsella but both of their desired reforms, more land and admission into the army, were rejected. Although at first many people were wary about Asen and Peter's proposed revolt, they were finally swayed by idea that God no longer sided with the Byzantine emperorship. In response to the insurrection, the emperor pushed the rebels back into the territory of the Cumans. This proved to not be advantageous to Isaac because the Vlach and Bulgarian people became allied with the Cumans. Fear and weak military foresight caused Isaac to return to his capital in Constantinople without creating any defenses. The returning rebel forces were surprised to find the area which they were prepared to fight and die for foolishly deserted by their enemy. In addition to the original tract of land, the rebels were also left all of Moesia. Isaac had become increasingly worried about the rebel forces but he never expected a betrayal by his own family.

After he appointed his uncle John as military commander of the Byzantine troops in the insubordinate region, John too decided to question Isaac's authority and began a revolt of his own. The brother-in-law of Isaac was then placed in charge. He proved to be faithful to the cause but unfamiliar with both the region and the people soon encountered failure and loss. Well-established governments often have trouble coping with the military tactics of guerilla rebels. Although the oppressor often has access to more weaponry and supplies, the local people's knowledge of the region usually proves as a major advantage. This was the case in both this uprising against the Byzantine Empire and in the American Revolution against the British Empire. When the rebels in the former began to retreat, faithful John began to follow them into the mountains, hoping to capitalize on his victory. Although his military strategy was usually sound, in this instance he charged into an ambush. Like the North in the American Civil War, the Byzantine

Empire changed commanding generals often. However, unlike the North, they never found the correct one. After the second John, came Alexius Branas who like the first John turned traitorous and attacked Constantinople. Although Alexius was defeated, the many failures of commanding generals had led to decreased focus on the original Vlach, Bulgarian, and now Cuman rebels. One last attempt was made at victory but after failing to attain the fort of Lovech Isaac surrendered the region. This was extremely satisfying for the Bulgarians seeing that they had participated in a rebellion previously against the same enemy. Although Isaac retreated, there were still repercussions against the rebels. Hostages had been taken by the Byzantine Empire which included Asen's wife and one of the rebel's brothers. Despite the unintended consequences, a certain degree of freedom was once again enjoyed by the people of this region although they were still ruled by a king.

Although not involved directly, the Holy Roman Empire through its support of the Teutonic Order attempted to suppress the local people living in the region of Prussia. These people did commit barbarous acts such as burning men alive in their armor, but they were provoked by the invading armies. In any case, the conflict began in 1226 AD after the Duke of Masovia gave the Teutonic Knights the authority to combat the "pagan" Prussians from the region of Chelmo Land. Soon after Emperor Frederick II of the Holy Roman Empire voiced his support for their campaigns due to the Christian plan to use Prussia as a military base for training soldiers heading to the various crusades against the Muslims. Although the offensives were eventually successful, it took over fifty years to complete the subjugation. The control by the Holy Roman Empire was political as well as religious. While having the power to decide which nobles maintained their position, the empire also executed and exiled inhabitants who refused to convert. In the past, the Roman Catholic Church had compromised by admitting certain pagan practices into Christianity. This was mentioned before with the example of icons. Even after this, they have been known to institutionalize aspects of pagan culture as is apparent with the holy days of Easter and Christmas. These holy days emphasize events important to Christians but are celebrated on days derived from non-Christian sources. Although these precedents show a general trend, leaders in the Roman Catholic Church were wary in the case of the Prussians. However, local rulers were far more lenient with religion. As long as they were baptized and "converted," many common religious ceremonies which had occurred previous to the invasion by the Teutonic Order became increasingly common again. In addition to religion, other aspects of Prussian culture were destroyed as well. This included the destruction, reconstruction, and renaming of important cities. All the dead Prussians had to be replaced and an importation of immigrants from primarily Germany, but the Dutch and the Flemish as well, from modern-day Flanders in northern Belgium, were also included in this.

The Teutonic Order later became increasingly powerful and still exists today. Directly after their campaigns in Prussia, they continued to attempt to forcefully spread their beliefs by attacking Russia, which associated with the Eastern Orthodox Church. While two Christian sects fighting may seem odd, it is not uncommon among well-established religions of this time period. As seen previously both Muslims and Jews participated in wars against each other, and in the case of the Jews this conflict came during a rebellion against the original Roman Empire. Despite their efforts, the Teutonic Order failed, as invaders of Russia often do, and became confined to the region of central Europe.

The Anatolian Peninsula once again became prevalent to the storyline of revolution with the rebellion of Baba Isak against the Seljuk Empire. A leader named Gıyaseddin Keyhüsrev II was placed in power after his brother's and father's assassination. Like Mazdak, Baba was a reformer of religion and society as well as politics. Unlike Mazdak he was not famed with any major victories. Although he put forth effort, Baba was eventually hung by the established government and the rebellion ended. Despite their failure, the foreign invaders called the Mongols were able to successfully defeat Gıyaseddin Keyhüsrev II. Even though the Seljuk Empire was supported by mercenaries from surrounding countries, they could not defeat their enemies. The Mongols however were not extremely interested in complete domination and they contented themselves with an annual tribute from the leaders of the peninsula.

Another revolt occurred in the Islamic world but this one spawned a revolution. A slave revolt, multiple assassinations, and the Bubonic Plague all collaborated to finally bring Ottoman rule to the regions formerly held by the Abbasids. It may seem counterintuitive but the Abbasid and Ayyubid sultans decided to import a large number of slaves, which were called Mamluks, and train them to be in the military. While the practice of slaves working with weaponry has been somewhat common throughout history, it seems that these slaves were given enough men and ammunition to turn and defeat their oppressors. Looking at this from a largely Westernized perspective, it may seem that these slaves were fighting an ideological war for freedom and a just cause. This assumption would be extremely false seeing that many of the slave leaders themselves had slaves of their own. Modern society would have seemed odd to them and it is doubtful that they saw their hypocrisy.

As seen in the case of Imad-ud-Din Zangi, the leader of Mamluk forces against the Abbasid, Karma comes back to bite. After obtaining the city of Edessa, Zangi caught a few of his slaves drinking his wine and before he had a chance to punish them, the slaves slew their master. This did not end the kingdom that Zangi had began however and his son Nureddin was successful in conquering Damascus. This simple story accompanies the much more complicated rebellion against a group of Mamluks Ayyubid rulers. After conquering Jerusalem from the Christian crusaders, the Mamluks grew in prominence around the region of Egypt and Syria. In 1250 AD, Shajar al-Durr won the prize of the worst mother of the year after murdering her only son to retain power over the region. After this, she married the leader of the Mamluks, Aybak, to maintain the peace, but eventually killed her husband as well. Although this is true, she, in turn, was executed and having no eligible successors, the kingdom was turned over to the Mamluks. After Aybak the province was ruled by a line of Mamluks which created the Bahri Dynasty. A man named Baybars rose to the highest position after his victory over the Mongols who were then undefeated in the Middle East. In addition to this, the Baybars repelled the crusaders. Not known for their love of Christians, after the defeat of Antioch all the one hundred thousand citizens, that had survived the slaughter of sixteen thousand people, were sold into slavery. As with many long-lasting dynasties, the Mamluks had a golden age. Theirs was short however due to the fact that the leader who ushered in this period of time was killed by the Bubonic Plague. A different party of Mamluks called the Burjis reigned after the Bahri and they became relatively powerful. A little over a hundred years after their beginning however, the Ottoman had been successful in their struggle for power.

The island of Sicily, which is now unified with the Italian mainland, once became embroiled in a revolt against its ruler Charles of Anjou. Charles was a stereotypical try hard and a power hungry man. Wherever he went he made enemies, but his friendship with Pope Urban IV helped him to secure power in Sicily. Although this is true, the island was of low importance to him due to the fact that he also had land holdings in Tunis, Greece, France, Jerusalem, and Albania as well. Although this list is quite impressive, Charles' main goal was to defeat the Byzantine Empire. The Byzantine Emperor, Michael, learned of this plot and was obviously dissatisfied. Although this was Charles' most threatening rival, his power was also contested by King Peter I of Aragon, whose wife Constance was seen by many Sicilians as the true successor. These two men conspired against the overly ambitious leader and began to formulate a plan concerning his removal. These two rulers were too slow however, and the people of Sicily revolted before a royal invasion of the island. This revolt was caused not only because of the questions concerning the legitimacy of Charles' reign but also because he had imported a significant amount of French people. This undesired immigration already caused discomfort, but Charles then decided to demote locals from positions of power in favor of the French. Tensions were high among the subjugated people and therefore a small spark was all that was needed to ignite the entire territory. This came through a somewhat odd occurrence in terms of the instigation of rebellions.

In the city of Palermo while waiting for an evening prayer service, called vespers, a French man decided to make a move on a married Sicilian. This was seen as extremely offensive and therefore the husband of the woman stabbed the wooer. The comrades of the French man were alarmed and attempted to aggress. The sheer number of the Sicilians was able to overcome the governmentally established oppressors and spread the news to the surrounding cities and countryside. In addition to this, the news reached the Kingdom of Aragon, and the Byzantine Empire and the rebels requested their help. Soon the only region of the island left in Charles' power was Messina, which is located by the strait with the same name between the island and the Apennine Peninsula. This with the help of King Peter and Emperor Michael was also taken from Charles and he lost the island. The far more popular Queen Constance was installed as ruler but she and her allies had to deal with a certain degree of threat until the death of Charles. Although the queen was a more popular leader, the lack of checks on royal power showed that government was still at a primitive state.

As mentioned earlier Scotland was independent from England, but during certain times the English crown exercised a fair amount of control over the King of Scotland. This was seen as a humiliation for many Scots and they sought a complete disassociation with their southern neighbor. Although this was their desire, Scotland was flung into chaos when their king, Alexander III foolishly attempted to begin a voyage to see his new wife while in the middle of a storm. In the end, his sex drive drove him to death and the autopsy on his body at the time said that he had snapped his neck. His death was extremely saddening and not only for the obvious reasons. He died without leaving any male heirs to the throne. Although he did have extremely young daughter in Norway, the people held out that his wife was pregnant from one her previous encounters with the king. This hope was crushed and the king's daughter, Margaret was sent for. A worthy suitor was searched for by the Scottish nobles and this was found in King Edward I's son Prince Edward. Although he was open to the idea, King Edward had some stipulations and created the Treaty of Salisbury. The main point of the treaty said that Margaret must remain in England until she and her husband were old enough to rule. These conditions were agreed upon but the Scots had some guidelines. In the treaty of Birgham, the English king agreed to several Scottish safeguards to their liberty and independence as a sovereign state. This included freedom of the Scots to have customs and religion separate from England. In addition to this the maintenance of borders was signed upon although Edward would eventually go back on his word.

All of these events became meaningless after Margaret died on her way from Norway. Although aggravating, it was not uncommon for children to die very young at the time and it is now believed that the young Queen may have caught pneumonia on the voyage. Despite the fact that Edward was no longer needed, the Scottish nobles employed him as an arbitrator in the fight for the Scottish crown. The nobles were unsuspicious of Edward's ulterior motives and therefore sought his council. This proved to be a major mistake seeing that Edward took the opportunity to cement his power in the northern territory. Before choosing a ruler, the English king had everyone submit to him. This was done because no man wanted to be left out of the chance for the position. John Balliol was eventually chosen and began his humiliating rule as King of Scotland. Although representatives of the king were usually sent, Edward forced John to travel and speak with subjects about complaints personally. This may seem very benign today but it was an act of subjugation by the English king. In addition to this, he/ broke the Treaty of Birgham by forcing the Scots to change their customary tax code and even the king's seal. This offense was taken aggressively and King John attempted to spread throughout Scotland the knowledge that the treaty had been broken by the English. After hearing about this attack on his authority, Edward made John publicly apologize for his speech and also state that the treaty no longer was in effect.

A territory conflict between France and England resulted in the chance Scotland needed for revenge. Instead of following the order of Edward to fight in the English army, Scotland created an alliance with France. Although this was of great concern to Edward, he was preoccupied with his attempts to quell a rebellion in Wales. This rebellion was led by Madog ap Llywelyn but was relatively short-lived. Although it served as a beneficial distraction for Scotland, the capture of its leader hastened its demise. After this victory, Edward was able to focus on his other rebellious territory. Scotland proved to be a weak rival for England because of their inexperienced military commanders. After the English victory at Berwick, the fighting moved to Dunbar. Falsely interpreting a shift in the lines as a retreat, the Scots under command, charged their opponents. Their ranks were completely dismantled and John had to plead with Edward for mercy. Although he was never executed, King John was once again publicly humiliated and eventually stripped of his power.

A rebel who has now been immortalized in film considered English rule loathsome. William Wallace's hatred was probably cultured by a couple instances of arrogant English soldiers. It is said that he killed at least a couple Englishmen before his lover, Marion Braidfute, was captured by his rivals. Although she was executed, Wallace continued to fight and the number of dead Englishmen greatly increased. Although many Scottish men desired freedom, they also feared King Edward. After Wallace won at the Battle of Stirling Bridge, he encountered a crushing defeat. This caused many of the nobles to reject him and he was considered a bandit with no governmental support in Scotland. Another Scotsmen loyal to the English crown became the cause of Wallace's death. While hiding from the English authorities, a Scottish knight gave Wallace over to the English. This was considered a great accomplishment, and Wallace was tortured before finally being executed.

Although he was no longer fighting, William Wallace was soon replaced by Robert Bruce who was chosen by the Scottish clergy. After years of fighting King Edward and his successor Edward II, the Treaty of Edinburgh was eventually signed by Edward III which established Scotland as free and independent. Edward I who placed much emphasis on the maintenance of English rule in Scotland stated that he would not be entombed elegantly until the kingdom was under his families command. To this very day he is buried in Westminster Abbey in a lead casket. This story has been somewhat romanticized by modern culture but it does provide some incredible insight. Rising in what now is the United Kingdom of Great Britain is a more recent move towards Scottish independence, but this largely depends on vote rather than military strength. A political chasm can be seen forming now between the two states. Should the largely liberal Scotland be forced to unite with the more conservative England? Many Scots believe that too much emphasis has been placed on London and that the inconvenience of the physical distance is overshadowed by the political differences. This issue has risen to the surface during the vote in the British Parliament to leave the European Union. This decision came partly due to immigration concerns. Although it is often dismissed by many as xenophobic, the threat of Islamic extremists is a major concern to many citizens. The European Union which allows for smooth passage of travellers around much of western and eastern Europe is no longer supported by much of the British population. Belief in this is vividly contrasted with the desire of most Scots to be members of the union. This poses the question: Should the union of the British Isles which came originally from subjugation by England be forced to endure? Should the former strength of men still be used as the political boundaries of nations? I believe that now advancing into the twenty-first century, the two states of Scotland and England should separate from the unions that no longer represent them; the former from the United Kingdom and the latter from the European Union. This subject will be discussed in more detail where it is deemed appropriate.

The capital city of Brussels, Belgium is interesting due to the fact that all road signs are printed in two languages. This situation can be traced back to medieval times. Today the northern section called Flanders speaks Dutch, while the southern section called Wallonia speaks French. In the capital the two regions collide creating an example of European multiculturalism. If history would have taken a more conventional path however, Belgium today would look very different and maybe not even exist. In 1302 a battle took place where the Flemish people fought France to remain independent. This victory for the low countries can be compared to what Charles Martel did for all of Europe. The Flemish victory was a great marvel due to the fact that commoners were able to defeat heavily armored knights. Although the French had more advanced weaponry, the tightly packed Flemish, armed with spears and a medieval weapon called a goedendag beat back several advancing ranks. The name of the Battle of the Golden Spurs is derived from the outfits of the French. Flemish commanders demanded that anyone with spurs be killed, and golden spurs signified the highest rank in the French military. This one decisive battle was enough to repel the French attacking forces.

Although this fight ensured the continuation of independence for Flanders, a more popular revolt would occur because of over-taxation and an increased French influence culturally. Louis I of

Flanders supported France but was caught off guard by a group of peasants who rose up against his policies. Looking for more help after the rebellion grew, Louis called on France. While not being able to defeat the Flemish government, they were able to defeat the Flemish people at the Battle of Cassel. This lack of a syncretic bond between the people and the government had been the norm for millennia.

In the next rebellion the Teutonic Order, which had previously defeated Prussia under the blessing of the Roman Catholic Church and the Holy Roman Empire, again became a dominant player. As with the previous war in Prussia, the Teutonic Order was once again working against the will of the majority of inhabitants. Valdemar, the King of Denmark, was looking to sell his rights to Estonian land to the Order. The ruler of Brandenburg named Ludwig was also compensated by the Order for the land-holdings that he had gained through his marriage. This regift of land did not go unchallenged however. The general population of Estonia did not agree with the decision of these foreign rulers who had little concern for their well-being. While foreign oppressors often are conscientious of the state of the people, this was because of their desire for rebellion prevention.

This is where the question posed by Machiavelli is applicable. Is it better as a ruler to be feared or loved? While Machiavelli considers fear to be the better option, there is room for disagreement. It is an important note that the general will of a people, provided that they are of a significant number, eventually will trump their oppressors. Therefore if a ruler has aligned himself with the general will and subsequently loved then peace will be maintained. For this argument a contrast must be made however between foreign and domestic rulers. As we have seen, domestic rulers are usually warmly received until they begin making mistakes, while foreign rulers of colonies are often hated even when concessions of the people are addressed. The American Revolution provides a good example in this case. This war, originally a fight for representation and not independence, was sparked by what is seen today as a tax that was monetarily insignificant. While the taxation without representation argument explains the explosion of this uprising, a general loathe of any foreign rule which is hard to express with the limits of language was the builder of internal pressure.

As America requested the aid of France, so the Estonians beseeched the Swedish. Their help came too late however and at the battle of Sõjamäe the popular army, composed of many peasants, was demolished. The Teutonic Order continued to increase their power over significant sections of European land.

Although the ever-changing circumstances of world politics demand new and innovative ideas, a consideration of past responses can also lead to resolution of problems. Due to this fact the modern classification of politics centered around the dynamic liberal and conservative scale is absurd. It is nearly impossible to find man who is purely for or against change, which is the implication of the classification. While conservative on constitutional theory, I believe that many modern social problems require change and am therefore a liberal by definition.

One man who modelled himself after a previous government's successes while addressing current issues was Cola di Rienzi. Although he possessed little knowledge concerning the importance of localized rule, he was still a very intelligent man despite humble beginnings. Gaining much of his knowledge and language from ancient Rome, he yearned for days like those of the Republic. In addition to his focus on the old world, he also was aware of modern problems facing the land in modern-day Italy. Some of these issues dealt with the grievances of common people against their nobles. One of these nobles had killed Cola's brother without any noticeable repercussions for his actions. In addition to this some of the women of the region were being raped and abused by the rulers' sons. When the leader of the nobles, Stephan Colonna, was absent, the followers of Cola declared a new beginning for the old Roman Republic. Although he was a great speaker, Cola proved to be a relatively weak and inexperienced leader. Taking money from the Roman Catholic Church caused him to lose religious favor and he was eventually excommunicated by the Pope with the charges of rebellion, heresy, and sacrilege. In addition to this the strong defenders of this second attempt at partially representative government were beginning to be irritated by Cola's actions. His extravagant spending style and consequently the higher taxes began to wear on the common people.

After an attack by Count of Peperino, Cola was captured and put in prison. The power of the nobles returned and so did the previous offenses. Cola escaped, but he was arrested again and given to the papacy. They, in turn, released him, and he went back to cause more trouble for the nobles. He tried to revive his old reign but it lasted less than half a year. While fighting in a skirmish, Cola was once again captured by the nobles. This time, they did not give him a chance at escape. First he was hung and stabbed. Then his body was burned and eaten by dogs. Despite the fact that he was not respected in his death, his efforts are now recognized by many in modernity. His views on political theory were advanced for the primitive medieval time he lived in and he was a strong voice for the common people of Rome. Although he was one of the best of his time, government still kept revolving.

Many times in social encounters, one wrong done by a party will be avenged by another more heinous act. Although this occurs neither party concurs that they have done anything wrong. From the pen of Jean Froissart an account is written about the peasant uprising called the Jacquerie. Although known for being an impartial historian, it is obvious that he takes the knights' side and does not bother to mention the reason that the peasants were fighting. Instead he dismisses their cause by saying that each one was following the actions of the others and had no personal provocation. The peasants may have had a cause, but its purpose was tainted by their egregious actions. While the instances of rape and murder are bad enough, many more atrocities were committed. One of the worst examples comes from a group of peasants who captured a knight with his wife and children. After roasting the knight over the fire in plain view of his family, they proceeded to successively rape the mother. Then they tried to make the family eat their father's flesh. Lastly they viciously murdered the wife and her children. There were other cases involving large amounts of violent deaths and even one where the rebels killed a pregnant lady. This they all did without guidance or leadership. It seemed that while they had a cause, which was killing all of those with noble birth, they did not have a practical plan for execution. This is just one example of how every movement must always have a form of leadership under a common cause. To succeed and implement the needed changes today, unification must be maintained until reforms are created that nullify this necessity.

The peasants were not united by any leader or realistic goal and therefore were put down in a couple of weeks. This sad and disturbing excuse for a rebellion was partially dealt with by Count of Foix. After a decisive victory in favor of the knights, a major peasant stronghold was burned and the rebels were routed. Some died by fire, not being able to flee from the burning city. In addition to this thousands died by the sword while others were drowned in a river. This finale only emphasizes the point that unity is key even if discussing a non-violent rebellion.

The Mongols, who were previously mentioned when dealing with the Anatolian Peninsula, had also taken over much of China and established a capital in modern-day Beijing. Although they had created a strong presence, a group of peasants was able to rebel and become victorious. Zhu Yuanzhang was hailed as ruler of China and it was he who established Beijing as a Chinese capital. Like Cola di Rienzi, he looked to the past for certain modern solutions. Imitating in part the Tang and Song Dynasties, Emperor Hongwu, as Zhu Yuanzhang was called after attaining power, made many reforms in the Ming Dynasty that he created. In addition to creating a more favorable tax code, he also incentivised the farming of previously mismanaged land. Overall his policies helped both the people and the economy. His empire would endure for nearly three centuries until it was replaced by the Qing Dynasty. Trouble was soon to follow in England.

There is a group of people in America today who claim that jobs and careers are "wage slavery" and that there bosses are "feudal lords". Their beliefs are not justified but there is a modern lesson from medieval serfdom. While these people complain about a system based on paper money, they miss the true backing. Some method of payment is required in all economic systems because people are naturally going to demand a reward for their work when there is no exertion or threat of force. A traditional economy where people are almost wholly self-sufficient eliminates the need for a currency, but does not allow society to follow the path of progress which leads to greater job diversity. While there are problems that need to be dealt with in a progressing society, such as pollution and overpopulation, there are also advantages. Increased options and happiness counter the downsides to prosperity. Although equalization through a primitive state is not practical or desirable, a modern system which controls people's amount of land and wealth are legitimate. Bans on monopolies and manors have already been active in America for quite some time. According to the Social Contract written by Jean-Jacques Rousseau, the modern idea of private property and possessions which are not based on anarchal strength owes its very existence to society. Therefore it can be inferred that society can regulate their distribution, but an incentive should be created for hard work and superior intelligence.

Although all of this political theory would be foreign to English peasants in 1381, the natural inclination for freedom guided society forward. The actual feudal lords had gained their land and power through personal strength and not the general will. This unjust system which served only a select few based on heredity was eventually dismantled by the people that it oppressed. Tired of pretentious nobles freeloading off of their miserable life, the peasants and other subjugated groups revolted. Over-taxation and a sense of value, which came from the decrease in the labor force as a result of the Black Death, were two immediate causes. Unlike the Jacquerie, the English rebels were more realistic and had a unifying cause and leader. After mass tax evasion by the general population, the government tried to enforce the same tax again. Eventually the people were pushed to the edge and began to rebel. The will of the people was at odds with the strength of the king and the immediate result of this rebellion was defeat.

When the government is in conflict with the people, it becomes the responsibility of the people to overthrow the shackles of tyranny. This predicament is extremely common in monarchical and dictatorial powers because they rule through personal strength and not the strength of the people. Due to this fact it is important to limit the government's power. It is also important however that a nation's government is strong enough to defend itself from foreign threats. The solution to this difficult balance will be discussed later. Although there were many reasons why the peasants revolted, there were also certain beliefs that held them back. The historian John

Froissart said, "The evil-disposed in these districts began to rise, saying, they were too severely oppressed; that at the beginning of the world there were no slaves, and that no one ought to be treated as such, unless he had committed treason against his lord, as Lucifer had done against God; but they had done no such thing, for they were neither angels nor spirits, but men formed after the same likeness with their lords, who treated them as beasts. This they would not longer bear, but had determined to be free, and if they labored or did any other works for their lords, they would be paid for it."

Many in the lower class at that time did not want to suppress the belief that their overly powerful leaders were divinely appointed. Although this was true for a while, religious beliefs as they relate to government evolved to the point where in the early United States it became the common belief that God protected liberty and supported representation. This dynamic between religion and politics continues to change and today it is believed by many that the belief in a deity is no longer necessary to support government.

Eventually the peasants overcame their presuppositions and revolted. It began in 1381 at Kent and Essex after the general population drove tax collectors from the cities. After this, certain goals were verbalized. Unlike the Jacquerie, the English peasants did not simply kill authoritarians out of anger, but set up a system of rebellion with the ultimate goal of the end to serfdom. After taking forts and points of interest, an oath was taken by defeated nobles. In addition to this documents, which tied peasants down to the manor, were destroyed and those in debtors' prison were released.
A leader, Wat Tyler, was chosen from within their ranks as the revolt continued. After a great degree of success, it was decided to attack London. There they found a great deal of support and were successful in battle. Although the people had expressed desired reforms in government, they still believed in the legitimacy of the throne. This proved to be their most apparent weakness. After gaining the domineering position within the city, King Richard agreed to some of the rebels' conditions. A meeting was planned between Wat Tyler and King Richard to discuss other concerns. Although Tyler had the utmost respect and trust in the king, he was betrayed by him. First the rebel leader was stabbed and his neck was

severed. Then the news broke of their leader's death and the crowds scattered. More of the rebel leaders were executed and the rebellion fell short of attaining any of its goals. It seems that this group of peasants was far too dependent on Tyler's leadership and without him they were far from what could be considered a cohesive group. This failure was followed by many more.

The creation of the Timurid Empire was a short-lived favor of large government to small. Regional rulers were subjugated and either demoted to local regent under royal power or removed and replaced by relatives of the emperor. In this account, the problems with regional rule become apparent. Although it is more tailored to the needs of the people, it leads to a great degree of fighting and instability in government. Strong leaders or established empires tend to exploit their weak state as can be seen through the example of the Roman defeat of the Grecian city-states. This also became true in the Middle East where nomadic tribes and individual cities were conquered, unified, and then separated. Then, for a short time, a great deal of the region was ruled by one man named Tamerlane. With the humble beginning of being a robbing bandit, he gained a following. After participating in a Mongol invasion of the region, he was rewarded with command over land around the city of Samarqand. From there he went to conquer the rest of the area which constituted Transoxiana. His empire was established and he ruled partially through the personally perpetuated perception that he was from the lineage of the great Genghis Khan. While he held control over Iraq and Transoxiana, he also invaded India and parts of Russia. His execution of plans and skill set were amazing but after his death, the empire fell.

Although history was slowly advancing towards the popularity of popular government, for a rebellion to be successful it often needed to be headed by royal blood. Without this leadership many people doubted whether their cause was supported by God. In the case of the Welsh Rebellion headed by Owain Glyndŵr this was not a problem. Tracing his lineage back to two royal families in Wales, the people were not hesitant in their decision to follow. Even though he is considered a hero by many for the cause of freedom, his military record was tainted. Fighting with Richard II of England in his war against Scotland, it may seem hypocritical to speak grandly about the importance of liberty. This was not considered by the Welsh people and after a brief battle with Reginald de Grey of Ruthin the skirmish developed into a full-scale war. The skirmish had been caused by an unfair judiciary headed by the English king who showed favoritism to personal associates. At first the rebels were successful in defeating the English forces through the use of guerilla units and fortunate weather. The English came back however with greater fury. The French, who have been England's historical rival, had previously supported Owain but began to seek peace. Although Owain was a strong independent leader, he was defeated without foreign support. He was never reported to have been captured but his movement slowly dissolved.

As balancing a scale takes some back and forth movement, the history of rebellions is filled with conflict until an equilibrium is reached. After the original goal of independence was reached, it has become quite common among the former rebels to attempt to deprive other sovereigns of their rights. Greed and need for resources caused these hypocritical actions Although this practice has become less common in recent times. It can't be seen with the United States' support of Latin American independence, but has persisted with the example of the Mexican War. In this situation the dictator, Antonio López de Santa Anna was supported by the US government in exchange for the promise of land. Still, these examples are now more of a rarity in modernity while older occurrences abound.

One of these older examples is the establishment of the Lê Dynasty. This revolution occurred in Vietnam after much popular hesitation which was caused by an ideology introduced by their Chinese conquerors. Although there are various obvious hindrances to mobilizing a people to fight and possibly die, the teachings of Confucius, which were then deeply rooted, taught about ruler's having the mandate of heaven. As mentioned earlier connecting a dynasty to divinity or even claiming that the ruler was a god created a greater loyalty to the government. To convince the people to rebel, Le Loi had to convince the general population that the Ming Dynasty of China had lost the mandate. Although this was quite a task, it was eventually accomplished and the many people risked their lives for an independent government.

This shows the natural opposition to change that can be seen even today. While conservatives often complain about the liberals lack of respect for tradition and liberals berate their belligerent brethren for living in the past. Both separate spectrums are necessary for healthy solutions. This situation is paralleled by the dynamic of millennials versus people of earlier generations. While the young people are generally prone to the adventure of change, the elderly serve as a necessary filter on unwise and blinded actions. As with all legitimate discontentment which surfaces and consolidates, this rebellion avoided large-scale disapproval by the people. For ten years fighting took place, until the rebel forces finally were successful in definitively deterring and defeating the Chinese. This was accomplished after the center of Chinese power in Vietnam, which was located in modern-day Hanoi, fell to the rebels. Although certain conquerors have been characterized by cruelty, Le Loi showed civility by allowing and even aiding surrendering soldiers in their return to their Chinese homeland.

Although this instance is looked upon with favor through the passage of time and the lens of modernity, later rulers in this dynasty were not so advanced in their social interactions and resorted to the guide of their primitive inclinations. As with many states of the time, the newly freed leaders of the people were far too eager to become an empire. Although they fell short of the domineering title of empire, a later leader named Lê Thánh Tông defeated the city of Vijaya and therefore the land of Champa. Although the control of the Le Dynasty continued for a time, it eventually collapsed. It is said by some historians that the demise of the dynasty was partially blamed on the power of the local governments. While this may be true, the power of local governments must be protected. A system of government should not be set up so that the most power naturally ascends to the top. Rather, like the atmosphere, every higher layer should aid in the stability of the lower layers. The constitution and social constructions should safeguard against the natural inclination of people to increase their control. This principle can not only be seen through ancient conquest but also through modern interactions.

While the authors of the Federalist Papers considered the attachment of the people to the more local governments as a strong enough bulwark against the rise of the power in the national government, the introduction of advanced communication technology has created a greater connection between those of lesser ideological difference rather than those of lesser physical distance. This change in society can be used as a positive tool but currently the full potential of these devices has not been utilized due to the lack of correct social arrangement. Usually those with similar circumstances and abilities group together to form homologous local groups. This does not form an argument for white nativists however, although it may seem at first that it does. The racial tension in the United States today comes not because of integration but because that integration has not been thorough enough. For pure and complete integration to occur it must be uncoerced and must originate within the hearts of the people. This causes the need for integration to be local matter although state and federal restrictions must be present to protect minority communities. Local and communal integration is pure, due to the fact that instead of different groups living together separately, the people join each other blend as a society. Although this is only a short preview, this issue will be discussed further in a later chapter.

Whatever the underlying causes of disunity, the most apparent instigation of the Vietnamese Divided Period was the rebellion of the Le dynasty's general Mạc Đăng Dung. This new ruler suffered the rise of various rebellious movements, the most influential being the reinstatement of the Le rulers through the power of Nguyễn Kim. Kim was succeeded by his son-in-law while his own son, Nguyễn Hoàng fled to the south. The kingdom that was started by Kim conquered the kingdom of Mac in the north while Hoang took over the south. Although the borders changed slightly, this is the beginning of the North and South Vietnam dynamic which continued until the dismal failure known as the Vietnam War. This and other modern wars will be discussed while plans to avoid future conflicts from being magnified by larger states.

As with many rebellions, the Hussite Wars were motivated by attempted control of religious movements which should be marked by political fluidity. Hindrances to religious freedom had been very common in the Catholic Church during the Dark Ages of Europe. Many reformers were imprisoned and died for their beliefs at the hands of the church. Although the Dark Ages receives its name for many reasons, the lack of genuine political theory probably contributed. The intermingling between the church and the state was appalling. While keeping the people from knowledge and learning, the popes often exercised much power over the life of common people. The ideas of religious liberty and freedom of speech which have now become staples of civilized society would have been mocked. Although this is true those who attempted reforms to the Catholic Church did so for religious reasons and did not always respect liberty either.

Whatever the case may be, the Catholic Church splintered in part through the work of an early reformer in the modern-day Czech Republic named Jan Hus who was influenced by John Wycliffe, the English translator of the Bible. This reformer hoped to make communion more communal while also undermining the power of the priest by attempting to abolish traditional confessions and saying that common people could interact with God personally. Although his ideas persisted, he died a horrible death for not denying them. As with the leadership of the English Peasant Revolt, Jan Hus had far too much trust in the authorities which opposed him. After receiving a message from church officials that he would be given a chance to defend his beliefs before a council and that he would also be given safety by the church, Hus headed for Constance. This proved to be a false promise however and he was thrown in jail on arrival. Later he attempted to defend himself but he was eventually burned at the stake.

Followers of Hus from eastern Europe, more specifically Bohemia, proclaimed Hus to be a martyr and began a rebellion against Emperor Sigismund of the Holy Roman Empire. A leader named Jan Zizka was chosen for his brilliance while the Catholics searched for support. To gain help for a crusade against the Hussites, as they were called, Pope Martin V and the emperor called upon the states in Germany. Although Catholic at the time, these people had little interest in waging a war against the Hussites. Due to this fact, many evaded both taxes and military service. The mood in this region quickly changed however when the rebels foolishly invaded parts of Germany. Although the pope began to gain more support in Germany, the Catholic forces continued to suffer defeats at the hands of Zizka. Using his revolutionary military tactics, Zizka once defeated a force of over seven times his number of men. After being demolished at the Battle of Taus, the Catholic forces changed up their strategy. After trying force, the emperor set up negotiations with the majority of the Hussites. He did not deal with the more radical Taborites who desired even more reforms. The more radical fringes of the Hussites were quickly defeated without support from its base. Some of the reforms of the moderate branch which were accepted included a certain degree of social and religious freedom in Czech lands, the sole appointment of Czech people for office in their lands, and the ability of commoners to participate in communion. Although these reforms were solid, they were of no importance when the Hapsburg Dynasty took over the region after Emperor Sigismund died. While at odds with the Holy Roman Empire, this dynasty too was a Catholic institution.

Although it is seen that to become a noteworthy rebel, the procurement of a great number of the general population is necessary, there seems to always be a group who is loyal to the established government whatever the former grievances may have been. This is seen in the rebellion of the American colonists against Great Britain through the actions of the Tories, but also further back in Jack Cade's rebellion in England. Although he had a great number of men and a list of grievances against the king, many did not support him. He did not help his case through some of his vicious acts which became extremely unpopular. Finally it was decided that when Cade came back from one of his almost nightly raids, the citizens would lock him out of his conquered city because of his horrible acts. The plan worked and Jack Cade was again on the run. Although this is true, he still had some of his fighting men. To deal with this fact, those high in English society granted indemnity to deserters from the rebel army. In addition to this a reward was granted for anyone who brought the body of this bandit to London. Although it took some time, his dead body was eventually brought in and hung from the London Bridge as was customary. This example implicates the necessity of general popularity in cases of rebellion, whether solely political or also militaristic.

Another example of a failed rebellion came from the land of England in 1497 AD. Although there are similarities, this latter example did not fail due to the desertion of troops. While trying to manage financing for wars against Scotland, King Henry VII decided to raise taxes in England. The region of Cornwall rebelled due to the fact that this ordinance was in conflict with the law. Although not as popular as the move for Scottish independence, certain groups in Cornwall are calling for an autonomous government today despite the fact that it is smaller than the state of Rhode Island. The leaders of the old rebellion, Michael Joseph and Thomas Flamank, summoned the aid of Lord Audley. Despite the fact that they had the support of a noble, the many angry countrymen who had insufficient weaponry were no match for the disciplined English army of around ten thousand. After this major defeat, the rebel commanders were captured and executed while the resistance slowly died.

While the Catholic Church of the Dark Ages was notorious for its acts against fellow Christians, many atrocities were also committed against those who aligned themselves with Islam and Judaism. Today, there is a debate about the "rightful" possessors of Spanish lands due to the fact that it had been conquered by the Muslims from the more original inhabitants. Either way, the actions of the Catholics in that era are indelible. The question of "rightful" ownership is seen through this example, and it also becomes apparent in the more expansive conquest of America by the Europeans. Although ideally this land would have been left to the natives, the undertaking to completely rid these continents of the effects of the invasion is absurd. In addition to the fact that mass deportation would be economically disastrous and literally impossible to administer with any sort of morality and fairness. The fact that many Central and South American countries are composed of a majority of Mestizos, people with a mix of Native American and European blood, adds to the futility of theoretical transfer. While the sorting of people is possible but ill-advised, the sorting of genetics is an absurdity. If this theoretical allocation of land to original inhabitants was imposed internationally the result would either be an overpopulated Europe or mass genocide. Certain radicals would claim that this be a just consequence for European acts of injustice, but it must be remembered by the more considerate members of civilization that these injustices were committed in the past and therefore by people who no longer exist. Disputes about who can trace their inheritance back the furthest are unsolvable due to the immense passage of time, and if a way to trace human existence accurately to every square mile, it would be found that most of the land originally was inhabited by no one. After human population spread across the world, the land was taken and lost successively by various tribes and people groups. Therefore, it becomes imperative that instead of reminiscing and longing for "the good old days," humans join together and choose a humane and logical approach to the problems of minorities in various countries. This problem and others will be discussed further later in this book.

Whatever your beliefs are concerning the rightful inhabitants of Spain at the time, it is obvious that the final outcome was still based upon principles of strength and not good government. In addition to good government, basic morality was thrown out during the Dark Ages. This is seen through the example of Catholic violation of the Treaty of Granada. After the establishment of Ferdinand V and Isabella as rulers in Spain following the Granada War, the surrendering people needed the promise of some protective measures. These included the protection of Moorish culture which included the Islamic faith. During the reign of Cardinal Cisneros these measures were thrown out due to the fact that the Muslim inhabitants held no weight in the government that wished to control them. Without the staple of good government which guarantees that rulers be similar to the ruled so that they are able to sympathize with their circumstances, the Christian government searched to subjugate the Muslims. This is evident through their various actions which included forced conversion of both people and buildings: Muslims to Christians and Mosques to Cathedrals. In addition to this forced baptisms were occurring while important Arabic texts were burned publicly.

Although the concepts of freedom of speech and the fluid transfer of ideology were not popular at the time, these actions obviously induced the anger of the Muslim inhabitants of Spain. Due to these injustices the First Rebellion of the Alpujarras commenced. While this movement garnered support from the suppressed subjects in Spain, in the end it's only accomplishment was the death of one of Cardinal Cisneros' agents. Despite this success, the repercussions of their actions overshadowed the victory.

Persecution of the Muslim inhabitants intensified. Although this punishment was meant to be a show of power by the Catholics, the Muslims refused to be subjugated that easily. Due to this fact, the Second Rebellion of the Alpujarras began for the same reason as the first. Although religious intolerance was the general cause of both, the more immediate instigation of the second was an ordinance by King Phillip II. While inhibiting the use of very common Islamic practices, the king also began to enforce an unpopular ban on the Arabic language. The second rebellion was a noble attempt at independence, but the end result was the same as the first. A ruler from Austria, Don Jon, was ruthless in his victory against the Moorish Muslims. After needlessly murdering two thousand and five hundred people, this ruler and others after him contemplated the logistics of a relocation of the Muslim population. Although it took some time, through the work church and political leaders alike, expulsion based on religion eventually occurred. The numbers of displaced persons are discussed by historians today with some estimates exceeding a half million.

This was a significant portion of the whole population of Spain and brings up some disturbing facts about the government of the time in much of Europe. While the state of politics at the time was decided by the power of individuals and not the consent of the masses, looking back on history from the advantageous view of modernity can help society propel forward by recognizing the pattern of mistakes. In this case it is important to notice the absurd amount of absolute power which had been absorbed by a sect of the population. The Catholics had formed such a strong connection throughout Europe in the church that even a rebellion by a significant portion of the population of one country could be easily quelled by members of different countries. This and other examples similar to it form a hysteria around powerful countries and especially the idea of global governance. Opinions like this are not baseless fears but rather are formed through intelligent analysis of past circumstances. Illustrating this point is simplified through present examples.

While the Chinese government has a relatively good handle on the principle of regional power, its federal government is detestable. In addition to this, the overly excessive power of the

Republican and Democratic parties in the United States can be seen as a major inconvenience to change and a hinderance to conforming government to the will of the people. However this two party system is far more advanced than the federal government in China presently. Although more parties, and therefore political options, are advisable, the discussion of a rational means of obtaining this objective will be discussed later. Currently however, the two party system serves certain functions even if in mediocrity. One of the most important advantages of any multi-party system is the fact that the conflicting groups tend to check the power of their opponents. In the United States, with a relatively even split in ideology and a strong constitution the citizens need not worry about one group having absolute control. However this is not the case in China where the whole region is governed by the Communist Party of China. Although this is true, the Chinese constitution did install a certain degree of power separation despite the fact that the legislative branch nominates the leader of the executive. In addition to these facts, changing the government is nearly impossible due to the harsh control of the people by the reigning party. Freedom of speech is not respected by the government because of their desire for conformity within the country. Another example comes from Russia where the president has no term limits and is not sufficiently checked by any other institutions. These more primitive forms of government and the path to change will be discussed in greater detail in a more appropriate section.

While the continents of Europe, Asia, and Africa have been the main focus thus far due to the fact that these places had been the epicenter of civilization, North and South America now come into the light. The general consensus of modern anthropologists is that the first creatures classified as homo sapiens developed in or near eastern Africa. From this point they spread across the world. Over time the Africans spread and settled also on the continent Australia where they are now known as the Aborigine people. From eastern Asia people migrated to the Americas where they remained relatively isolated. From northern regions of modern day Alaska and Canada, where natives including the group known as the Inuits live, the migrants slowly spread south. Settlers were slightly disturbed in eastern Canada by a brief incursion by Europeans, possibly by the men of Leif Erickson from Iceland. After the natives quickly destroyed this settlement, foreign threats were ended for quite some time. Although tribal warfare existed as it did in western Europe until the rise of the Roman Empire, the original American way of life was not threatened until European expeditions in the fifteenth century.

Today it is thought of as having minimal influence in the world, but the country of Spain was once at the forefront of exploration and colonization. This can be seen through their support of the Italian explorer Christopher Columbus and through the conquistador Hernan Cortes. The latter of these two men instigated rebellion in both senses of the word. Cortes not only fought a rebellion against a Spanish commander but also forced a Aztec rebellion through his unfavorable rule.

The story began when Cortes travelled from Spain to Hispaniola, the second largest island in the Caribbean, which had been previously rediscovered by Columbus. Although this is true, the real adventure began when Cortes joined Diego Velasquez in his attempts to conquer Cuba, the largest island in the Caribbean. This they accomplished, but it was hardly a feat due to the fact that the indigenous peoples in Cuba were far less advanced in terms of weaponry. Thinking in terms of fame, one would assume that a man who played an influential role in conquering the largest island in the Caribbean would be remembered for these actions. Even so, it was after this role that he participated in a scheme so grand that it overshadowed his previous accomplishments. After spending some time in Cuba, Cortez became anxious for more adventure and glory. This is when Velasquez was asked by Cortez if he would be supported in an attempted conquest of Mexico. To this Velasquez consented and the famed conquistador began his journey. Landing on the Yucatan Peninsula, the Spaniards immediately made contact with a hostile native tribe. This tribe, however, was not a major force in the region, and therefore this defeat was deemed relatively unimportant militarily. Despite this fact, Cortes' crew obtained a translator from the skirmish.

Sailing west from the peninsula, Cortes landed at the city of Veracruz and defied Velasquez by declaring himself to be under the direct command of the King of Spain. Although many Native

American groups today are praised for their peace and oneness with nature, it is seen that in politics they were still relatively primitive. This fact is not demeaning to the natives due to the fact that even though European government was changing, the men of that continent also had not figured out the general principles of good government. The differences between these two groups perfectly illustrate the current conundrum of modern government. The more tribal tradition of the natives was more suited to the people's preferences but was prone to internal conflicts. The European model had the potential to lessen fighting but was inconsiderate of the general public. It is said that it had the potential because conflict in Europe was still extremely common due to divides in the church and crusades against other religious groups. In addition to this, small conflicts were able to escalate very quickly into large-scale wars which led to increased death. For this reason I believe that the Native American system was better, but also that the European system was doomed to dominate due to advancements in weaponry and a larger population. The question of federalism which has been posed and also that of immigration will be discussed later.

So after Veracruz, Cortes began to search for the key player in Mexican power. This he found in the Aztecs and he began to plan his course of action. After gaining an ally in the tribe of Tlaxcalans, Cortes headed towards the capital of the Aztecs in Tenochtitlan. Instead of being met with an warring group of natives, the Spaniards were welcomed as honored guests. Although this may seem strange, a prophesy from the Aztec religion said that their god, Quetzalcoatl, was preparing to return. The pale skin of the Spaniards confused the Aztecs and their trust in superstition proved to be fatal. Entering the city with an escort, the European invaders quickly took over the city. The leader of the tribe, Montezuma, was spared but no longer held any true power. This is when the succession of rebellion began. First, Velasquez sent a force from Cuba to quell the rebellious actions of the new leader of Mexico. Cortes left the city and defeated the Spanish force sent by Velasquez. While he was gone however, the Aztecs had regrouped and began a rebellion of their own. To regain the lost territory, Cortes again attacked Tenochtitlan and once again took the city due to the spread of smallpox amongst the natives. These and other incursions formed long European campaigns against the natives which eventually led to the complete conquest of North and South America. This brief journey to the story of New World rebellion is followed by a return to Europe.

As with many revolts, Kett's rebellion was only appreciated long after its end. Although two of its leaders were brutally executed by being hung, now plaques are located around the rebel's homeland honoring their deeds. The rebellion was named after brothers Robert and William Kent who became somewhat unexpected leaders. The main cause of the insurrection was a general discontentment with wealthy and influential men closing off sections of common lands. It is odd, therefore, that Robert had previously been tried in court for that very offense. Another wealthy landowner named John Flowerdew was being threatened by a mob, which had formed from a segment of the population that was dissatisfied with the closing of common lands and had the intent of tearing down his fences. Previously, Flowerdew had made enemies with Robert by proposing the destruction of a local abbey. To deflect the angry masses, Flowerdew reminded the crowd of the offenses committed by Robert. For this reason, the mob scurried to the Ketts' and demanded compensation. Instead of disregarding the mob, Robert decided to become its leaders. It is still not known to this day what happened to change Robert's mind. A few of the proposed theories include the intimidation of the mob, a sort of revenge plot on Flowerdew, or maybe even a sincere connection with the pleading of the common people.

After becoming the mob's leaders, Robert quickly wanted to change the rag-tag bunch into a unified resistance to arrogance of the nobility. After the meeting at the new leader's residence, the group reconvened at a place called Robert's Oak. It is here that you will find one of the aforementioned plaques, praising the spirit of rebellion. Also here, people come to remember the inspiring words from Robert which served to give the rebels a sense of hope and identity: "I refuse not to sacrifice my substance, yea my very life itself, so highly do I esteem the cause in which we are engaged." If the leader of the rebellion which had so much to lose was willing to fight, the commoners would gladly unite around him. The first major success was the capture of the city of Norwich. Due to the great threat the rebellion now posed, an army was raised from Suffolk,

London, and Essex to deal with the Ketts' army. This proved to be a successful plan by the English and the rebellion was quickly quelled. The two rebel leaders were captured and hung as a reminder against future rebellions.

It was seen through the former example of a Welsh rebellion that many times people who should have had no troubles uniting under a common enemy, fail to consolidate. This can be seen again through the example of Native Americans. Many tribes allied themselves with European groups for revenge on their enemies, but it is now seen that while tribal differences were divisive, the rule of white men was destructive. Eventually it did not matter to the European subjugators whether or not a tribe had been previously friendly to them or not. All Native Americans were grouped into one category while their land was slowly taken, and their religion and culture forcibly destroyed.

The beginning stages of this common occurrence can be seen through the example of the Acaxee Revolt. In this case, Jesuit missionaries had infiltrated the region and were beginning to force what they considered a superior culture on the natives. Along with taking away their religion, the Spanish dictated how the natives dressed and cut the long locks of hair which came to symbolize freedom and resistance to European occupation. The natives of that region united under the leadership of Perico who promised salvation from the invaders. However, this did not come to pass. The Spaniards with the help of several different native tribes, were the final victors. After killing only around fifty settlers, the rebellion's leaders were executed and many of its participants were sold into slavery. Enslavement of the natives was a relatively common until the practice of importing Africans became more cost-effective. Now the current largest country in the world will be discussed.

The country of Russia is a great anomaly for some people today. While it is not nearly as densely populated, this large country now holds approximately three times the amount of land that had been possessed by the Roman Empire at its height. Although much of its land is still considered relatively worthless, the feat is still awe inspiring. While the most noteworthy threat to Russia was the German attacks in World War II, there was a string of domestic insurrections that developed in the seventeenth and eighteenth centuries. One of the larger examples is that of Bolotnikov's Rebellion which began in 1606 AD. The underlying causes included a previous war which had weakened Russia and a severe famine. In the capital of Moscow alone, over one hundred thousand people died due to lack of sufficient food supplies. In addition to this, a man called False Dmitry rose to the throne under the pretense that he was the true son of Ivan the Terrible. His reign lasted only a short while however and he was promptly assassinated. Replacing him was Vassiliy Shuysky who ruled during the rebellion. With the support of close to two hundred thousand men from around seventy separate cities, Bolotnikov marched on Moscow. A couple battles were won against the established government but the czar finally was successful through the help of hired commanders taken from the rebellion. Although the rebellion still captured the city of Tula after this loss, it eventually ended. Its leader, Bolotnikov, was captured and died the old-fashioned Russian death of being forcibly drowned in icy water.

Peasant rebellions were relatively common in Russia and feudal Europe but they also occurred in other parts of the world. The accounts of Africa and Asia are often excluded from the works of American histories due to the fact that the foundation of the United States is based mainly on principles and people coming from Europe. Although this is true, the spirit of liberty is transcendental across all religious, racial, ethnic, and political groups and an accurate account will be given of the significant struggles of these groups towards freedom. One such struggle called the Shimabara Rebellion occurred in Japan and started in 1637 AD. While it is relatively well known in terms of rebellions, there are very few reliable primary sources from the time. Even with this fact, certain things can be extrapolated from the available information. In the past it was thought that the rebellion had a more religious origin. Although these claims come directly from the the pens of people who lived during that era, it can be seen that there viewpoint came largely from bias. Both the rebel leaders and the established government preferred this narrative. While the rebels, some of whom had been persecuted by the government for their Christian faith, wanted the commoners to unite around a cause greater than themselves, the Japanese government wanted to hide one of the main causes. While some of the leaders were fighting against religious persecution, it is now believed that a majority of the peasant resentment came from an overbearing tax load. Although this is true, the immediate instigator is widely believed to be a murder by a local government official. Discontent centered around the region of the Shimabara Peninsula, where it is estimated that around half of the whole population participated, although it spread to the islands of Amakusa as well.

While their causes were very different, the condition of the peasant fighters can be compared to that of the Confederate army in the American Civil War. A general ammunition deficiency and sometimes severe malnutrition among the troops plagued both rebel armies. Although this similarity exists, it seems that the Confederate army was more fortunate in terms of adequate leadership. The legend of the Shimabara leader Masuda Shiro is largely believed to be fabricated and the realistic stories surrounding him if true do not prove advanced tactical analysis or military prowess. Contrast this with the combative genius and discipline of Robert E. Lee, who instigated a linear succession of victories and was complemented by greats such as Thomas "Stonewall" Jackson and cavalry commander J.E.B. Stuart, and it facilitates the formulation of understanding. While the beginning of the rebellion accomplished the holding of almost the entire peninsula, this success did not last for long. The government forces eventually caught up with the resistance and painstakingly captured the stronghold at the Castle of Hara. Although its end result was failure, this rebellion proves the inherent diversity of the independent spirit.

Through the ages, very few conflicts have become more confusing than the English Civil War. Although an internal conflict, certain external factors further complicated the issue. As with the Shimabara Rebellion, there were certain religious factors. The English Parliament was Protestant and suspected King Charles I of sympathizing with or even being a Catholic, partially due to his marriage with a Spanish woman. The religious factor will not be focused on however due to the importance of the politics. Even though many great political thinkers have come from England, most notably John Locke, at this time the country was still vastly controlled by the sometimes wavering and unstable personality of hereditary monarchs. King Charles I did not look upon Parliament favorably and hardly ever called it into session. This changed however when wars with Spain and Scotland drained the treasury. After King Charles turned to Parliament for funds, this branch of government was determined to created reforms. These reforms were consolidated into a document called The Grand Remonstrance. Although it sought to increase the power of Parliament, it passed only by a slight margin. The king considered this an act of defiance and had warrants for several leaders including John Pym. He and others had already fled however and were being protected by the people of London.

      After these events, the army split, some choosing to follow the "divinely appointed" king and others joining the Parliamentary ranks. The fighting went back and forth with no clear victor so Parliament employed the help of the Scots in the fight. In the ensuing battles, a man named Oliver Cromwell proved himself to be a serious threat to the royal forces. The fighting continued for awhile but ended when the Scottish army captured King Charles and handed him over to Parliament. With an extreme amount of power at their fingertips, the leaders of Parliament only proposed relatively moderate reforms. After commanding the army to disperse, Cromwell refused. A coup had begun and the army now demanded that certain members of Parliament be arrested. The army arrived in London and a fierce debate occurred about not only this particular situation but also political theory in general. In this fierce discussion, now known as the Putney Debates, the very foundation of civilization was questioned rather Socratically. Although an insignificant amount of the total gathering, the Diggers proposed a total restructuring of society. Not only did they promote the abolition of private property but also that of present government itself. Their ideas of communal lands and others will be discussed later but their questioning of fundamental principles of government and society showed real progress.

      Another group which would no longer be deemed radically liberal was silenced by Cromwell for advocating the freedom to think differently, the annual election of Parliament, and the voting right of every non-poor man. Despite the grand potential of the meeting, nothing of importance came from it due to the fact that the only noticeable outcome was increase of Cromwell's influence. Eventually King Charles was executed by vote of Parliament although he would be replaced by one with even more unchecked power. Acting largely as a king, Cromwell both dealt with internal disunity and foreign affairs very decisively. Dissenters were executed while the attempt of Charles II to fight with the Scots to take England was thwarted. Parliament was dispersed by Cromwell and he became what he called "Lord Protectorate," but what historians would call a dictator.

This fact illustrates the point that a rebellion must safeguard against the unwarranted usurpation of power. Although history is sometimes stained by names such as Julius Caesar and Oliver Cromwell, there are examples like Cincinnatus and George Washington that restore hope. Cromwell remains a relatively common term and is sometimes used as a political insult during mudslinging. People from both sides of the very limited United States' political spectrum sometimes use it to describe their opponents. It is sad that although the claims are exaggerated, both sides usually have at least partial truth in their argument. There no longer is any party which proposes the end to the unconstitutional actions by the federal government. This and other offenses of the party system will be discussed, but now back to the history.

Cromwell was a ruthless ruler and spent considerable sums on his many wars. Due to this fact when Charles II decided to return, large groups of Parliament sympathizers joined his ranks. After Charles was instated as king things went back to the way they were before the civil war. Although this persisted for a time, King James II tried to undermine Parliamentary authority and paid the price. After this tyrant was deposed, King William from Holland was invited to rule. This deal was beneficial for both sides because Parliament received more power and William gained an important cache of resources for war. Around this time the English Bill of Rights was drafted and politics on the British Isles continued to advance. On the Asian continent, however, things began to spiral in their continual change of dynasties.

The Ming Dynasty that had lasted in China for almost three hundred years was put to an end through a long series of unfortunate circumstances many of which were outside of the emperor's control.

Although the effect of the plague in Europe was far more drastic and memorable, it also spread throughout much of Asia. In addition to this, an environmental occurrence shortened the Chinese growing season. The situation became more severe with the ongoing feud between Japan which resulted in a drained treasury. As is often the case, the high aristocratic class did not bear much of the burden but rather it was placed on the lower peasant class. Although there were ideas such as Confucius' "divine mandate" that served as checks to constant rebellion; due to certain events, commoners were beginning to feel that it had been lost by the succession of Ming rulers. An earthquake hit the city of Xian which is estimated to be the deadliest in history with eight hundred thousand people killed. Compare this to the San Francisco earthquake in 1906 AD, which only killed around three thousand people and was declared one of the worst natural disasters in United States history.

In addition to this event two other severe earthquakes hit China and this coupled with the aforementioned environmental cooling furthered doubts among the general population. Eventually the starving and overtaxed peasants were avenged by a rebellion with the leadership of Li Zicheng. After this rebel placed pressure on the capital of Beijing and the Ming Emperor Chongzhen committed suicide, a famed Ming general named Wu Sangui was prepared to cede. Although the leaders of the revolt could almost taste victory, one from among their ranks still succeeded in messing up the almost guaranteed success. After a rebel took his concubine, General Sangui decided to seek revenge. Although not ideal, the general decided to hand over the kingdom to the Manchus by opening up the Great Wall of China. The Manchus, which composed a whole different ethnic group, ruled China for quite some time under the general discontent of the Han people. This only further illustrates the point that it is extremely difficult to rule such a large area of land and amount of people without advanced government and regional checks.

King Philip's War is the perfect story of revenge and betrayal. How an award-winning film has not been produced with its storyline is frankly surprising. Contrary to the general first impression, King Philip was not a European monarch, but rather a local native chief of the Wampanoag Tribe. The war began in

Plymouth Bay Colony after the first generation, which had been friendly with the natives, died out. The brother of King Philip, Wamsutta, was the reigning chief until he died after rough treatment by the colonists. This obviously was not popular with the natives and many united around Philip. While the movement quickly was depleted of food and other important resources, certain tribal members deserted and joined the colonial force. Without the complete support of the whole Wampanoag Tribe and no strong allies, the colonists under the command of Josiah Winslow defeated the rebels. The rebel leader was killed and the native people of that region were subjugated. Although not killed, those natives that had sided with the colonists were sometimes still deported or sold into slavery. The weak position of the natives and the increasing power of the European population started to become extremely apparent.

Although many of the accounts so far have been purely historical and ideological, Nathaniel Bacon's rebellion has several more direct applications for today. First, it teaches the need for a well-educated public. Although some founding fathers such as Thomas Jefferson saw this as a possible governmental objective for the states, it is now seen that their control in this area has been evidently negative. There are candidates such as Bernie Sanders who in the past have supported measures of the federal government to make public colleges and universities free but the many flaws in this proposed reform are relatively easy to see. In his past Sanders has gained some of his support by pandering to those who want more things provided by the government. As a way of justifying his proposed unconstitutional abuse of federal power, Sanders often misuses the term of "right." A right as determined by the U.S. Constitution and its predecessors is an often generalized concept that protects the people and smaller forms of government from larger ones. Although this is the original meaning, Sanders and other politicians distort this meaning by allowing it to encompass not only true rights, but also reforms which would give more power to the federal government. General social issues such as education and healthcare are no longer seen as services and this has killed competition. Making state colleges free would not only reduce competition by serving a major blow to private college attendance, but would also be anything but just, due to the fact that those who

choose to go to private college or a trade school would be paying for
those who opt for public education. While it can be now seen that it
is impossible to force a people to be educated, a new system will
later be discussed that would serve to protect against conscious
ignorance.

Whatever the case may be, ignorance by the colonists was
deadly in this example. The European colonists were as
unknowledgeable about the American natives as most modern
Americans are about the political situation in the Middle East.
Although there are more educational opportunities now and certain
safeguards in place, these did not exist to the same extent earlier and
the colonists suffered because of that fact. The dynamic between the
two rivals Governor Sir William Berkeley and Nathaniel Bacon is
extremely interesting to study. They actually were related through
Berkeley's marriage to one of Nathaniel's cousins and although
friendly at first, soon they acquired the now stereotypical in-law
relationship. After Nathaniel's father sent his son to the "New
World" because of his arrogance, Berkeley offered him a place in the
government of Virginia. Differences of opinion quickly emerged
with Nathaniel taking the side of a large percentage of the common
people. Even though the common people are often seen as the
oppressed, it is seen in the case of the South in the American Civil
War and this example that they can also hold the position of
oppressor simultaneously.

As with the end of the Ming Dynasty in China, hard times
and natural disasters ushered in the Bacon Rebellion. Economic
problems were accompanied by a series of hurricanes. In addition to
this precipitation seemed to come sparsely or in access without a
middle ground while hail tore up crops. With colonial frustration on
the rise, a scapegoat was found, as it usually is, in a weaker group. In
the case of Nazi Germany this group was the Jews, but in this
example it became the vastly overly generalized Native Americans.
The Doeg Tribe was unhappy with the apparent absence of payment
from a settler named Thomas Matthews and conducted a raid in
which several of their tribesmen were killed. To make matters worse
a rowdy group of settlers created a revenge plot against the natives
but attacked the wrong tribe. Although Berkeley's absence of true
authority, due to the fact that he was appointed by an overly

powerful king who was not responsive to the will of the people and had a general apathy towards the native causes, he was more informed and correct than Bacon. The Bacon Rebellion is sometimes praised for certain aspects such as its fight against an English ruler but more is now known about it. There were certain reforms that he accepted to gain support of people like the voting rights of all freemen, but his main focus was his attacks on the natives. After Bacon attacked a couple groups of friendly natives and burned Jamestown, he died of lice and flux. His name would be remembered until today while Governor Berkeley would be relieved of his position and sail back to England. The rebel in this case fought largely for power and not popular ideology.

Although it often becomes difficult to apply largely Western principles to the change of Eastern and Middle Eastern governments, the spirit of rebellion is universal when people are pressured into precarious situations. The series of rebellions which led to the end of the Safavid Dynasty and the reign of Shah Solṭān-Ḥosayn form, as usual, a story of dissatisfied people bringing about change. Despite this fact, the increasing effects of globalization are also easy to see. While rebellion against absolute rulers is basically inevitable, inept rulers only serve to increase the rate of change. The shah mentioned earlier was anything but a brilliant commander. As a Shiite leader, he began the institution of the more radical religious reforms of Moḥammad-Bāqer Majlesi. In addition to a statewide ban on alcohol, the Zoroastrian, Hindu, and Sunni population began to be discriminated against. This came partly from the mismanagement of more local rulers which only served to exacerbate the negative inclination to Shiite rule. After more unpopular policies and inactions by the shah, the dynasty hastened to its end.

Members of the military began stealing from the people while the shah continued to spend their money on extravagant purchases such as a "pleasure garden." Finally after more than a decade of rule, things began to break down for the shah. After several cities were attacked and the land around them taken, a more serious problem surfaced, and the shah's mismanagement of it brought his dynasty down. A governor under the Safavids named Gorgin Khan suppressed a rebellion by capturing its leader, Mir Ways. The prisoner was sent to the capital and somehow convinced the shah that Gorgin Khan was in the wrong. Due to this fact, Mir Ways was released. After he was out of prison he murdered Gorgin and took over command of that region. He and his son ruled officially for some time. During this time they attempted to take more Safavid land while an Afghan group infiltrated the country. This group was finally successful in taking the dynasty's capital of Isfahan and they became the major power. During this turbulent time however, the Russians and Ottomans took advantage of the situation. Fighting amongst themselves and with other more local rulers, they eventually divided up much of the region for themselves. This point emphasizes the importance of a stabilized revolution which proves to be impossible under absolute authority.

It seems like a simple enough concept but rebellion is often preceded by war. The definition of war in this case is a conflict between two established governments. Although there are various examples of this concept, the aftermath of the French and Indian War is a more simple one. In contrast with a general misconception of ill-educated Americans, this war was not fought between the French colonists and natives but rather was a contest between the French with their Native American allies, and the English. The war will not be focused on due to the fact that it is not a rebellion, but the victory of the English caused a sort of political revolution. After the French defeat, almost all of their territory, including much of modern-day Canada, was taken through the Treaty of Paris. Although this was extremely humiliating, the country was allowed to keep its holdings on the western side of Hispaniola. This war quickly had both immediate and long lasting effects. The more lasting effects include a whole redirection of world history while the immediate effects include Pontiac's Rebellion. This insurrection was caused by native resentment concerning the loss of French rule which had been friendly to them. Although there has been a thorough history of rebellions from native tribes in America, this one stands above the rest. Instead of single tribes attacking European forts, this example shows various tribes cooperating against a common enemy, thus illustrating a modern political concept.

When election time comes closer, both major parties in the modern United States experience a large move towards party unification. This can be seen in 2016 when the hesitation of many

Republicans voting for Donald Trump and the resistance of Sander's supporters turned into the convention speeches involving party propaganda. Although it has been demonstrated earlier that unification is a beneficial concept, it must be against a common enemy. In today's case the enemy is not the Democratic nominee or the Republican nominee, but the two party system that only allows for those less than ideal choices. During the 2016 presidential race, both major party candidates practiced in mudslinging. Businessman Donald Trump was called irresponsible and irrational by his rival while he called Clinton "crooked Hillary." Surprisingly, in this case, both politicians were correct. Citizens of the United States will soon have an opportunity not to unite over the old orthodox system which has remained unimproved for years but rather a new version of politics that can produce a broad spectrum of possibilities. A full plan of execution will be discussed later but now back to the rebellion.

Although five different tribes corroborated, the main one was the Ottawa which were led by Chief Pontiac. Sandusky, the only garrison in Ohio, was only guarded by thirteen men and was easily conquered. Two English colonels were sent to subdue the natives and were successful for the most part. Most of the rebellious tribes surrendered due to the lack of food and ammunition but Pontiac's tribe persisted until 1766 AD. This defeat was a major advancement in the complete subjugation of the natives and it continues into today.

The change of government often brings about a change in names, whether that be of cities or natural landmarks. This principle can be seen through the example of the failed protection of South Vietnam. After the North Vietnamese were successful in taking the South Vietnamese capital of Saigon, it was renamed Ho Chi Minh City after the northern leader. In the case of Pugachev's Rebellion, Catherine II of Russia renamed both a city and a river after the insurrection was quelled. The hometown of the leader was renamed Potemkinskaya from its original name of Zimoveyskay while an important river was given the name Ural. Although the rebellion was eventually quelled, the increasing amount of popular disturbances shows the problems of overly large governments. In the decade leading up to the rebellion, it is said that over one hundred and fifty disturbances occurred. These were nothing when compared to the real threat of Pugachev's Rebellion. In this case, the modern "happily ever after" fairytale storyline was not followed. Pugachev was believed to be Peter the Great's relative, although this is now known to be historically false, and was supported by a very diverse group of people. His ideals of religious freedom were strongly countered by Catherine II's belief in government control of that institution. After several victories including against Major General Vasily Kar, the rebels began to suffer defeats. Colonel Ivan Ivanovich Mikhelson was more successful and the rebellion was quelled. As was the norm, after Pugachev's capture he was executed in Moscow.

I don't know what you have thought so far, but this book has been severely depressing for me. The extreme magnitude of failed rebellions with just causes is disheartening, to say the least. Through the period of recent rebellions, the destruction of the traditional tribal government can be seen. Although there were certain advances such as the Magna Carta, the English Bill of Rights, and a great degree of independence for Scotland, most of the world was not making much progress. The power of government increased in much of the East, not out of the people's will, but out of an increasing power of individual rulers and aristocratic groups. These would later form the countries of China, Saudi Arabia, and Russia that still require a revolution. World-wide reforms are needed to encourage freedom of speech and a system of peaceful exchange in government.

In continental America things were quickly worsening. The fact that the influence of Britain spread to the "New World" had many beneficial side effects including the establishment of the United States, but the treatment of the natives was truly appalling. Their previous system of government may not have been as "advanced" by modern Westernized terms, but it allowed for a harmonious relationship with nature and provided for the needs of all inhabitants. Whatever the case may be, European victory was inevitable. The white invasion was bound to happen once Europe became more populated and powerful. In the beginning Leif Erickson's mission from Iceland was a dismal failure due to native resistance, but at this time the conflict was nothing more than a relatively weak Viking tribe without contact and communication with their homeland against the better established Native American population. Europe began to grow at a faster rate, and as fluids naturally move to an area of lower concentration through diffusion, so Europeans moved to the more open and available lands of America. Their military advancements and weapon upgrades coupled with important Asian inventions such as gunpowder placed the settlers at a high advantage.

Certain governmental principles can be extrapolated from this past situation. First, that hindrances to the free flow of immigrants is sometimes necessary. This is contrary to the ideological lyrics of "Imagine" by John Lennon: "Imagine there's no heaven. It's easy if you try. No hell below us, above us only sky. Imagine all the people, living for today. Imagine there's no countries. It isn't hard to do. Nothing to kill or die for and no religion, too." In fact the only theoretical place where such a system could be implemented is heaven whose existence was contested in the song. No matter how evolved human social interactions become, it seems that evil is bound to follow in some form and protection against this will always be sought after. As the natives had reason to be wary of white settlers threat to their society, so modern societies need some sort of protection and an immigration policy.

Debate about how strict or lenient limitations will be should be discussed openly without fear of derogatory titles such as "libcom" or "xenophobe." Although impractical and racist people can be found in today's parties, these are fringe movements and not a just representation of those involved. Secondly, this brings up the points of conservation and the threat of overpopulation. While many support the former, the latter is of scoffed at and control over it is feared. Naturally, conservation is being threatened by the simple principle that people will never be inclined to living in cramped spaces when deforestation provides more room and is incentivized by monetary gain. While the free market can be utilized as a useful vehicle of betterment for society, it must be remembered that the people hold the true power. An example of a pure free market flaw is the hypothetical of a factory on the river. This factory provides both negatives and positives to the community. The jobs it creates and the system it participates in allows for more free time and therefore more scientific and philosophical advancements. The pursuit of knowledge has always been better suited to societies where survival is not the main objective but is taken largely for granted. While these many positives to private enterprise can be seen, this factory expelling toxic chemicals into the river and killing fish negatively impacts the enterprise of private fishermen. It is seen that without a government ruled by the people, these two groups would resort to war and other means to settle the conflict. With the general population, which has no vested interest in the conflict, a fair arbitration can be performed.

Thirdly, the white infiltration of America brings up the question of defense; both governmental and individual. The natives had a system that was more helpful than has been let on by many historians. While it did not aid in expelling the foreign European attackers, its internal checks were outstanding. In this world where advancements in weaponry did not pass the status of primitive hunting tools, a government could not function without the will of majority, due to the fact that the people were equally as strong as those who governed them. Internal conflicts between warring tribes never amounted to dangerous and deadly wars that involved whole continents. However the introduction of more deadly weaponry caused a change in the balance of power. The Second Amendment served to maintain this equilibrium but has run into certain problems in the last centuries. Due to globalization and dangerous advancements, many people find themselves longing for the simplicity of the well balanced system of pre-Columbian America. Whatever the case may be, society will continue to search for knowledge, therefore rendering a reversion back to those simplistic times of global ignorance impossible. Although this is the case, a plan will later be established in this book that deals with the changing world. This will be done with a detailed analysis of the problems possessed by both systems but also the benefits of each. Whatever one's personal beliefs may be, colonization marked a whole new chapter in the sphere of government.

Chapter 3: Modern Revolutions

Millennia of political history have built up to what was to become one of the greatest experiments of all time. Questions existed worldwide about whether a people could be self-governed without the help of a "divinely appointed" family or ruler. This question was coupled with the questions of great free thinking minds such as those of Charles de Montesquieu. In his book, Spirit of the Laws, Montesquieu states: "It is natural for a republic to have only a small territory; otherwise it cannot long subsist. In an extensive republic there are men of large fortunes, and consequently of less moderation; there are trusts too considerable to be placed in any single subject; he has interests of his own; he soon begins to think that he may be happy and glorious, by oppressing his fellow-citizens; and that he may raise himself to grandeur on the ruins of his country." The founding fathers addressed these two problems and others by calling on the works of men from the Age of Enlightenment. With these great minds as guides for their work, America's greatest men created what Montesquieu later described in his book as a Confederate Republic. This form of government addresses the two problems of protecting against internal and external threats as Montesquieu explains: "If a republic be small, it is destroyed by a foreign force; if it be large, it is ruined by an internal imperfection. To this twofold inconvenience democracies and aristocracies are equally liable, whether they be good or bad. The evil is in the very thing itself, and no form can redress it. It is, therefore, very probable that mankind would have been, at length, obliged to live constantly under the government of a single person, had they not contrived a kind of constitution that has all the internal advantages of a republican, together with the external force of a monarchical, government. I mean a confederate republic." With great minds at the helm and the free spirits propelling politics forward, the American Revolution had all the needed factors to become a successful endeavor with meaningful change. Government would never be the same.

Due partially to oversimplification by those in the United States, the American Revolution is largely misunderstood. The beginnings of the revolution were not an immediate attempt at independence from a wholly corrupt and liberty hating empire. Instead, rational people on both sides sought reconciliation. Lord North's policies of subjugating the colonies were contested not only by Edmund Burke from the House of Commons, but also by the Duke of Richmond who stated: "You may spread fire, sword and desolation, but that will not be government. No people can ever be made to submit to a form of government they say they will not receive." In addition to this Benjamin Franklin was considered to be more of a moderate until his unfriendly conversations with British officials radicalized him.

This discussion was initiated after the Britain's Parliament passed the vastly unpopular Coercive Acts. These created a strong control of the colonial economy, including an enforcement of exclusive trade with Britain while also forcing Americans to quarter soldiers. Although the latter problem was dealt with through the Third Amendment in the United States' Bill of Rights, the former present more of a problem. The Constitution of 1778 gave the power of restricting trade between the states to the federal government, but the main difference between that and the British control of America is the fact that the people are now represented more fairly. In this case, it becomes difficult to explain the modern territories of Puerto Rico, American Samoa, and the U.S. Virgin Islands. However, the apparent hypocrisy can be cleared up with the fact that if these territories truly desired to be free, U.S. military resistance would be extremely unlikely.

Whatever the case may be, the point is that a majority of American colonists did not primarily desire freedom, but only to be treated with the status British citizens. For this reason, the Declaration of Rights was created by the First Continental Congress for the purpose of listing the offenses of the established government. The vast majority of people still hoped for peace but Massachusetts was soon fighting with radicals such as John Hancock and Samuel Adams at the lead. With their leadership, the physical fight began at Lexington and Concord. Although Massachusetts was a major instigator, the states were already largely united against a common enemy. When British ships blockaded Boston as punishment, both northern and southern states sent food as support. In addition to this once fighting broke out, the message was sent and received warmly. Paul Revere aided in this task and soon enough a large militia of minute men were marching.

Even before the Declaration of Independence was signed, the Second Continental Congress began to deal with foreign affairs. This governing body of America would later negotiate an alliance with

France but began by speaking with Native American leaders. An interesting fact about these meetings is that a Fourteenth colony composed of natives was proposed. However, this was never acted upon and the United States would eventually expel natives from almost all of their lands. Whatever the case may be, the war continued but the colonial armies were still loyal to King George III of Great Britain. Due to this fact, the Olive Branch Petition written by John Dickinson was sent to but immediately rejected by the king. The odd connection that remained between the "united colonies" and the power hungry government of Britain is extremely difficult to comprehend through the lenses of modernity. It can be seen however that there was still a strong tie culturally, and the fact that they would be pioneers was sometimes frightening. Despite these psychological hindrances, independence was finally chosen in part through the work of Thomas Paine in Common Sense. Many states began to declare independence from Great Britain before the Declaration of Independence was written, revised, and ratified.

Now it became the responsibility of General George Washington to unify the army. Mutinies and resistance to men from other states occurred but Washington implemented discipline appropriately. In many histories the state of British unity is not discussed. Enlistment was often a weak attempt due to the fact that many Brits also shared the connection mentioned earlier and the use of German mercenaries became increasingly common. These would later prove to be ineffective in the Battle of Trenton.
Although the recruitment of foreigners often harmed the British cause, natives of France, Poland, and Prussia all aided in the American cause. The difference largely lies in the motivations of both groups. While those on the British side fought solely for the high pay and therefore were not willing to risk their lives, the foreigners who fought for Washington were motivated by glory and the ideals of freedom, both of which transcend death. Baron Friedrich Wilhelm Von Steuben from Prussia was instrumental in the disciplining of troops and was partially successful in his emphasis concerning the importance of army issued bayonets for close combat. In addition to this important addition, Marquis de Lafayette was praised by General Washington for his contributions to the early American cause.

The war continued and the Battle of Trenton proved to be a pivotal victory for Washington. Often times in war, overall victory can be procured without great skill through the inaction of an opponent. Washington, now considered by many a military genius, obviously had skills but was aided by the cautious personality of General Howe of the British command. Many aspects of Howe's demeanor can be seen throughout history, including many northern generals in the American Civil War. Before the rise of Ulysses Grant, many commanders such as George McClellan were plagued with indecision and often shied away from fully engaging the enemy forces. Although Grant was criticized by many in the north for high death rates, the loyal states could replenish relatively easily and he is now remembered as a great leader.

Whatever the case may be, General Howe was eventually replaced by Sir Henry Clinton, who was hopefully going to be more successful. While the war raged on in the New World, the political scene in the Old World became just as important. The British after years of fighting were finally willing to cede to the demands of the colonists. In addition to the coercive acts being repealed, the only power that would be held by Britain over the colonies in the proposed treaty would be the right to conduct foreign and military policy. This concession was too late however due to the fact that an alliance had been struck between the United States and France through the brilliant work of Benjamin Franklin. He had established in France the fear of a reconciliation between the rebels and Britain and the United States, and gained the pivotal support of the established French Navy. Despite this important ally, defeat was becoming common for the rebels. The city of Charleston was taken and the attempt of Horatio Gates to reconquer the Carolinas was met with overwhelming defeat. In addition to this, Benedict Arnold, who was severely underappreciated, especially when it came to his victories at the First and Second Battles of Freeman's Farm, decided to desert and join the British ranks. America's most famous traitor decided to give West Point to the British and even though his plan was foiled, the British still gained an impressive military commander. Arnold later became successful and defeated the Virginian capital of Richmond.

Eventually, through the help of the French at Yorktown, the English began to negotiate a treaty. One was finally signed recognizing the independence of the "Thirteen United States" and a great republic was born. Although the principles of the nation still needed to be discussed, their government was now free and independent. This feat would lead the way for other American nations to fight for freedom from their European masters and change the history of government forever. Despite this enthusiastic and patriotic attitude, it must be remembered that while government was advanced, society for a time regressed with the oppression of the native people and the acquisition of their land.

Back from the huge success of the American Revolution, we return to the less successful revolutions that are often dismal failures despite the good intentions of both the leaders and the people. The United States policy of the Monroe Doctrine that was later adopted served to aid in continental America's independence from European subjugation. In addition to this great and successful leaders rose up like Simon Bolivar who possessed the independent spirit. However, both of these benefits were not awarded upon the Tupac Amaru Rebellion which proved to be unworthy of the distinguished historical name of "revolution."

This rebellion had a great potential due to the fact that it was fought by native Incas and could, therefore, provide the indigenous Americans a true homeland once again. Tupac Amaru II respected the Roman Catholic Church and like the early "united colonies" claimed to fight in the name of the subjugator, in this case, the Spanish King. The local authorities took care of the insurrection relatively quickly however and many of the leaders were captured. Both Tupac Amaru and his wife were dragged behind horses. After this, they were forced to witness the death of family members and friends before it was their turn. After his wife's tongue was cut off and she was strangled to death, Tupac was cruelly tortured. After this ordeal, he was beheaded in front of his young son. With this, the rebellion was pretty much quelled although fighting continued for some time. The story ends sadly but it was not forgotten. Now the rebellion's leaders are honored in South America with the men who later actually obtained independence for different colonies.

After some hesitation, Shay's rebellion has been included in this historical account although it was no more than a skirmish militarily with little more than ten people killed. The rebels were quickly dispersed and their leader Daniel Shays, who previously had fought in the colonial army, fled to the territory of Vermont.

The insurrection started when poor farmers were placed in jail after they were unable to pay state taxes. Hard economic times after the American Revolution fell especially hard on the poorer class in Massachusetts. In this situation, it is important to see the perspective of all involved. This was different from many of the previous rebellions because it occurred against a republican form of government. While this might be considered odd, a popular government can still have defects. A rumor was spread that those in the large cities of Massachusetts were attempting to acquire rural lands through the imprisonment of the poor and this further encouraged the rebels. While this was the perspective of the rebels, many in the federal government were frightened by their actions. Their overreaction was contrasted with Thomas Jefferson who upon hearing the news of the rebellion from Paris stated: "A little rebellion now and then is a good thing; the tree of liberty must be refreshed from time to time with the blood of patriots and tyrants. It is its natural manure."

One of the most applicable and irritating opinions was from the old Tories who pretentiously viewed this event. As with many revolutions, it may take awhile for the economy to adjust to the change of conditions. Also, many of the Tories failed to acknowledge the vast quantity of historical revolutions in absolute governments and constitutional monarchies. They saw the event as a failure of the new government. In many ways, this assessment of the situation was just, but it was a failure of the current application and not republican government. The rebels were treated kindly, with most of the leaders pardoned, but the question that they and the people involved in the War of the Regulation in North Carolina brought to the surface would permanently change the United States. This event caused a convention which would end the reign of the Articles of Confederation in favor of the modern U.S. Constitution.

With the obvious success of the newly created republic in America, certain nations attempted to follow suit. The free thinking of many Frenchmen would not allow the rule of absolutism for very long. While the system of nobility and peasantry was not popular with the rebels, it proves to be an important lesson for modern society. First, it provides support for the importance of property limits and the dissolution of monopolies. In governments based on strength and not the intellect of population, the government is itself a monopoly. It holds power through fear and has no true authority. While today private property and enterprise has provided an effective means of governing the economy and building wealth, it also is a social enigma. A theoretical pure capitalistic society would not work for the majority of the population because wealth would be continually passed down through the same families and it would be close to impossible to get a foothold in the market without knowing the right people. However, through a popular government's control of the economy, ideally innovation and not family connections prevail. In addition to this, different levels of the global community have the ability to control natural resources such as lakes and streams from pollution, which is inevitable when wealth is the sole objective.

Secondly, the nobles provide a primitive example of the need for separation of powers between different governmental levels. Even if a king was considered an absolute ruler, the nobles checked his power. Popular power is usually needed for meaningful revolution, but nobles also provided a check on national power. Whatever the case may be, the French were overtaxed, partially from their support of the American Revolution, and were tired of the present monarchy.

Although many of the reforms were needed, the rebels did not have strong enough checks on power and soon a different type of absolute ruler took over. In addition to this, some radical revolutionaries began to hinder free speech by punishing religious people instead of focusing on protesting the overly powerful Roman Catholic Church. With the motivations of a hate for multiple overly powerful institutions including the church, manorial lords, and monarchical government, thoughts began to boil over into revolution.

After certain groups refused to pay taxes, the king called into order the Estates-General. The three groups that composed this assembly were the clergy, nobles, and commoners. The commoners, also known as the Third Estate, formed a revolutionary group that was joined by some members of the other two estates with the intent of writing a constitution. The National Assembly, as they now called themselves, was forced to meet on a tennis court. Their response to the King Louis XVI's messenger has remained legendary: "Go tell your master that we are here by the will of the people, and that we shall be removed only at the point of the bayonet." In addition to burning manorial documents, a famous prison named the Bastille in Paris was destroyed. The rebellion held a great degree of potential after the constitution was created which abolished the entire feudal system and severely limited the king. In addition to this, the Declaration of the Rights of Man provided the freedom of expression and reformed the tax system.

After these great successes, however, the revolution fell apart. Instead of freedom being the main player, the guillotine took over. The king was the first to be killed but his death was within reason. Problems and wars with other European monarchies quickly began and executive leader needed to be chosen. Sadly Maximilien Robespierre was chosen and he quickly became a dictator similar with Oliver Cromwell of the English Civil War. Mass amounts of executions were performed with the guillotine often without proper trial. After Robespierre was arrested and sent to the guillotine, more problems arose and Napoleon Bonaparte became the dictator. This revolution that held so much potential at the beginning soon fell due to the French dependence on greedy leaders.

Slave rebellions often accomplish little more than killing masters and instilling fear. This was not the case with the Haitian Revolution. In this conflict, the second recognized nation in North and South America was created by a group of slaves which many considered more "primitive." Despite the obvious moral and political high ground of the rebels, support from the U.S. was extremely wavering and nonexistent at times. During both the Washington and Jefferson, the United States was either not involved or was a supporter of the white colonists. John Adams supported the rebel leader, Toussaint Louverture, for a time due partially to his antislavery sentiments. Although it was one of the most profitable colonies for France and in America, the leaders of the French

Revolution mentioned earlier supported it for a time as a way to control sympathizers of the king.

After the British attempted to take the Hispaniola for themselves, Louverture submitted to French rule under Napoleon and became the colonial governor. The ministry in France began to believe that the governor was becoming too powerful and captured him in an attempt to reestablish slavery. While he died in a French jail, new leaders took his place. The once slave colony finally gained its independence with the help of Jean-Jacques Dessalines. The country was split after his death but slavery was ended. Although it did not create a republic, the Haitian Revolution proved that a people's desire for freedom transcends race and that the principles of many great Age of Enlightenment thinkers were not inventions but discoveries. This also provides an example of the disunity of the movement of freedom in the eighteenth and early nineteenth centuries. Today, disunity is not an option.

Religious persecution has persisted from earlier times until today in China. Today, horrifying accounts are coming out of China in concern to their organ harvesting programs. It has been alleged that so-called "prisoners of conscious" are being held in camps and then executed for their organs. Their bodies are incinerated after the process is done. The stark comparison between this and Nazi Germany is appalling. Former Canadian Member of Parliament, David Kilgour, with David Matas, conducted an investigation in 2006 and found that the practice is likely occurring. This practice is one of the most horrible modern stories of violence and it needs to be addressed by political leaders around the world. The harvesting of organs is not only horrible due to the fact that it monetizes and gives an incentive for execution, but also because the vast majority of the executed are imprisoned because of the expression of their religious beliefs. This assault on human rights needs to be met with resistance. Although this example is horrifying, persecution has been going on for quite some time in China. In 1796 a rebellion broke out due to religious persecution. The White Lotus Rebellion, which is named after a religious movement that encompasses Falun Gong, fought against the Qing Dynasty's policies. Although it continued into the nineteenth century, the rebellion was quelled through harshness. This rebellion may have failed, but their cause must continue and be applied to the current Falun Gong crisis.

If a person studies history for long enough, patterns begin to emerge. One such pattern is the power of addictive substances. The Opium Wars in China and the Whiskey Rebellion in the early United States are two examples of this. Although there were other motivations involved such as an aversion to taxes, the point still stands. Another case of this pattern in history is the Rum Rebellion. This was not a fight about the legality of rum consumption but rather an attempt by wealthy citizens of New South Wales in Australia to gain more power over the colonial governor. It started when the land grants of John Macarthur, who had become rich through the sale of rum, were contested by the new governor, William Bligh. George Johnston, the commander of the militia in the colony took Macarthur's side and had the governor arrested. For a time this persisted and the governor was shipped back to England. Lachlan Macquarie was then sent to be the new governor and trials for the rebels took place. Nobody was executed but their previously honored titles were stripped. Macarthur proved to be a rebel without a sufficient cause and was defeated without one.

This type of power would again be seen in leaders such as Al Capone. While Capone's murderous deeds needed to be accounted for, the system that allowed him to rise to power also needs to be destroyed. Prohibition on a federal or even a state level is absurd. A punishment for those who risk other's lives should be established, but a certain level of personal freedom must be maintained. This system of banning alcohol only served to create gangs and increase violence. While this is considered a historical fact, the Drug War in America still persists. Does it not have the same consequences as the Prohibition? Drug raids and the militarization of the police has decreased both freedom and security. A large incarceration of nonviolent criminals is disturbing and is being paid for by taxpayers. While state restrictions on child abuse should remain, adults using drugs with other adults affects no one outside of that group. The need for reform will be discussed later.

The countries of Venezuela, Colombia, Ecuador, Perú, and Bolivia all have a common story for independence. One man, Simon Bolivar, led all of these countries against Spanish colonial rule. As with many modern revolutionaries, Bolivar was influenced by many works from the Age of Enlightenment. Before war broke out, Napoleon Bonaparte was establishing himself as ruler of France. Bolivar, as an idealist, saw this as an offense to the originally sound principles of the French Revolution. Soon these two contrasting leaders would be fighting against one another to see what type of government would rule the continent of South America. After Bonaparte was successful in his homeland, he took over the country of Spain. This served to convince some who were still loyal to the Spanish throne, to join the rebellion. The Spanish, now under the control of Napoleon's brother, successfully repelled any attacks by Bolivar.

After the original line of kings returned, however, there was some success. Many attempts and defeats had not discouraged the young idealist, and Bolivar decided to attempt a daring feat. The comparison between Bolivar and General George Washington is already apparent but it is aided by the battle for Bogotá. Much like Washington crossing the Delaware River to attack Trenton in the dead of winter, Bolivar started his journey across the Andes Mountains during the rainy season. Starvation and disease plagued the rebels but they were finally successful in their mission. The large tract of Gran Colombia, which includes much of northern South America and parts of Central America, was freed and his homeland of Venezuela was completely conquered after the Spanish defeat at Caracas. Peru was then taken and many of the large colonies which had gathered so much wealth for Spain were now prepared to provide for their own citizens. Eventually, disunion separated the large area of Gran Colombia into many of the nations in modern geography.

Many great cultures, for a time, are left without a national identity. After Roman conquest of Peloponnesus Peninsula, the Greek and more specifically the Athenian culture, survived, but was never protected by a specific nation or government. After the Roman Empire split and the Eastern side fell, most Greeks lived under Ottoman Turk control. One major problem that faced a bid for Greek independence, was their comfort and standard of living. The same problem, to a certain degree, faces the United States today. Famous comedian George Carlin once said, "Nobody questions things in this country anymore. Nobody questions things. Why? People are too fat and happy. People are way too (explicit) prosperous for their own good... Nobody wants to rock the boat. People have been bought off and silenced with gizmos and toys." This has a lot of truth to it. Local elections, which should be the most important, are now shrugged off. It seems that the only time a mass amount of people participate in politics is during the general presidential election.

As a counter to this conjecture, some might say that even federal level elections have lower turnout than should be expected. These political commentators are the same people who wear around their sticker which says "I voted" and urges the general public to do the same. If people are never involved in politics or discussion, why should they be encouraged to make an uninformed decision? Politicians and the system in which they are involved pander to the ignorant by creating a simple two choice option. In the new government, a system must be set in place to guard against the willfully ignorant.

Whatever the case may be, learned and cultured men made the Greeks reminisce about former glory. The question of nationalism that this poses will be answered at a more appropriate time. The planners of the militaristic revolution created three different fronts that began simultaneously in Istanbul, formerly Constantinople, the Peloponnesus Peninsula, and Moldavia with parts of modern day Romania.

The Great Powers, which included Russia, Germany, Austria, France, and Great Britain, were committed to a balance of power in Europe after their Congress of Vienna. They were wary of any revolution after Napoleon, but the fact that they were preoccupied elsewhere benefitted the Greek rebels. The peninsula was the only point of success, but even that did not gain much ground at first. Civil War broke out between the classes and the Great Powers contributed a limited military presence. The French, British, and Russian forces became more concerned however when the Ottomans struck a deal with their ruler in Egypt. Mehmet Ali, who ruled Egypt under Ottoman control, was encouraged to quell the rebellion in Greece by being offered all the land he conquered as compensation for his efforts. This was seen as intolerable and much of the Egyptian fleet was sunk. After this, Russia attacked the Ottoman

Turks and forced a treaty. Part of this agreement was a separate Germanic king who would rule Greece. Although a certain degree of independence from Islamic rule was nice for the Orthodox Greeks, the situation was still not ideal. A series of military coups caused political changes in favor of democratic and republican principles but instability continues to this day.

Different revolutions are doomed before they even begin. This is evident from the example of Denmark Vesey's slave rebellion. This highly intelligent and educated former slave organized a large resistance, but was quickly defeated through betrayal and lack of communication. After a couple members were arrested, the date of the planned insurrection was changed but was not communicated with the thousands of potential participants. In addition to this, several slaves snitched due to the fact that they did not want to participate in the killing of masters. These people gave authorities Vesey's name and he was arrested and executed. This ended one of the shortest rebellions to date.

Although native resistance is often focused on as it relates to the Americas, the Aborigine people of Australia also were involved in various rebellions to protect their land and culture. The Bathurst War, which was fought between the Wiradjuri people and the British Empire, has recently stirred up controversy after protesters desecrated a monument honoring imperial troops. While the importance of the monument as a historical marker is important, the anger of people is reasonable. Like the Native Americans, the different Aboriginal groups are now only allotted a small fraction of land which was once ruled by their leaders.

Another interesting story to come out of resistance is from the Nangoon people. After killing several settlers, Yagan was forced to go into hiding. A young man named William Keates, who had been trusted by the native, shot and killed him for reward money. Yagan's head was severed from his body and the skin from his back was stripped for the tribal markings. Almost two centuries after the event, the remains were recovered from an unmarked grave in the United Kingdom and buried with the rest of his body in Western Australia. The different insurrections were noble but were doomed to fail because of weakness that can be partially attributed to disunity.

Without a significant threat or presence of force, nations are allowed to divide and diminish in size. This can be seen through the breakup of much of eastern Europe extremely recently. In addition to this, stability in western Europe during the balancing of powers in the nineteenth century allowed for the creation of Belgium. Without fear of invasion for the purpose of land acquisition, Belgium rebelled against the Netherlands. Before this, during the Congress of Vienna, these two regions had been united under the rule of King William I. Tensions began to rise due partially to economic reasons and the Dutch therefore began to occupy Brussels. This action unified the all Belgian parties against a common enemy and they were eventually successful. The provisional government that had served during the revolution was replaced with a more stable constitution that protected many cherished rights. In addition to this, it implemented Montesquieu's principle concerning separation of powers between the three branches of government: executive, legislative, and judicial. Due to its interesting past, the government had to account for the country's biculturalism. To this day, the northern region of Flanders with its Dutch culture continues to be united with the southern region of Wallonia and its French ties. It is said that civil war is unlikely, although there are obviously going to be some tensions.

The Texas Revolution is often both praised and vilified. While the revolution was not a pure cause due to the fact that it had ties to slavery and Anglo-American expansionism, neither explained the Mexican government's resistance. After the former colony of Mexico was freed from Spanish imperial rule, a debate ensued about what type of government should be created. Generally, the people who were involved are placed into three different groups: confederalists, federalists, and centralists. The confederalists believed in complete regional autonomy, the federalists believed in a separation of powers between the regional and national levels, and the centralists believed in no regional power. The two groups vying for regional power were split and defeated by the centralists who were led by Antonio Lopez de Santa Anna. This leader was also not a republican and therefore under his power, the original constitution was trashed.

Due to this dangerous usurpation of power, several different groups rebelled. The most successful group was the Texas Revolution. A declaration was printed outlining the causes of the conflict as an attempt to reinstate the constitution and make Texas an independent Mexican state, instead of a territory. Soon, however, it was evident that the people of Texas would be far more willing to risk their lives for a completely independent nation. Therefore, the Texas Declaration of Independence served as a more appropriate replacement. The opening paragraph states: "When a government has ceased to protect the lives, liberty and property of the people, from whom its legitimate powers are derived, and for the advancement of whose happiness it was instituted, and so far from being a guarantee for the enjoyment of those inestimable and inalienable rights, becomes an instrument in the hands of evil rulers for their oppression." Later after a lengthy list of offenses, a statement concerning the abolition of the Mexican government's power in Texas is made. Soon after this new declaration, two massacres served to further invigorate the cause.

Much like the insubordinate actions of Richard Ewell during the Battle of Gettysburg concerning Robert E. Lee's call for pursuit, which may have cost the Confederates both that Battle and the war, the commander of the fort at Goliad failed to follow Sam Houston's call for retreat. After this unfortunate decision, Mexican troops captured these men and under command of Santa Anna executed the majority of them. Many modern historians would liken the participation of the Mexican troops to the situation of slaves in the southern United States when certain masters forced one captive to whip another, but there is a key difference. The Mexican soldiers were involved in a previous decision in which they all chose to follow the leadership of a dictator. If the rule of such a government is accepted, one must be prepared for sporadic and irrational choices without the influence of law or tradition.

Around the same time, another massacre occurred at the Alamo fort. In this battle, prominent men such as James Bowie and Davy Crockett were killed. After the Mexican forces were successful, a similar decision by Santa Anna resulted in the death of most anyone who surrendered. The fame of the phrase "remember the Alamo" continued through the war and into modern times. Over time, many Texan commanders and soldiers lost patience with Sam Houston's plan of small attacks followed by retreat. Although this is true, it was eventually successful and culminated at the Battle of San Jacinto. It was here that Santa Anna dressed as a common soldier signed the Treaties of Velasco which ended the conflict. Eventually, the "Lone Star" nation would enter into a union with the United States which would be only shortly interrupted by their involvement in the American Civil War.

Sadly before times where principles of freedom of expression, assembly, and speech were widespread, new ideas were often introduced and spread by force. Therefore ideas were not judged by their merit, but by the strength and trickery of their followers. Although these principles spread through much of the world, in China they are still refuted by the Communist Party. The free spread of ideas is a firm basis of society which should be adopted universally. During the Qing Dynasty, the Christian Taiping Rebellion under leader Hong Xiuquan occurred and succeeded in obtaining about a third of China. Revolutionary reforms such as an abolition of private property, an end to slavery, and equality of women were accepted. With more equality came the end of footbinding within the controlled regions and the opening of administrative roles. In addition to this religious policies such as a ban on opium, tobacco, alcohol, prostitution, and polygamy were implemented. Teenagers were given an important role in society and even received land. Whatever the case may be, the rebellion eventually failed. The established Manchu Chinese forces looked for help from the Han through Zeng Guofan. This plan failed however and he began to rebel himself. Only through the combined forces of Europe and imperial China was the rebellion quelled.

Most people know the major events of one of the most important conflicts in modern times: The American Civil War. First, shots are fired at Fort Sumter. This was followed by the Battle of Bull Run. After a lot of victories on both sides, the Union soldiers take both Vicksburg and New Orleans securing the Mississippi. At the Battle of Chancellorsville, Confederate General Thomas Jackson is mortally wounded by one of his own men. The Confederate's had a major loss at Gettysburg which could have forced Lincoln into a treaty if the North was threatened. This was followed by the fall of

Richmond and Sherman's march to the sea. Finally, Lee surrendered at Appomattox with his rag-tag group of soldiers. This was an extremely shortened version of course, but the causes behind the Civil War are more important to discuss. Now some have argued that the South was fighting for state's rights and not slavery. While an argument could be made for previous abuse of the Constitution by the federal government, the South was really fighting for a state's right to continue slavery. The Texas Ordinance of Secession states: "Texas abandoned her separate national existence and consented to become one of the Confederated States to promote her welfare, insure domestic tranquility and secure more substantially the blessings of peace and liberty to her people. She was received into the confederacy with her own constitution under the guarantee of the federal constitution and the compact of annexation, that she should enjoy these blessings. She was received as a commonwealth holding, maintaining and protecting the institution known as negro slavery-- the servitude of the African to the white race within her limits--a relation that had existed from the first settlement of her wilderness by the white race, and which her people intended should exist in all future time."

Now, while the beginning of this declaration is a beautiful testament to sound principle, the last part can only be seen as an affront to Enlightenment thinkers. A second myth propelled by Confederate sympathizers is disbanded in the ordinance. While some might say that the institution of slavery might come to a peaceful conclusion, the above statement says otherwise. Men from the South had gone from believing that slavery was similar to holding a "wolf by the ear" like Thomas Jefferson to believing that it was an institution from God. Again we see the abuse of religion like it was used during the Middle Ages. However, the North was not a pure and holy fighter against slavery either. Several Northern slave states had remained loyal to the Union. It becomes difficult to fight against slavery while retaining a certain number of them. The Emancipation Proclamation did not come until over a year of fighting had taken place and it was protested by Northern factory owners. Around the Civil War time frame, the only group which promoted the untainted ideals of freedom were those who participated in slave revolts. In addition to this if the South had surrendered before the proclamation, slavery might have continued.

In a letter to Horace Greeley, Lincoln stated: "If I could save the Union without freeing any slave I would do it, and if I could save it by freeing all the slaves I would do it; and if I could save it by freeing some and leaving others alone I would also do that." Lincoln eventually turned against slavery only because "a house divided against itself cannot stand." It is seen that neither side was fighting for a pure cause, but the end result was beneficial. Although this is true, an ideological blow to federalism took place and that part needs to be recovered. No society should be able to forcibly hold members, but different levels of government lead to greater option and freedom if the principles are applied correctly.

Due to the great complicity of the situation, many wonder how such an event should have been handled with today's more advanced perspective. I say first that the pre-civil war Union had been protecting the evil institution. If the South was left to fend for its own, the hope would be that enough masters would be killed by slaves to instill fear upon the masses. It is seen If slavery persisted until today in an independent South, it would never leave due to the increase of national power and the subsequent aversion to war. Therefore an international alliance limiting the power of higher levels of government is needed. Another principle that is illustrated is the need for more limited large governments. Modern nations such as China and Russia do not follow this principle. Whatever the case may be, for all the things that could have gone wrong, the outcome of the American Civil War was relatively good.

Another very notable failed revolt is the Boxer Rebellion. It was crushed but the questions that it poses are very important. Many of the "Great Powers" mentioned earlier with the addition of the United States, Italy, and Japan had carved up the once great empire of China into spheres of influence. Through the influence of many of these countries, Christianity was spread throughout the territory. The Righteous and Harmonious Fists or Boxers wanted to return to a more orthodox culture. To accomplish this they raided different villages and harassed missionaries. Chinese government under the Manchurians did not hold much power but condemned the attacks. This changed however when the alliance of European powers and

Japan started to take different cities. The Chinese forces with the Boxers failed relatively quickly and proved some disturbing points. First, it proves the power of alliances. In addition to this, it highlights the need for a mechanism of cultural change. The fact that over three million square miles of land and the people within are supposed to share a common culture is absurd. This question will be further addressed at a more appropriate time. New problems began to rise now in the new countries of America.

Turbulent times struck Mexico after it gained its independence from Spain. Dictators usurped power and destroyed attempts at constitutional republics. Under these circumstances, creoles dominated social and economic life while poorer Mestizos suffered. The account highlights the importance of the masses control of lands and the economy. If an economy does not work for the general public then reforms must take place. Although this is true, the idea that this should always come from the federal level is absurd. A system where people can choose is best and that system must emphasize local power over everyday circumstances. While many times anarchy and monarchical control breed overwhelming inconsistencies, a misinformed republic can also create monopolies and a manorial economic system.

Whatever the case may be, a line of dictators tried to take power away from the general mestizo public but all would fail. After Porfirio Diaz resigned and the revolutionary Francisco Madero was assassinated. One of Diaz's relatives Victoriano Huerta tried to take power. After the United States had broken their trend of isolationism, they intervened and helped the revolution. Venustiano Carranza, then supported by the United States, started to sway from his promises of restoration. This necessitates a mechanism of punishment for those who abuse power and break promises. In the United States today a president holds all executive power, but has no clear check on his power except impeachment, which is now deemed impossible due to the partisan nature of politics. Anyway, General Álvaro Obregón rose to the position of president and unlike his predecessors, he did not wish to rule for life. Politics in Mexico had just made a large step forward.

The modern situation in China is completely disgraceful. After the Qing Dynasty was overthrown due to corruption and popular discontent, a republican system was implemented. The leader of this revolution was Sun Yat-sen and he spoke for many of the people's demands. Due to his system, the Han people were no longer subjugated by Manchurians. After his rule, however, more discontent grew. Economic problems arose similar to those before the Mexican Revolution. Instead of instituting meaningful reform under the newly created, the Chinese Communist Party hijacked the government. The general will always come to the surface in untainted republics without the aid of unwise measures. While many of the reforms were recommendable, they should have been instituted at a more local level. In addition to this if the reforms were truly representing the will of the people then closely monitoring the media should not be necessary. The principles represented in the first amendment need to be the basis of any modern culture. Without an open exchange of ideas, the people cannot be represented correctly. The social and economic systems of communism and socialism are still important to discuss today.

The rights of workers and the movement towards better wages has been recently introduced at a federal level by former presidential candidate Bernie Sanders. Through his work, his rival Hillary Clinton adopted many of his reforms. While his calls gained him a lot of millennial support, many did not agree with his stances. Many on the right and some on the left called him radical. While I do not believe that calling something radical is a legitimate argument, some are saying that his plans would be disastrous for the economy. While some believe that the goal would be worth the economic impact, others do not. This poses the question: What levels of government should have the most influence over the economy? Although local governments are a good option, during modern history they have held very little power and therefore cannot execute plans appropriately. In many states during the early twentieth century, the stability of the economy was emphasized to an extreme and strikes were prohibited or discouraged. In West Virginia, coal miners were harassed by their employers after walking off of the job. Peaceful protest did not seem to be possible. After men were shot by detectives before a trial began, tensions rose. Multiple deputies were shot, but the insurrection was quelled after President Harding sent in reinforcements.

In the first half of the twentieth century, Germany, China, and Ireland all created independent democratic systems of government. None of these accomplishments have been more influential than the creation of an independent India. What is now called the largest democratic system in the world was created. The East Indies Company and the government of Great Britain ruled the area now including Pakistan, India, and Bangladesh for quite some time. Ethnocentrism and even racism dominated British culture at the time and therefore colonial policy. The Indian people and culture were thought of as inferior and the decision was made to educate a select few in that country to spread the ideals of their white subjugators. Instead of this going as planned, one educated Indian named Mohandas Karamchand Gandhi protested in favor of independence. He and his system of nonviolent protest were adopted by many reformers including Martin Luther King Jr.

One of the largest wars ever, World War II, caused a great amount of rebellion. From resistance movements in France, Italy, and Holland, it seemed many were doing their part to remain independent and reinstate the balance of power. While this was occurring a more simplistic and carnal fight for freedom was taking place in German concentration camps. One such rebellion at Auschwitz resulted in the death of several German guards. Ironically, one German, who had previously been very cruel, was burned alive in the crematory. The Germans had a system within extermination camps where those captured would be rewarded for participating in the execution process. This not only included burning the bodies but also leading groups into the gas chambers. Due to the fact that these groups of helpers knew the inner workings of the system, they only worked for several months before being killed themselves. The workers found out about this and began to organize. Women in the munition plants would smuggle gunpowder to the men in the extermination business where they would make small explosives. Although the rebellion was a failure, a significant amount of guards were killed in a sort of kamikaze style suicide attack. All the explosives were detonated and everyone around both prisoners and guards died. The prisoners who did not benefit from dying in the skirmish were publicly executed while others were tortured for information. Some of the men informed the Nazis of the female companions who had helped them, while the women in return did not give any new names. This point proves that sometimes resilience of spirit is more important than strength or size.

The conflict in Vietnam has been largely vilified by many people today. While I do not agree with the idea of the United States being the "police of the world" or the sole fighter for liberty, the principles behind South Vietnamese resistance are sound. There is no problem with a people voting to contribute to a communist or socialist government, but many times throughout history communism has been forced on too large of a scale. When Ho Chi Minh spoke of a unified Vietnam, he really was advocating the subjugation of the southern people. The war was unconventional in the fact that the forces of the Viet Cong were guerilla fighters and challenging to pinpoint. While an international treaty of noninvolvement would have been preferable, the Soviet Union and China supported the communist cause. The real fight was not Eastern culture versus Western or communism versus capitalism, but freedom of choice versus subjugation. Hardly any American would have pledged their lives to the idea of controlling another nation's economy knowingly. This soon became the longest war in the United States' history and was protested during the later stages. After tens of thousands of deaths and numerous injuries, Richard Nixon ended the conflict. Communist tanks rolled into Saigon and renamed it Ho Chi Minh City after their infamous leader. The fight for freedom had fallen for a time in much of Eastern Asia.

While peaceful protests' successes from people like Mahatma Gandhi and Martin Luther King Jr. are inspirational, the importance of mass strength cannot be negated. While the bloodless People Power Revolution in the Philippines may be placed in these ranks, there was a strong element of force that allowed for a change to be made. When President Ferdinand Marcos was rumored to have assassinated prominent resistance movement leaders including exiled senator Benigno Aquino Sr, Filipinos forced a new presidential election. This was severely rigged however and the situation escalated. Much of the military sided with protesters and Marcos peaceably stepped down. The wife of Benigno, Corazon Cojuangco-Aquino, was elected president. This proved the overwhelming power of popular movements.

Singing has a powerful meaning to many groups yearning for freedom. The lyrics of the negro spiritual "Let My People Go" still resonate for many today: "Go down Moses way down in Egypt land. Tell ole Pharaoh to let my people go. When Israel was in Egypt land, let my people go. Oppressed so hard they could not stand, let my people go. 'Thus spoke the Lord', bold Moses said. 'If not, I'll smite your first-born dead', let my people go." Music serves not only to protect one's culture, but also to instigate change.

In a very modern attempt at independence, the Baltic States, especially Estonia used music as a means of rebellion. After the Soviet Union took control of the once independent country, the Estonian flag and national anthem were banned while Russian was instituted as the official state language. At a popular music fest, many disobeyed these restrictions. In addition to this, some set up an independent Estonian government which served as protection to the capital and a radio broadcasting station. A human chain stretching for nearly four hundred miles was created throughout all three Baltic States. Eventually, Russian independence was declared by Boris Yeltsin and the Soviet Union disintegrated. This meant a restructuring of many regions in eastern Europe and independent rule for many ethnic groups.

While rebellions destroyed the Soviet Union, they also brought democracy to some Middle Eastern countries. In addition to this, it served to protest negative effects of a globalized economy in Chiapas Mexico and to break up Africa from European control. From ancient times, rebellions protested and plodded the progress of empires. From the Frankish and Celtic tribes of western Europe against the Roman Empire to tribes like the Sioux and Delaware in North America who fought partly against the descendants of the Franks and Celts, the spirit of independence has proven universal. After social awareness increased, popular movements and legitimate governments largely broke down the size of primary governments. Although this was beneficial, the advantages of more organized government cannot be forgotten. The orchestration of peace agreements and trade deals became more simple while science and the arts flourished. A fusion of these two systems is ideal, a system based on the principle of federalism. Now the building blocks of a well-functioning global society are in place and a plan of execution is now necessary. Revolutions must continue to change government both around the world and in the United States.

Section 2: Needed Realistic Revolutions

There are three different sections in politics that are going to be discussed in this book: historical, which was just discussed; practical, which is now the topic; and ideological, which will be the last section. Often the middle section is not focused on enough. History has been viciously defended by great scholars such as George Santayana who stated: "Those who cannot remember the past are condemned to repeat it." This is true and a thorough study concerning the history of rebellions has just been conducted, but discussion dealing with the application of principles that are gathered from history are equally important.

In addition to this, there have been great men, especially from the Age of Enlightenment, who have adamantly advertised pure concepts of freedom and virtuous government. Their efforts were courageous seeing that their very lives were sometimes threatened by the monarchies which they protested, but their plans were never acted upon during their lifetime so they did not have to deal application. Pure ideology is a topic of importance, but the procedure by which society advances towards better governance is of more pertinence. Therefore, throughout this book, all three levels will be discussed.

Due to the globalization of government, changes must now often be universal. A few examples will be necessary as sufficient evidence. One of these examples deals with nuclear weapons. While many Americans fret about the programs of North Korea or Iran, the very existence of nuclear weapons should be thought of as absurd. In many cases, reports have shown that stations within the United States are poorly equipped with sometimes negligent management. All that is needed to for a full-blown nuclear catastrophe is the ill-advised or unstable decision of one world leader. Executive command is all that is needed to launch the U.S. into such a conflict.

Although conscious decisions to detonate these weapons are a concern, accidents seem also to be important. Comedian John Oliver was discussing this issue on his show Last Week Tonight and he brought up two long forgotten events in U.S. history. One was called the Goldsboro incident and it happened in 1961 at the height of the cold war. This event, and any events like it, has been said to be clouded in classification. During a flight mission, a plane crashed and fell apart in mid-air with a nuclear weapon of relatively high strength. It is said by one former government agent and other sources that the only step that was needed for detonation was the flip of a switch in the cockpit. Part of the weapon was not recoverable and is still located in the soil around the town of Goldsboro, North Carolina. Comedian John Oliver remarked, "Yep, you dropped an armed nuclear bomb on your own country and it is frankly amazing that you don't talk about that more often." In a separate case, a socket was dropped from the top of a nuclear silo in Arkansas and caused a fuel leak and subsequent explosion.

Now these are horrifying cases and the number of nuclear weapons are being reduced daily, but a practical plan of execution must be put in place. First, major powers need to collaborate and simultaneously deplete their supplies. Then an international alliance against nuclear weapons must be created, maintaining a strong position of negotiating primarily through economic sanctions but also through an underlying threat of war. This is deemed an area for international control due to the fact that no single ruler should have the power to end civilization. This plan of action is dependent on a number of factors that necessitates universal cooperation in meaningful change.

For both stages of complete nuclear disarmament to be completed and maintained, all governments must become transparent. In today's political world, Americans who would prefer more information, force themselves to live with less due to the fact that the United States is competing with nations such as China and Saudi Arabia. These nations are ruled by an individual leader or party while having less experience and connection to the ideals of personal freedom. Ideally, all nations could be transparent, not only for its citizens but also for international affairs like nuclear investigation. A future could be created where "weapons of mass destruction" would not be a reason to invade a country, but only the subject of a routine international investigation. In addition to this, the investigation would not be tainted by the fact that the United States still has nuclear weapons which are often mishandled and not cared for properly. A transparent world with transparent governments, a place where conspiracy theories can be discounted on a regular basis due to increased information. While this paints a pleasant picture of the future, the execution of a plan proves to be more difficult. Slowly, nations must together negotiate the declassification of documents. This will be considered as sufficient evidence for the complexities of globalization

Saving the most interesting and applicable case for last, several foreign governments will be analyzed. Needed reforms and plans of execution will be set in place. After this, a description of the situation in the United States will be given. This will be separated into two sections. One will be focused on the need for reversion in certain areas of politics and the other will be based on the ideals of pure progress. My conservative side will show through the support of a restitution in federalism and a love for the Bill of Rights. My liberal side will show through ideas dealing with campaign finance reform and a change to the two party system. Liberal and conservative, in this case, do not hold anything of the usual political definition but from the actual dictionary definition. These terms are absolutely absurd when used to describe oneself politically due to the fact that no one is purely single sided. If you believe that everything should change or that no change is needed then you would fall under a category, but that is extremely unlikely. Instead, a careful examination of both sides will be given in a non-partisan fashion.

Above of the reforms is a desire to bring political discussion back to the United States. A people who do not understand the political process or the history and society of America are not going to be able to have any basis for a decision. It is time to bring back open conversation about issues, not hindered by modern vocal etiquette or restraints. Many who endorse a politically correct vocabulary do not understand what they are doing. Using social pressure to silence opposition is legal, but problematic. Ending racism does not begin with a ban on discriminatory or offensive language, but a true change of heart. In addition to this anger cannot be allowed to grow like mold in the shadows but must be brought to light and dealt with. Many notorious racists from John Calhoun to Adolf Hitler believed that they had a scientific argument that backed up their claims and actions. It is absurd that people today do not use information to combat this argument more readily.

In addition to this people should not be dismissive of a person's beliefs. If a person believes that "a big, beautiful, powerful wall" is necessary, why would an honest discussion with this person be unwanted? A person with strict views on immigration is not inherently racist. To add to this argument, even if a person was racist, a conversation with them is not a horrible idea. These people no longer hold much political power and as long as threats do not ensue, a conversation could even change their opinion. An absolutely horrible rebuttal to the ideas of open discussion is: What if they change my opinion? If a person's beliefs are that fragile then more learning is necessary. People should not be afraid of ideas but rather the application of them. Therefore, instead of labeling, practice the forgotten art of arguing. With all of this information, it can be seen that a political and social revolution is about to occur in America. We must go back to the past, but look onward into the future. Not throwing out the wheat but only the chaff. This is the mission which we are now embarking on and I believe that Americans will once again be up for the challenge of bearing real political reform as was the case during the revolution. We not only as Americans but also as citizens of the world can shape our own destiny and find a way to live together in harmony with ourselves and with our surrounding.

Chapter 4: Reform in Other Nations

While the story usually revolves around the United States, there are many reforms that need to occur around the world. Dictators and powerful monarchies still exist, and people are being subjugated under foreign rule. Instead of turning a blind eye to the suffering of these people, a thorough analysis of their situation must be given. Reforms with plans of execution must be given to eventually free all of the world from the yoke of tyranny while creating stable governments that respond to the will and desire of the people. Here many of the offenses of overly powerful leaders will be listed.

The terms of Western and Eastern have been used in the historical section to highlight the thought of many philosophers, both past and present. This contrast between the Eastern and Western worlds has been overly propagated by the Communist Party of China to diminish the cause of freedom there.

To understand the situation it is important to realize that substantive discrimination occurs worldwide. An idea should not be rejected based on the section of the world from which it came. Just because a group largely composed of Europeans discovered sound political principles during the Age of Enlightenment does not mean that they should be dismissed. It is not a point for Caucasian supremacists due to the fact that the European continent had just been immersed in the Dark Ages, which was a bleak time for learning and government. Would the leaders of the Communist Party reject the concept of gravity for the sole reason that it was discovered by an Englishman? In addition to this point, no claim can be made by the Chinese government that their system is purely Eastern. In addition to the fact that both the East and West have no cultures, the region is actually extremely diverse with differing cultures.

It may be this extreme generalization that allows for many different religious and ethnic groups under the Chinese government. The one party system currently in China is not a representation of Eastern culture but rather an example of how tyranny was once universal. People in China should rise up and demand that the government conforms to their wishes. The members of the Communist Party have disgraced the country by effectively saying that they think the Chinese people are not intellectual enough to choose their own leaders through a more direct method.

In addition to the monopoly that the Communist Party holds, many different cultures are held under the rule of one unresponsive government. The region of Tibet has been occupied by the Chinese ever since an invasion by the Communist Party soon after the end of World War II. The communist party of the region is known for its great propaganda and this has been used against those seeking independence. A whole new history of eastern Asia has been constructed to "prove" that Tibet has been united with China for centuries. While both were unified for a short time under Mongol rule, this barely constitutes anything meaningful due to the fact that this was purely military conquest. The Communist Party is trying to undermine Tibetan culture by participating in several guileful acts. The autonomous region called Tibet in China, which is controlled by the central government, is only one part of historical Tibet. Through this change, they are able to retain some of the land even if the modern day region with the name rebels.

Many do not see the urgency of the situation in Tibet. In addition to the previous act of subjugation, many Han Chinese people have been transported to the region. Soon the Tibetans may become a minority. While atrocities like the acquisition of Native American land by Europeans are now deemed irreversible, there is still time to reverse this. In addition to this, in China federalism is not a well-established principle but is rather a result of lacks centralized power. This regional power can be usurped without a constitutional infraction. All in all, for China to survive in the new world, they must conform to sound principles and not dismiss political discoveries based on the region in which the philosopher was born.

In addition to the problems with organization in the nation of China, there is also extreme corruption. This seems to be impossible to change due to the very structure of the government. The central authorities and Communist Party has been extremely opaque. The problem of this reform has been discussed earlier, but the Communist Party is at a whole new level. Change is also deemed nearly impossible due to affronts on free speech and expression. While protests and demonstrations are commonplace for anyone from a large city in the United States, the Tiananmen Square protest was considered revolutionary and tanks were sent in by the Chinese government.

A true republican form of government is dependent on open information and free speech. If the public does not have access to most or ideally all government records, then how are they supposed to be able to make an intelligent decision? How are changes going to occur if discussion is monitored and limited by the establishment? Tibetans are not allowed to express many aspects of their culture or protest the government. This is sharply contrasted by the fact that discussion about the rights of Mexico to much of the southwestern United States is open.

Perhaps the most devastating offense to free speech and human rights comes from the example of the Falun Gong persecution. As mentioned earlier, Falun Gong is a religious group that is imprisoned for their beliefs. Allegations have been brought up by various human rights lawyers and political activists that these prisoners are executed for the harvesting of their organs. These disturbing reports have added to the long list of abuses. Sex-trafficking is rampant in the country while prisoners are forced to produce items for the government. In addition to this, accused prostitutes are not given due process and sweatshops have become almost a staple. It seems that nothing now from China remains untainted. Many of the things which have made them famous in today's market including clothing, organ transplants, and pornography are all the result of abuses. An investigation needs to be carried out by a coalition of nations and economic sanctions placed in accordance with the findings. Reforms should be encouraged that break up the monopoly of control in Chinese government. Although the Chinese Communist system is horrible, there are also many problems with the two-party system in the United States and other countries like Great Britain and Australia. The more available choices the better when talking about politics.

Another example of an extremely secretive government is Russia. These two countries with the addition of the United States provide ample support of the need for international declassification. Although this is an important lesson, there is a more specific principle that the Russian government has ignored. While there are legislative and judicial checks on executive power, the president holds his office for life unless if it is unexpectedly interrupted. This is important because the will of the general population is bound to change during the course of a lifetime. While it does allow for more coordinated foreign policy, if that foreign policy is not supported by the people then it is likely that it is not for their benefit. In addition to this, as social awareness increases, people tend towards wars only that benefit all of civilization.

As the importance of strength on the international stage decreases, the emergence of purer government not based upon the natural fight for survival will occur. In the United States there is a similar problem. While the main executive office of president has term limits, members of Congress can be re-elected for life. There are very frequent elections, but the tendencies of people tend towards the incumbent. While it may be said that the general will is still being sufficiently expressed, term limits serve as an effective means of exercising the minds of citizens. If the policies of the established figure are still fully supported then a person with the exact same plan can be found relatively easily. Most likely however, there will be a few problems found with the member's record. The election cycle without personal connections to a specific person serve as a great stage for debate. Discussion should be welcomed and public involvement praised.

This reform is suggested but not entirely necessary. One reform that is absolutely necessary is the limiting of executive power. In this story the need to increase the party options around the world also become apparent. Executive powers have practiced usurpation for centuries. One modern example from the United States is that of Franklin D. Roosevelt. He attempted to deceptively encourage an increased number of Supreme Court Justices so that he could fill the positions and influence more decisions. He could not make it through this loophole however and the issue ended. With the example of Russia however, a loophole was considerably wider and Vladimir Putin forced his way into increased power. After his two terms collectively of eight years had been completed by Putin, the now former president searched for a way through the constitutional term limits. The United Russia Party with which he held much control, nominated Dmitry Medvedev as president. The new president nominated Putin as Prime Minister and under his power constitutional term limits were amended. Putin then regained control of the presidency and continues to lead today. Many consider him a dictator and his actions prove the dangers of strong party affiliations.

In America the party affiliations often cloud people's judgement. Many of the founding fathers were aware of this fact and John Jay in the tenth publication of the Federalist Papers stated: "But it could not be less folly to abolish liberty, which is essential to political life, because it nourishes faction, than it would be to wish the annihilation of air, which is essential to animal life, because it imparts to fire its destructive agency." While this is partially true, parties unlike fire do not serve any useful purpose. While fires allow for the destruction of the old and renewed growth, parties hinder needed change. If it is believed that parties are like fires than it has become apparent that the United States needs to take part in some political fire management. They have been allowed to grow too powerful and a plan will be detailed about how to break up the binopoly they hold.

Much like the subjugation of Tibetan people under the Chinese government, the Russian government due to its large size participated in much of same practice. When the Soviet Union broke up in the early 1990s, the region of Chechnya tried to gain its independence. This attempt failed after many rebel deaths and the destruction of the region. Many people from the region had been angered by World War II era offenses including the mass deportation of its people to Siberia which resulted in an estimated fifty percent death rate.

However, recently the movement has become tainted. The loss of whatever international sympathy they had gained, came after a series of terrorist operations. Russian schools and subways were targeted and innocent civilians were involved. While some claim that this terrorism is due to the fact that the region is largely composed of people who practice Islam, examples similar to this come from a variety of sources.

One historical account comes in the form of William Tecumseh Sherman's "march to the sea." His actions were not only unnecessary but also unlawful in the sense of many military customs. Not only was the city of Atlanta bombarded with cannon fire and artillery killing many civilians, but they also displaced a lot of the remaining members taking much of their property. In addition to this there are allegations of rape and other offenses among Sherman's ranks. While he can not be blamed for all of these events personally, it is the job of the commander to control the actions of one's troops.

Any action of scorched earth or total war should have been considered ignorant due to the fact that the war was winding to a close. It seems that this front of the war did not only accomplish the defeat of the deep southeastern section, but also stirred up bitterness which would last until long past the war. The fact that a civil war was being fought in which reconciliation was the ultimate objective had been forgotten. During this final stage of the war, resentment should have been avoided at all costs. Not everyone was as forgiving as Robert E. Lee and after the war this action was remembered by many southerners. Whatever the case may be the Chechen terrorism largely ended when its leader Shamil Salmanovich Basayev was killed by the Russian forces. The movement continues until today and many people are now hopeful. Without violent and radical leaders as the picture of the rebellion, members are now hopeful to gather international support for their cause. Instances of religious and ethnic toleration within the country exist but are rare. In addition to this, forced subjugation of a minority should not be risked for diversity. If social obligation on a scale larger than local is to be enforced, a system based on stable coexistence and not the whimsical activities of politicians needs to be established. Whatever the case may be, many lessons are still available from other countries.

While both of these countries need reforms, the Middle East is an even more tricky area to deal with. Although there have been attempts at more democratic forms of government in many countries, some are still ruled by a dictatorship or a religious leader. Terrorist organizations have run rampant in the area and anti-American sentiments have grown. Some claim that this is due to the area's hatred of freedom while others point to mishaps during bombing raids and extremist propaganda. The region was largely taken through conquest, although there have also been cases of non-forced conversion. Religion is a serious topic both socially and politically. Many people today attempt to claim that almost all the evil in the world stemmed from these institutions. As mentioned during the introduction, I believe that it is often used as a mask for evil intentions. From way back in ancient Egypt, pharaohs were claiming to be the sons of the gods. This assertions helped to cement a ruler's power through uniting a people under something greater than them. Rome continued this practice throughout its existence. First, it was often claimed that the Roman Emperor or local ruler was related to the gods. After time past and Constantine I accepted the doctrine of the formerly cultish sect of Christianity, and wars and conquests were carried out for a supposedly heavenly purpose.

In the same way Islam was used many times, and it seems that the ancient practices of the pharaohs had also been used by the Native Americans. While the merits of any particular religion will not be discussed, it is important to remember that radical leaders have come from almost all ethnic and religious backgrounds. Even if one believes that a religious text specifically incites violence, it can not be banned. Rather the adherents of the religion will be judged individually by their action from a political perspective. Radical interpretation can be said to play a role in the Middle-Eastern chaos, but other factors are important as well.

Historically, this region has been ruled by various ethnic and racial groups. The lack of history and self-identity that this has caused can be thought of as negative. While diversity in a nation can be maintained peacefully, it is important that there is something else for the people to rally behind. Often times this becomes a religion. In this sector of the globe, however, the differences between Sunni and Shiite Muslims deeply contrast so unification becomes even more difficult. Due to the odd hate Caucasians in the United States often have for themselves, many solely blame the effects of European conquest. This can be thought of as an important factor, but it must be remembered that Arab and Ottoman control could also be thought of as conquest from the perspective of ancient times. Europeans and especially the British handling of the situation can be seen as an oddity due to the fact that historically it has remained uncommon. Instead of trying to maintain control of the vast empire, the nation began to give land back to the people. This occurred not only in the Middle East but also in North America with Canada and in Australia. Although this action was in the best interest of global government, errors did occur. It seems that many of the borders were created by the lines of European control rather than ethnic or religious borders. This stirred up confrontation in the recently formed countries with newly created minorities feeling the negative effects.

In addition to this, it seems that the creation of an Israeli state has also caused anger. Whatever the case may be, Israel brings up a question dealing with regional protection of minorities that will be discussed later. As with China, the United States policy towards this region should favor republican government and democratic principles. Although this is true an international policy of non-interventionism needs to be adopted during internal strife. Unlike the Chinese or Russian governments, the Middle Eastern governments are weak enough so that they can be brought down by a sizeable popular resistance without international aid to the established government. In many cases the old saying "you can lead a horse to water but you can't make it drink" proves to be applicable. Religion obviously plays a large role in the region, but if the people honestly believe in what is being taught, then in a republican government politicians would be elected with an emphasis on religion. This may seem as too great of a power for religion but if freedom of speech and expression persist, people can choose for themselves what is correct.

In this circumstance nothing can be forced by outside sources. The people have the power to rebel if they choose and they will cherish the principles more if they come from a localized source. The pain and sacrifice that is given will be remembered and a true nation will be born. The words that Thomas Paine wrote in The Crisis are still applicable today for people suffering under absolute rule: "These are the times that try men's souls. The summer soldier and the sunshine patriot will, in this crisis, shrink from the service of their country; but he that stands by it now, deserves the love and thanks of man and woman. Tyranny, like hell, is not easily conquered; yet we have this consolation with us, that the harder the conflict, the more glorious the triumph. What we obtain too cheap, we esteem too lightly: it is dearness only that gives every thing its value. Heaven knows how to put a proper price upon its goods; and it would be strange indeed if so celestial an article as Freedom should not be highly rated."

It is now seen that a distinction must be made. There are two different goals which usually characterize rebellions in history. One is the desire for local rule and the other is for liberty or the betterment of government. The former must usually be achieved before the latter, as many of the more radical leaders of the American Revolution came to realize. While almost all the world is now free from foreign colonization, the fight for liberty and good government continues. In the country of Venezuela, the "president" Hugo Chavez has been involved in corruption. Spending in that government has gone through the roof and the partial dictator tried to make his term for life. The world can now learn a lesson from the Venezuelan mistake. The people of Venezuela were put in a precarious situation. With the created constitution in effect, citizens were not satisfied. Therefore, Hugo Chavez, who had promised change, was elected into office. Once there, he dismantled the established government, and without sufficient checks on his power, took control of the country.

While the people had legitimate concerns, it important that these are addressed with the initial constitution. Every issue with unification under a single government in a particular region must be discussed and dealt with before, if at all possible. Slavery was this divisive issue for the Americans, and the effects proved to be fatal. Although this is true, if any decisive action was taken in respect to slavery, the country may never have been created. The first U.S. constitution, The Articles of Confederation, proved to be a failure because it did not give sufficient power to the federal government. Fortunately, there were men dedicated enough to the cause of liberty and the pursuit of intellect that the usurpation of power did not become a threat. This proves the importance of having a committee rather than an individual instigate this type of change. In an ideal situation however, a constitution will have a method of amending which partially conforms to the winds of change but also checks the overstepping of reasonable boundaries. Whatever the case may be, none of these guidelines were followed and the people of Venezuela paid as a result.

Before any more examples are given, a few general misconceptions about government need to be cleared up. Many of the more complicated systems of the United States government may seem unnecessary. While many governments in South/Central America and eastern Europe are relatively small or divided up by different ethnic groups, this country is not. This country has been famous almost since it beginning for its extreme diversity in both religion and race. In my ideal organization of the globe, many of the previously mentioned smaller states would be considered only overstretched local institutions. In the United States, there are obvious reforms that need to be seriously considered, but many of the overall structures which define the government are ingenious.

When the "general will" was mentioned earlier, its definition was left relatively vague. Now it will be elaborated upon. The general will is often misunderstood as the "majority wins" mentality. This is not the case however and it is a lot more complicated. While the majority always rules in a hypothetically pure democratic society, this government is not fit for anything above a local level. As the size of a government increases so should the checks and balances placed within the system. Therefore, under an ideal system, a federal government's application of general will is going to look different. People's desire once they become informed should lean towards increased social discussion and understanding. There should be a couple of principles that they can unite around which obviously give an advantage to all involved.

In addition to this, the concept of federalism must be instigated to place a greater importance on smaller forms of government. All people from throughout different communities and points on the globe should be able to realize that it is to their benefit to reject the urges to seek extreme amounts of control over other groups and instead focus on themselves. There are important functions for larger governments like the definition of life and a protection against local coercion, but most aspects of culture and society should be controlled by government that is more responsive to popular needs.

This is not the case in the United States, however, where every group seems to run to the federal government for unimportant reforms, apparently for personal fame and the primitive urge to control others, rather than justice and liberty. Power hungry people seem to rise to the top and even more checks are needed to hold them back.

One more negative effect of people's urge for overly simplified government is applicable to the Venezuelan case and most governments around the world. It is now seen that the branch of government most likely to usurp power is the executive. When dealing with federal governments, people must resist the urge to unite around one leader like Russia or even one party like the ironically named People's Republic of China. The latter isn't controlled by the people, a republic, nor wholly composed of Chinese territory due to the subjugation of the Tibetan territory. A system of singularity is simplistic but dangerous. It is possible that this system can showcase the general will, but volatility and usurpation are too probable. Therefore checks are needed. Sadly some of this has been lost in the United States, but this will be discussed later. Now back to the foreign reforms.

Foreign aid has been a topic of discussion in many different publicized political debates. Probably the most important aspect of the argument against foreign aid is the mounting debt and the lack of money. Although the budget must be considered, there are other problems with the United States' current policy. In certain countries where we ship food and other essentials to, the aid is given to the leader or government of the country instead of directly to the wanting people. This becomes a problem when instead of helping those in need, they take much of it for themselves or sell it to the highest bidders.

In North Korea, there are many starving people. It is said that the northern half of the Korean Peninsula was extremely dependent on the southern farmland and now has no dependent source within their country. Foreign aid has been given to this nation by various nations and institutions like the United Nations. While helping the people of this poor region should be important, true prosperity can only be brought about by a popular revolution. A dictator with no real connection to the people cannot be expected to provide for their needs.

From a military perspective, it is almost impossible to carry out a successful foreign campaign against this country. An extreme amount of destructive weaponry is pointed at the South Korean capital of Seoul which makes any attempt dangerous. The best chance for success comes from a hypothetical guerilla operation from within the country against the government. The people must band together and fight against a government that no longer provides for their needs and has no concern for them whatsoever. This proves to be tricky because of the many restrictions on speech and expression, but it is possible. The first step is convincing people that their leader is an ordinary man. The idea of Juche, translated as self-reliance, was introduced by Kim Il-sung to separate North Korea from other communist countries. This established Il-sung's family as the interpreters of this leading philosophy and put them in absolute authority. It seems that this ideology stresses the importance of individuality, but its application is hypocritical. If the individual is going to be valued in a society, why would they not be considered intelligent enough to choose their own government. The type of government in North Korea showcases a total misunderstanding of genetics and sociology. Just because one person holds great negotiating, administrative, or intellectual skills does not that their children will express those characteristics as well.

In fact even if they do inherit such skills, they will still most likely become a terrible leader. Jean Jacques Rousseau stated in The Social Contract, "When someone is brought up to command others, everything conspires to rob him of justice and reason. Great pains are taken, we are told, to teach young princes the art of ruling; but it does not appear that this education does them any good. It would be better to begin by teaching them the art of obeying." Many monarchical or hereditary rulers become out of touch with reality and start to consider their own interests above the public. This can happen in republican forms of government to a certain extent, but term limits serve the purpose of minimizing the sense of entitlement. Popular government is further proven to be beneficial when Rousseau continues: "But if there is no government more vigorous than monarchy, there is also none where the particular will has more command, and more easily dominates the other wills. Everything moves towards the same end, it is true, but the end is not public happiness; and the very strength of the administration operates continuously to the disadvantage of the state." Niccolò Machiavelli says that it is better to be feared as a ruler, and that is why republican governments have set up a system where one must first gain the love and trust of the people. Then, and only then, is the norm reversed for the benefit of the citizenry.

It is extremely sad to say, but sometimes the United States has competing interests on the world stage. This government should take every rational approach to promote liberty and popular power around the world without extensive military involvement. While it may seem idealistic, international treaties of disinvolvement in the national affairs of other countries would provide a fundamental step. If no major powers choose to be involved in a conflict, then several different broad objectives can be reached. First, the destruction of the hypothetical war will be severely decreased. Local conflicts should remain small and need not be magnified by large foreign powers. This can be clearly seen through the Russian and U.S. action in Korea and Vietnam, but is also evident with the example of World War I. The Korean and Vietnam Wars did have noble objectives of defending attacked nations, but greater planning could have led to a better outcome. For freedom to be defended on an international scale, it must not come from one country but by a large coalition of almost all major powers. It can be said that Russia and the U.S. equalized both sides but in all reality the only effect was a magnification of the conflict. If at all possible the two major nations should have come to an agreement to neither fight in the war nor send aid or ammunition.

In the case of "The Great War," which was soon eclipsed by an even greater war, nations did not have time to act rationally. Small regions unknown to many of the general public had somehow involved the whole world in a devastating conflict. Instead of leaving the regional authorities and The Black Hand to fight, everybody had to become involved to balance out those who were joining the other side. This brings up the important point that the international community should make alliances based on principles and not with countries.

Another adverse effect of the magnification in conflicts through the actions of world powers is the environmental factor. Many self-defined conservatives would mock this, but the threat is important to investigate. Former Central Intelligence Agency Director Michael Morell was mocked by many for saying that oil wells within ISIS territory were not targeted in part because "environmental damage" concerns. While ISIS needs to be wiped out not only for their humanitarian atrocities, but also for their destruction of historical sites, saying that the environment is a concern should not be thought of as radical. Keeping conflicts small can help to minimize this environmental threat.

Another reason why world powers should stay out of regional wars is that they can not be blamed for any ensuing problems. When I said that liberty should be promoted, I did not mean that the United States should be involved in various conflicts and ammunition drops around the world. Rather, we need to use our influence to keep other powers out as well. Many political activists today, attribute many of the problems in the Middle East to American or, even more vaguely stated, "Western" intervention. As stated earlier, European powers often did not draw political borders by ethnic or religious boundaries and therefore created instability. What should have been done after this is often not addressed by these activists. Should Europeans and Americans retake control of the Middle East and redraw the lines? Instead, a rational plan of principle must be laid out to guide the actions of future leaders.

I believe that the region must be left alone for some time to determine the most stable situation. Borders can be redrawn through rebellion and internal dissatisfaction while these now smaller countries form together to make larger more homologous institutions. While diversity is a good goal for modern society, in more unstable circumstances it becomes safer to avoid large national minorities. As is obviously true, a people cannot be forced to become open-minded.

Whatever the case may be the real question is the state of Israel. While the United States should try to avoid local conflicts, if a coalition of Middle Eastern nations rise up to force the state into submission, then a coalition of great powers should negotiate a noninvolvement pact with the threat of force. The policy of noninvolvement should not only apply to the United States, but also to large countries in the Middle East as well. In addition to this situation, the question of international terrorism should be discussed. A sound policy should only use direct involvement when the homeland or American people are attacked. It is not that the local people do not matter, but rather that they must involve themselves first in the fight for their own freedom. If they are not willing to sacrifice, then the cause of liberty in the region is currently dead. While these two are good reasons to limit direct international involvement, there is another one

While it is not the quickest method, the "scenic route" of politics will yield the most stable results. When the people become writers of their own destiny and not tag-alongs on a foreign journey, then the populous will become truly free. While the United States claims to fight for freedom abroad, their policies are rarely uniform. The plan above should be accepted to avoid unneeded hypocrisies.

These hypocrisies can be partially seen through their support of the established government during the Sandinista Revolution. The revolution was successful and created a more popular government. Recently, the government has become more corrupt. Through the work of the judicial system, the constitution in this country was adjusted to eliminate term limits. This has become common in many nations around the world and proves that the system of amending needs to have safeguards. The current president, Daniel Ortega, was once a populist revolutionary, but now he has become more of a dictator. Invading legislative areas of power proves this point. While there are examples of meaningful change, it seems that the country of Nicaragua has proven the words of Peter Townshend in the Who hit, Won't Get Fooled Again, "Meet the new boss. Same as the old boss," to be at least partially true.

Although it is ranked at nineteenth in land area, Mongolia is not very recognizable. This may be true, but there are several lessons that can be learned from this country. While not all communist or socialist governments are corrupt, many examples in the northeastern hemisphere perpetuate a damaging stereotype. Like the Communist Party of China, the Mongolian government is dominated by a singular party and choices are limited by it.

These examples do not accurately represent the entire ideology however. The important thing is not that a government ascribes to a certain social or economic system, but that the government remains accountable to the general will. Socialism has spread through more popular means to different parts of the world including the Scandinavian countries. Armed with these positive examples, certain politicians in the United States have attempted to introduce several reforms. The former presidential candidate, Bernie Sanders, was a major advocate for free state education, free healthcare, and enforced paid maternity leave. Many of his supporters believe that the American system of government is extremely rigged and that the "top one-tenth of one percent" have total control of politics. While there are obvious reforms that need to be considered, the very fact that Sanders garnered so much support proves that the political system is relatively fair when compared to the world. A plan of execution will be detailed later about how to continue the American political tradition of excellence, but the current situation must first be elaborated upon.

The words communism and socialism today stir up hysteria and often heated debates. However, this reflex is not purely negative. The topic that is being discussed could change the direction of the third largest and third most populated nation in the world. While conversation should never turn ugly, the controversy is understandable. Bernie Sanders speeches about the wealth gap between the rich and poor classes and the offenses of certain large bankers is partially true, but his plan of action is somewhat disturbing. Not only would many of Bernie's policies further entrench the nation in debt, but they would represent an extreme power shift towards the federal government. His proposed centralized education program would serve to move that sector closer to a government monopoly and would further the infractions on the principle of separation between government and education. This separation is virtually nonexistent in countries like Mongolia, and although this change may seem benign, it can turn cancerous. Especially in a one party system like Mongolia, but also in American politics; education can be used to quiet dissension and obstruct fair discussion. The place for education in an ideal society will be discussed later.

Whatever the case may be, many of the reforms proposed by Sanders should be instituted on a state or local level due to the fact that more conservative states should not be forced to accept unnecessary and unwanted change. However, Mongolia definitely needs certain reforms. Revolutions have occurred but it seems that in many ways they mimic the elliptical pattern of the earth revolving around the sun and not real political change. While certain advances have been encouraging, there is still a long way to go until more choices are brought before the Mongolian people.

The situation on the continent of Africa is not as complicated as the Middle East due to the lack of a severe nuclear threat, but it still presents political problems for its people. While European colonization did benefit the large region by introducing important ideology, it also had many adverse effects. Some pre-independence offenses by the Europeans and the long, bloody wars that often ensued, caused hatred to be stirred up against Europeans. In many cases, a mental rejection of all aspects of the oppressor's culture was subconsciously adopted. As a result, trends towards "traditional" African government were often preferred to more popular institutions. In the ancient African government kings were rulers for life and this tradition has continued with elected officials.

This perception of African tradition is incorrect however seeing that this more primitive system of government was originally the norm in every highly populated continent. Keeping African people under oppressive rule is not natural and it will eventually be destroyed. Rebellion, even if it is only psychological, needs to be based off of facts and rational thought. Therefore, while the goal of independence from Europe is noble, a political truth should not be rejected because of the place in which it was discovered.

One good example of an under-checked elected official in Africa, is Robert Mugabe who rules Zimbabwe. He, like many modern day rulers in simplistic governments, was formerly a prominent fighter for independence. After his guerilla missions were successful however, he began to rise to power. He was not checked correctly and the country soon became an example of John Emerich Edward Dalberg Acton's statement: "Power tends to corrupt, and absolute power corrupts absolutely. Great men are almost always bad men." For this reason great men such as Cincinnatus and Washington are considered historical anomalies.

Whatever the case may be, in many ways Mugabe began to prefer loyalty to him over loyalty to the ideology that he had previously fought for. His reign has not been marked by all negatives however. After centuries of subjugation, the poor Zimbabweans were ready for change. One important reform that took place was the redistribution of land from many European landowners to the general populace. While the two words "land distribution" are seen as dirty in the United States, Zimbabwe was a much smaller country and the native Africans needed to start out with a chance for success. While it is seen that the African-Americans in the United States definitely were not given a fair opportunity once freed, a more complicated and larger political system will require a more detailed plan that will be discussed later.

One cannot reject the hypothesis that a lack of land, general wealth, and literacy after emancipation did not at all contribute to the current situation of crime and poverty in many of the black neighborhoods. Whatever the case may be, the Zimbabweans enacted these reforms and continue to be a socialist government. In addition to this reform, education has been promoted by the government. In this small and developing country this is not necessarily a negative but it can still be used to garner support for the incumbent in a simplistic system. Political scientist Masipula Sithole said that in essence, by educating the general population, Mugabe is digging his own grave. Hopefully he will finish soon and allow the citizens to create a government that is more responsive to their needs.

While all of these examples are disturbing, the situation in West Papua is extreme. After years of Dutch subjugation in Indonesia, the decision was made to free the former colony. The United Nations was peacefully involved and a deal was made to place West Papua under Indonesian control. Due to the fact that the United Nations was involved in the creation of the problem, pressure should be placed on Indonesia because of human rights concerns. Videos have surfaced of torture and committees have found examples of rape committed by government officials. Most of these atrocities were against indigenous groups and many of their villages are subjected to raids in which people are imprisoned for apparent "offenses." These offenses include peacefully protesting Indonesian rule. It can now be clearly seen that replacing colonial rule with other forms of foreign government does not help the people. As stated earlier, good government cannot precede independence. It has become criminal in this region to raise the West Papuan flag or report on government corruption. Without the freedom of expression, government cannot be expected to change peacefully. In this region the indigenous tribes are often treated as sub-human and all support for Indonesia should be cancelled until reforms are made or independence for West Papua is achieved.

While many examples of needed reforms to governments can be found in both history and modern times, a philosophy which has gathered much support in modern times also presents a potential revolution. Anarchy is an age old cause that has much of its foundation in the work of Thomas Hobbes. Its core beliefs include a consensus that less government equals more freedom, therefore no government equals complete freedom. To sufficiently settle this issue, a better understanding of freedom must become common. Absolute freedom in society is not the final objective, but is rather based on the overextension of solid principles. If a society is composed of purely good people, completely void of greed or selfish ambition, then this goal can be attained, but government cannot be based on hypotheticals without a degree of reality.

It is also seen that if a society could completely shun personal desire, then how could the desire of other societies be controlled. An international pact could be formed but this would need strength to back it up and if administered, this would infringe on freedom. The freedom which is discussed in this literary work and others describes not absolute personal freedom, but rather the ability of a collective group to choose what is best. Hobbes once wrote, "It is not wisdom but authority that makes a law." This has a certain truth to it during the time in which Hobbes lived, but in many countries today, authority and wisdom can be intertwined. When the general population is allowed to vote, issues do not personally involve most of those registered. Therefore instead of voting based on personal gain, most vote based upon sound principle or matters of policy. Today's culture of questioning everything and valuing intelligence further aids in attaining this goal. Obviously certain freedoms must be preserved to keep society advancing forward like the freedom of speech and expression, but a no restraints society is not desirable.

If one looks into anarchist discussions through books and the internet, one sees that under their system it is not even possible to have absolute personal freedom. After being asked about what one would do after seeing a dog being beaten or a businessman cheating an old lady, many anarchists would respond that their response would consist of either torture or death. If these events were to take place, what would stop the family of the dead from coming and killing the other man. This system does not seem rational to me. Misinformation and passion would rule instead of a justice system that allows time for consideration. Some anarchists may argue that this does not speak for their cause but in a system without government how would they control those who believe this. Would not those who attempt this control be considered a hierarchy?

When studying the words of many anarchists, one becomes even more confused. In the world of anarchy there are hundreds of sects and divisions. If one browses through each group, one might see that many of the groups hate a good portion of other anarchists. Christian anarchists, which are comparatively rare, would have to fight against those with atheistic beliefs who believe that religion is a hierarchy. Are self-imposed hierarchies fine? What happens if this hierarchy becomes too powerful? As with many movements, there are those calling for unity against a common enemy. While movements do require unity, this movement will never attain that goal. One cannot blindly follow the belief that once government is destroyed all these problems will disappear. Primitive anarchists, who believe in living a simplistic life with nature, are not going to enjoy anarcho-capitalists destroying nature to build giant industrialized cities. How are land disputes between groups going to be settled? It seems that anarchists are not only in a fight against government, but also the acts of social obligation which it enforces. Many in this group want to be completely free while also having the ability to control others and this is a bad mixture.

Others are joining for the apparent reason that they are tired of the hierarchy within their workplace or as they call it "wage slavery." While reforms are sometimes needed when monopolies are held or abuses occur, aversion to work would not be acceptable to even an anarchist society. Work is not an imposition of modern society but rather one of nature. The people within this movement are well-meaning, but it seems that this belief system is not based on good judgement. It would definitely change the world but not in a good way. A revolution would occur, but it would only serve in reverting society back to the days of tribal warfare. As stated earlier, this time period had some advantages, but also some severe downfalls. In addition to this, if this system was implemented who could argue that the naturally course of events would not bring the world back to a time of feudal lords. This, by the way, is one of the most detested historical hierarchies in the anarchist movement. It must be remembered that it was not anarchism that ended this system but rather popular movements with ties to republican government.

Anarchism would only serve to create a power vacuum that would be filled by tyrants and dictators. If this type of anarchist doesn't sound like you, then in reality your belief system probably more closely parallels a small government republican (as in the type of government and not the United States' political party). It is important that as society advances forward, we do not give up on the goal of good government. Trying to mimic The Other Guys by attempting to "aim for the bushes" after jumping off of a skyscraper is not a mentality that works for government. In all likelihood, many in society would end up dead. Reform and intelligent changes will continue to advance society forward. As Jean-Jacques Rousseau says in The Social Contract, "We all know that we have to put up with bad government when it is bad; the problem is to find a good government."

It is now seen that throughout the world much reform needs to occur. While the instances of abuse throughout the world are extremely appalling, this should not stop advancements within our own country. Contrary to the lessons of many elementary school teachers, the policy of contentment does not work in every circumstance. While the United States should be proud of various accomplishments as they look out among the countries of the world, historical and modern day offenses still plague this country. This nation must learn from its mistakes and adopt a plan for reformation. What children should be taught through early education is that incessant complaining and sometimes force are needed to instigate real change. Asking whether the glass is half empty or half full does not accomplish anything. Rather, people should be asking why the glass is not completely full. After the cup is overflowing, then one should ask why the capacity of the glass should not increase.

Once one advances past the years of formal education, most will discover that there are bullies in the real world as well. If not a boss or coworker, they can be found in Xi Jinpings or Castros. The goal is not to end their existence but rather to reform the system in which they came to power. These leaders are not leaders but rather a disgrace to their countries of origin. Instead of being ashamed, people need to stand up and work together to oust these people from power.

Chapter 5: Back to the Past

As mentioned earlier during the discussion about anarchism, reverting to the past does not always have a positive connotation. In the case of anarchism, reversion means a lack of protection against tyrants and in many cases a possible return to feudal states. While neither fully apply, the terms conservative and liberal both apply in part to my governmental philosophy and this section will be devoted to the things that do not need change. This will of course have a strong connection to constitutional principles and guidelines, but also to nature. Before a people can advance toward the future, a better understanding of their roots is beneficial. This goal will be accomplished in the following pages.

While the policy issues that will be presented are extremely important, it must first be considered how one should receive them. Public discussion is of course encouraged, but it should be conducted in a polite manner. When speaking about the government and reforms, lines based on principle can sometimes be relative or arbitrary. Therefore, when discussing such matters, a level of intelligence as well as calm composure are needed. Arguments should not be based on a need for a socially perceived intelligence because this can often detract from the true purpose of obtaining good government. In addition to all this, an open mind should be had by all who participate.

Due to the fact that the ideals of open-mindedness have been diluted in today's modern culture, a more thorough explanation is needed. At its core, this philosophy supports free and open conversation within a subject area. Words should not be reciprocated with violence and escalation of conflict from verbal to physical should never occur. While violence should be avoided so should interruption and, as much as possible, prejudice. If one is talking to a white supremacist and does not let him speak, then they are not practicing open-mindedness. Not allowing this man to speak is not going to change his opinion, and the best chance for a change comes through rational argument, not indignation. In this case, the racist's hate for different people is not cancelled out by one's hate for him. The ultimate end to hate and violence does not come through force but through information and understanding of another's positions. Agreement, while it is the final objective, should not be obtained through coercion. Following the same concepts, places for communication should be adopted that make this possible. Coffeehouses or living rooms provide a soothing environment for friends to congregate.

In addition to this, people should challenge the relationships that they have and see how deep they really are. Socrates once said, "Strong minds discuss ideas, average minds discuss events, weak minds discuss people." This is a deep thought, but I do have a critique. It is not what people discuss that usually determines their intelligence but rather what they think. Discussion does aid in gaining new information, but some of the most intelligent people, like Socrates, gained much information through observation. What they do with it afterwards is not a matter of intelligence, but rather a matter of connection.

If all the people in the world were intelligent, still not everyone would discuss ideas. This is due to the fact that some people do not have strong enough relationships. In this circumstance strong relationships discuss ideas, average relationships discuss events, and weak relationships discuss people. One is not going to divulge their most cherished ideas with people who will not treat them with a degree of respect.

Also this quotation does not account for the fact that intelligent people can use a discussion about a specific person, to bring up an issue or event. Likewise, a discussion about an event, like a war, can begin a dialogue about the ideas that are also combating. Whatever the restrictions to free and open conversation may be, a way must be found to advance forward. Instead of having a friend base consisting of coworkers and schoolmates, begin to meet people from political events or scientific lectures. Agreeing totally is not a requirement, but the instigation of deep conversation at the beginning of the relationship will bypass awkward stages of growth. Psychologists have compiled lists of questions that can serve to propel romantic relationships forward, and the same sort of policy can be extrapolated for use in ordinary friendships as well. Instead of talking about the football game or what Lucille did on the bus, find deep people for real conversation. While sporting events and schoolyard gossip are insignificant, religious beliefs and politics have a major effect in society on a daily basis. Now that the stage is set, let the discussion begin.

In light of the theme of "back to the past," important ideas will be gathered by previous events or ideas. Although somewhat general, the importance of maintaining the spirit of rebellion cannot be negated. Spirit of course has no religious connotation, due to the fact that the discussion must remain on politics in this country, but rather references a sort of feeling or emotion. In many ways the stability of government has allowed people to take peace for granted. This has of course allowed for the advancement in learning and the creation of new ideologies. Many of these beliefs are important to discuss, but the price of liberty cannot be forgotten. From the rebellion of peasants in Russia to slave revolts in the American colonies, millions of lives have been lost. In certain cases the leaders of rebellions would have considered their freedom fighting counterparts of different backgrounds to be less than human, but despite this irony the world kept on marching forward. Different people, not always in agreement, fought around the world for many of the principles found now in the Constitution and Bill of Rights. Many participants did not even have a chance to better their own lives, but rather fought for their descendents or even for the descendents of others. The effects of their sacrifices can be felt now even centuries later after many generations have come and gone. The glory and wealth that could have been involved have now faded or been weathered by the effect of time, but the principles now stand just as solid as ever before. The application is often still discussed, but the foundation need not be questioned.

The spirit of rebellion not only demands a respect for these predecessors, but also a degree of unity. Fighting between individuals no longer is the major force for freedom in this country, but now a battle between ideologies is taking place. Once common sense plans are found, unity within the movement is required for the execution. Leaders will no longer be chosen based on party affiliations but rather by adherence to these plans. Another aspect of the spirit of freedom includes an understanding of those around. Politics often no longer revolves around the clashes between tyrants and wanting peasants, but rather tries to solve the problem of living in harmony. Aversion to coercion is a major force for this, but checks against the overly greedy must also be established. When people understand each other, this goal will be achieved. However this is often a slow process and as Nelle Harper Lee illustrates in her novel To Kill a Mockingbird, government cannot attain a higher level of excellence if the people are not ready. Sometimes it is not the system that is broke but the society which controls it. Now that the platform for discussion and needed mindset have been covered, the proposed reforms can be highlighted.

While much of the focus of this section will be about reverting to certain constitutional principles, first an analysis of the original state of humans as it relates to modernity must occur. The term natural may be the most misused word in all of history. This word has several different social definitions and it is important to understand each one. First, it can mean something similar to predestined as in it was natural that the Native Americans lost due to the spread of disease and lack of advanced weaponry. What is natural in this sense can be negated by human reason and rational expression. In many cases, what this definition entails is determined by human interference.

The next definition of natural can be closely translated as original state. This can be further divided into two different categories. The first includes all the uses that reference a situation with the hypothetical nonexistence of humans. This is used often by the scientific community but it is relatively useless when discussing politics. The other category does not include the nonexistence of humans, but rather refers to the animalistic desires of humans without the interference of our more advanced minds.

It is now important to go back to the distant past of the original state of human interaction and apply what is learned for today. While politics often serves to control natural desires of revenge and greed, certain aspects of nature should never be eliminated. Natural desires for clean food and water should be accounted for, but there is one example that needs special recognition. Although it used to be considered an inappropriate subject, through the influence of the media and more personal sources, sex has become a high topic of discussion. Even with this being the case, political policy and social conceptions as they relate to sex are still far from natural.

This may be coming from a largely biased source, but teenagers and young people in general are one of the most oppressed groups in modern American culture. Oppression in this case does not come through the unauthorized prohibition of voting rights or the torture of this group's members, but through a more unusual method. While the voting age of eighteen is a fine choice, the current age of marriage is not. The modern concept of monogamous marriage comes largely from religion, and most of the dominant religions in American society require the establishment of this institution before carnal relations occur. Females are usually sexually mature by the age of fourteen while it takes males sometimes a couple more years. When it is seen that the marriage age is eighteen in many states, problems start to appear.

Although there is a negative effect with the governmental involvement, a deeper problem is also apparent. It is seen that the average age of marriage in the United States for the year 2010 was over twenty-six years for women and over twenty-eight years for men. If it was only the government holding people back then many would be married at eighteen. While there are those who voluntarily commit to celibacy, they do not make up a significant portion of society. A good many bypass the institution of marriage and initiate carnal relations at a more natural age, but what if one's conscience has denounced this option.

A greater hindrance to this practice than a person's conscience is usually social pressures or awareness. Today's culture does not promote the natural age of sexual instigation as seen through the setup of the educational and economic systems. One rarely is able to commit when the whole direction of life is not decided until a while after college. By that time, one is often approaching their mid-twenties and it usually takes some time to find a mate. Sexual deprivation in today's society is disturbing. It is seen through this example that the Native Americans culture often considered "primitive," was often more successful in providing basic needs and desires.

Whatever the case may be, a better system should be created. The first step in fixing the problem of sexual deprivation is fixing the problems within the modern education system. The first important point to bring up is the fact that education should be a more local function. While larger institutions should still be established, they will not be continued through state and federal taxes. This change would result in a breakup of the current monopoly in education. While this is a good plan, some politicians have risen partially due to the fact that they promised to expand this current system. The effects of Bernie Sanders plans on a large scale can be also applied to state levels. Why should those choosing to go to trade schools and private colleges be forced to pay for those who go to public colleges? However true this may be, Sanders brings up various good points. One of his most important ones being that the poor in America need to be given a fair chance. His fight for this class is noble, but I don't believe this policy would help them. Free tuition would further monopolize that level of education as it did to the lower one. While the price would be lowered for the poor, the cost would be increased and this would be paid by the taxpayers. A more efficient method of easing the burden for the poor would be to directly cut taxes for the poor while making the higher classes compensate. Whatever the hypotheticals would be, as mentioned earlier, education should be a local function and therefore taxes need not be gathered for this function on a large scale.

Another problem with the modern education system is the monopoly held not by the government, but by the current educational model. The latter can be connected to the former, however. Large governments at the state level enforce many requirements that limit less conventional options when compared to public, private, and home schooling which all have problems of their own. While a purely capitalistic society is not to be desirable, competition can form very beneficial results. Why is it not the businesses that are doing the hiring, that choose their own requirements?

One might pose the concern that the science and arts would not be accurately represented in the minds of the young. As insinuated earlier, people are naturally going to be inclined to the advancement of society and this tendency does not need to be enforced by the government. Modern social society places great emphasis on both charity and science and while those who donate are not rewarded monetarily, people reward them with a sense of respect or gratification. If a people does not value knowledge then they cannot be forced to through government.

In addition to these problems, common sense combats the current educational model in certain ways. There are almost an infinite amount of questions could be asked about problems that arise as a result of this system. Why does modern day schooling take children who are excited about learning and leave many feeling depressed? Why are more formal careers enforced on those who already have decided to participate in more hands-on careers? Why are those who are more intelligent or who have greater traditional learning abilities not more easily advanced forward? Why is so much of their time wasted? All of these are important questions, but there are other reforms that need to be focused on.

Charles de Montesquieu said, "It is natural for a republic to have only a small territory; otherwise it cannot long subsist." These words echoed through the chambers of early American political discussion concerning the new Constitution and seemed to doom the new experiment as a dismal failure. This problem was solved through one of Montesquieu's other ideas however when he discussed the possibility of a confederate republic. In addition to the constitution, a Bill of Rights was added later. The first two rights listed bring up an interesting point. First, the freedom of speech, expression, and congregation should all be unlimited. These are all necessary as stated before for the peaceful change in government. Although the text is filled with phrases such as "shall make no law" and "free exercise," former politicians have wished to break, not "bend" this rule. With this legal document there is no middle ground, it is all black and white.

While the Civil Rights Movement accomplished many important objectives like open voting for blacks, certain reformers went too far and began to take away the rights of all citizens regardless of race. "Hate speech" is a ban that should not even occur on a state level. It becomes increasingly dangerous when the government is left to interpret who is an offender. While it may seem safe in the stable United States, it must be remembered that many other republics have fallen due to the slow erosion of the citizens' rights. As seen today, reforms in race relations are still rendered volatile. Many black activists even from far back have commented on the situation. Booker T. Washington said, "The indiscriminate condemnation of all white people on the part of any member of our race is a suicidal and dangerous policy. We must learn to discriminate." This quote may seem ironic in the context of modernity but it was applicable to the time.

Obviously there are larger problems facing this community today like poverty and crime and these need to be accounted for. Poorly administered federal welfare programs are aimed at helping all poor, but they are merely poor attempts to cover up a deeper problem with the structure of society. The concept of land has always been important as seen by John Locke's famous saying "life, liberty, and property." Why is this now considered a null point? Even if one believes in a strict communist state, land is still a main focus. After the Civil War in both the North and South almost all land was owned by whites and as seen through history, land in terms of a fluid has a very high viscosity. Those freed either stayed and worked for their former master or moved to the cities in droves. Obviously the economic effect of this would be negative and many could not find good paying jobs. Poor areas then became home and it has been hard for people to be liberated from this system. Much of the black community had been placed in a pit after the Civil War and no major political party today addresses their problems. Liberal policies of Affirmative Action and the expansion of welfare have the effect of keeping this group down in the pit, while conservatives barely converse about the problems faced by the black community. When people do talk about it, they only discuss the situation and not any meaningful solutions. Instead of throwing down food into the pit, bring down a ladder.

Unlike many political analysts today, I do not believe that either political party is based on racism but only that they are both inept to solve the problem. Racism will be vanquished only when the black community rises from the economic shadows. Frederick Douglass' words are important to note at this moment: "What I ask for the Negro is not benevolence, not pity, not sympathy, but simply justice." He then continues later, talking about the black community, saying, "Let him live or die by that. If you will only untie his hands, and give him a chance, I think he will live. He will work as readily for himself as the white man. A great many delusions have been swept away by this war. One was, that the Negro would not work; he has proved his ability to work. Another was, that the Negro would not fight; that he possessed only the most sheepish attributes of humanity; was a perfect lamb, or an 'Uncle Tom;' disposed to take off his coat whenever required, fold his hands, and be whipped by anybody who wanted to whip him. But the war has proved that there is a great deal of human nature in the Negro, and that he will fight." Even though the pure policy of inaction did not accomplish anything, the idealistic plan that will detailed during the last section will serve to elevate not only poor, minority communities but all humans.

While the First Amendment is obviously stated as being unlimited and this should not change, the Second Amendment poses a few more problems. In contrast with the more strong language of the first, the second leaves some room for compromise. Instead of a "shall make no law" tone, it rather states that the "right of the people to keep and bear Arms, shall not be infringed." What is to be categorized as arms is still up for debate. It has been stated earlier that no government should have the power to end all of civilization, but this point also applies to a greater degree when discussing individual citizens. Nuclear weapons provide an extreme that allow for a more rational perspective.

Even though there is a legal ability to limit, the right of citizens to defend against government tyranny should not be scoffed at. Former president Barack Obama does not understand what this amendment means, but this is sadly true of almost every politician in both political parties. The Republicans ramble about an area in which they are not educated, while Democrats like Obama say citizens should not fear the government because the "government is us." This quote from Obama is a very pathetic attempt to minimize a serious concern. Every student of history is bound to find examples of popular governments that have deteriorated. While ideally force will not be the major check on government, if the checks within the several branches of the institution or between the different levels fail; then popular force should be able to take matters into their own hands. The checks within the system are not to more accurately represent the general will, but rather to protect it from power hungry rulers. When this bulwark fails however there must be a backup plan.

As mentioned earlier, the decrease of federal power should be instituted internationally and simultaneously with other governments. The power of the government should never exceed the power of a majority of the citizens. Therefore in an ideal society, nuclear bans would not only be put in place, but also bans on other explosives and even tanks. The weapons of the government should never be of a higher grade than the arms of the citizen, but this plan will take some time to execute.

The modern debate about gun control does not consider this balance and rather is a contest between fear-ravaged people on both sides. Under the current system, gun control on a federal level is ridiculous. As mentioned earlier, people always run to the larger governments whenever they have a potential reform. Why cannot those states which consider "high capacity magazines" or more lax background checks unsafe place restrictions while those who value these items maintain their existence.

In all reality, this is a non-issue. One of the things that glorifies the system based on federalism in America is the competition between states. If one state has a high death rate by guns, look at the example and base your government on a different model. It's that simple. In the days after a Orlando massacre at a gay nightclub, there was mass hysteria. During this time, I found peace in parts of the system that I saw at work. Many became frustrated at the lack of movement in Congress and other branches of government, but this brought me new faith. Political decisions should not be made when emotions are still running high, if possible, but rather they need to be based on rational debate and sound policy.

One piece of evidence for the dangers of hysteria from this event came from a proposed "common sense" reform. It was really unintelligent and that is now seen by many. During arguments many suggested that those who are on the FBI's "no fly list" should also not be allowed to buy a gun. At a surface level this may seem rational, but a further investigation must be conducted. Who would be making this decision to take away one's constitutional right? It turns out that they would be officials not directly elected by citizens and no legislation would need to pass through Congress. Indirect decision making is part of the problem facing the corrupt Chinese government, and Congress, while sometimes slow and indecisive, guards against the tyranny in government from which the Second Amendment is a guard.

As Rousseau says in The Social Contract, "I believe indeed that one can lay down as an axiom that when the functions of government are divided between several commissions, those with the fewest members acquire sooner or later the greatest authority, if only because the facility of dispatching business leads naturally in that direction." Although business deals or legislation may run more smoothly, tyranny is also an increased likelihood. The passage of power to the executive branch can be easily seen in American government and the citizens must fight against it. The first step in doing this is spreading the idea so that people can recognize what is taking place. After social awareness is increased, these ideas can be reflected in the polls. In addition to self-identified "liberals," conservatives took part in some of the hysteria, and talk show host Bill O'Reilly recommended that the federal government should become involved. As mentioned earlier every part of the system has a reason and none of it should be discarded without due consideration.

Before returning to constitutional principle, the debate must turn to the purely idealistic and hypothetical idea of open borders. Now, once again, a distinction must be made between different vocabulary and definitions. When the term idealistic is used to describe one of my proposed reforms it is obviously not meant as an insult. Instead it refers to something that has not yet been put into practice. Now when the words idealistic and hypothetical are preceded by "purely" then an argument is usually being made against something. This is due to the fact that if something is described as such, then it is considered to be inherent under the current human condition which includes hate, violence, and prejudice. Even if these emotions are buried by every citizen, a lax in political rigidity would most likely bring them back for potential personal gains of power or wealth. For this same reason, the term "ideal society" is used in the place of the sometimes misused term of "utopia" which often is meant to include the inference of purely beneficial social relations.

Now back from the vocabulary to the political conversation. One argument that often accompanies the belief in open borders is that it is the natural order of things. From the set of definitions mentioned earlier, it will be decided which ones are applicable. An argument can barely be made for any of the three definitions that were previously described. First, it can not be considered predestined because society always tend to instigate some form of limited immigration. Second, it does not conform to either or the "original state" definitions of natural. In a world without human influence or existence, many creatures such as wolves would still mark off territory. These arbitrary borders would be defended through force and any trespassers would likely be attacked if they posed a threat to the pack or shared a similar food source. The other category of this definition in which humans interact with each other and their surroundings with a purely animalistic response also does not provide a justification for the open borders argument. If humans maintained only a narrow view of existence then borders would still be created. It has never been a need of humans to walk all territories without restrictions so this can barely be put in a category with hunger, thirst, or sexual desire.

Rather, humans must use their intellect to determine what system is best for themselves and their surroundings. When it is looked upon in this perspective, then the open borders argument cannot stand on its own. One of the arguments of open border advocates include an economic aspect. If a certain region is rich in natural resources or experiences great wealth, then people will naturally flock there and balance the needs of all the world's citizens. While a system in which resources are assigned fairly to communities is important, borders still serve a purpose. If success through innovation or spectacular social organization lead to general happiness and the well being of all citizens, then this system should not be forcibly changed by unwarranted immigration. The people coming over did not participate in the creation of this society and control in the hands of those who did is not an absurd idea.

This is not an argument of white supremacy however. This ideology can be applied to the example of the Native Americans whose insufficiently guarded borders led to the destruction of their culture and mass genocide. The Europeans often used the argument that the land was not being used to its full potential, but this belief does not hold up. New settlers were not entitled to the land just because they had begun the process of overpopulation and now felt crowded on in their own continent.

In addition to the disease and large wars which accompanied unhindered immigration, the Europeans instituted a new social system of large cities and colonies. It can now be seen that the consolidation of people, like the mismanagement of livestock manure, can cause environmental problems. In the case of humans it can also cause social disorder. It is the city that keeps many minority communities away from the raw material that can create primary wealth. Also local politics becomes tricky when people do not know and do not care about those who may live only fifty feet above them.

Remember, there is also an environmental impact. Water purification becomes more tricky and human waste disposal does also. One may say that society has taken care of all of these problems, but the real question is: What are we advancing towards? If natural needs are met more easily in a less populated society and with less environmental concerns, intellectuals and scientists can focus on more important questions. For local testing, both cities and more rural communities should be held to the same stringent regional guidelines regardless of their population. How is this fair? This can be easily explained with a futuristic plan which both protects the environment directly and curbs population overgrowth.

Many people attempt to mistakenly dismiss the concern of overpopulation by saying that the desire for offspring is natural. While this is true and in accordance with the evolutionary model, natural desire must be sometimes sacrificed for the desire of society to function correctly and the preservation of nature itself.

What is unnatural is not borders, but rather the large-scale forced integration of modern society. A system must be discussed which would address all of these concerns. First, at the communal level a minimum number of citizens must be required through the national government. In addition to this an environmental policy must be adopted to prevent the abuse of natural resources like air and water which are used by all communities. The dynamic of these two stipulations would serve to control population growth because a society would be held personally accountable for the effects of pollution caused by overgrowth. The federal government would grant available lands to different groups through a commission which is not informed of the race or unrelated background of the group to avoid unfair discrimination. To determine the overall aptitude of existing communities, a psychological evaluation of its residence will occur. If the results go under a determined point then the government that no longer provides for its citizens will be dissolved and replaced by new group. As this system advances, a higher level of performance will be expected and those communities which do not achieve the happiness of its citizens will be sorted out.

Failing the psychological evaluation or environmental inspection would open up opportunities for new communities to take over. This would solve many different racially related social problems. First minorities would be able to collectively acquire land and therefore bypass the adverse effects of being born into some of the problems that were not addressed after the Civil War. In addition to this, racism could be effectively filtered out on a local level. Coerced integration would no longer be the policy. While this policy may be compared by some to Jim Crow, it is completely the opposite. Unlike these abominable laws, the proposed plan would provide a level playing ground for all people. In addition to this minorities would be allowed to control their own fate as opposed to the southern system that was dominated by those of European descent.

Once humanity becomes more advanced, integration will become more popular on a communal level. Of course precautions would need to be taken to guard against state level racism, but these are clear to see. A separation of information between those who grant land, conduct psychological and environmental tests, and decide expulsion needs to be maintained. The powers of the communal level will be discussed further in respect to other levels. It can now be seen that the benefits of the human's tribal beginnings can be combined with the onward march of globalization. A stable system of federalism is the key.

Talking about race and culture does not always end up being constructive. Ethnocentrists and racists combat those who glorify diversity with little progress. Arguments on both sides are extremely flawed. While it is seen that borders are necessary to filter out potential threats, racists often have the wrong reasons. Politics can not be the arbitrator for an argument deciding the most intelligent or able race because no unbiased judge can be found. Instead of this constant bickering, learning to live around other cultures peaceably should be the goal.

While this is true some on the left have overly emphasized the concept of racial and cultural diversification. First, those who advocate for open borders must admit that their policy will not allow for individual cultures to survive, so one belief must be chosen. In addition to this many have supported different cultures to an extreme. Culture should be response to generally accepted beliefs and the environment around. Each culture has something to offer, and these items should be saved, while society advances forward as conditions change. On a communal level diversification of culture and race should not exist. Rather when the groups form, for true integration to occur both culture practices and genetics will be fused together. When the Spaniards came over to the Americas, they did not totally destroy the natives, and mestizos, who have a mix of native and European blood, remain the most populous group today. Although this provides a good example, integration should be voluntary and not forced like this example.

Also, homologous groups are less likely to encounter problems based upon suspicion. This occurs presently in both the black and white communities of America. There are suspicions that whites hold when walking into a largely black community, but this is coupled with black suspicion of institutions that they believe are largely controlled by whites. If these two groups combined into a homologous group then much of that suspicion would be lifted. Israel Zangwill once said, "America is God's crucible, the great crucible where all the races of Europe are melting and reforming." In an area as large as America, this is not and should not be the case. However, Zangwill does bring up an important point. It used to be the case in the early days of the United States that immigrants like the Irish were discriminated against. They were more quickly assimilated into the society however due to the fact that the differences were not as noticeable. All whites, who had previously created various different groups in their homeland, formed a more singular race in America.

Although it may take more time, other differences will be overcome and this will eventually occur with other races as well. Former president Jimmy Carter created an appropriate rebuttal by saying, "We become not a melting pot, but a beautiful mosaic. Different people, different beliefs, different yearnings, different hopes, different dreams." On a national level this should be the case, on a communal level it should be the opposite.

While reverting back to certain aspects of more tribal and natural government is important, constitutional principles from the beginnings of the United States must also be saved. There have been many offenses to the concepts of federalism and separation of powers in the national government and these need to be addressed. First, an understanding of the destructive path the U.S. has been on is required.

There are two debated passages within the constitution that allow for certain misinterpretations. The preamble of the Constitution has been assailed by certain groups, but it can be clearly seen that it was only meant as an overview and does not grant any legislative or executive power over the items listed. Instead it only introduces the reader to the reason for creating the new government, and it provides an explanation for the powers enumerated later in the document. Another contested passage comes from Article I, Section 8, and states that Congress will have the power, "To make all Laws which shall be necessary and proper for carrying into Execution the foregoing Powers, and all other Powers vested by this Constitution in the Government of the United States, or in any Department or Officer thereof." This does not allow any law to be made, but rather only enables the execution of laws. As stated in the forty fourth publication of The Federalist Papers by James Madison, "Few parts of the Constitution have been assailed with more intemperance than this; yet on a fair investigation of it, no part can appear more completely invulnerable. Without the substance of this power, the whole Constitution would be a dead letter. Those who object to the article, therefore, as a part of the Constitution, can only mean that the form of the provision is improper. But have they considered whether a better form could have been substituted?"

While ignorance and willful misinterpretation have played an effect on the expansion of national power, so have certain reforms.

At the beginning of the twentieth century, it was decided to end the power of state legislatures to choose Senate members. While these reformers had the decency to amend rather than trample the Constitution, I do not believe that due consideration occurred. The Constitution was meant to be both a federal and a national government. Federalism meant that the rights of the states would be protected while national power represented the general population directly. Indirect means of election have plagued countries like China, but the system set up by the Constitution differentiates itself. The popular branch of the House of Representatives guarantees that states alone cannot make any meaningful changes. The forty-fifth publication of The Federalist Papers by James Madison states, "Thus, each of the principal branches of the federal government will owe its existence more or less to the favor of the State governments, and must consequently feel a dependence, which is much more likely to beget a disposition too obsequious than too overbearing towards them. On the other side, the component parts of the State governments will in no instance be indebted for their appointment to the direct agency of the federal government, and very little, if at all, to the local influence of its members."

A key part of the Constitution cannot be cancelled without some form of replacement. State power needs to be represented in the federal government because like the nobles in the more primitive monarchical system, the states provide an important protection against national usurpation. If the national government becomes tyrannical, the states provide an organized resistance which would prove more effective than mere individual soldiers. State legislatures previously ran into corruption however and this called for reform. Certain states did not choose any Senators because of deadlocks while others chose corrupt members. A more comprehensive plan of voting in the legislatures and public knowledge of corrupt officials would have taken care of many of these problems but the movement continued. The movement passed the Senate in the form of the Seventeenth Amendment, showing that corruption was not that large of a problem. A major component of the genius system of the founders was lost.

The large amount of national agencies which need to be dismantled necessitates a dialogue based on principle and not specificity. Although this is true, examples will be given in each case to support the generalization. Consideration will not only be placed on what is ideal, but also what is constitutional. First, the case of science and remedial medicine must be examined. While both of these are current social goals, the level of government at which they are addressed is still up for debate. The national government as mentioned earlier does not need to force this on a large scale because most in society already support advancements. However, those who wish to live in a more primitive society should not be forced to share in this goal.

In addition to this, the national government has proved itself inept at handling funds and its responsibilities should be limited. There are many examples that would be placed under these categories, but institutes within the District of Columbia would not be included. Smaller items like the Arthritis and Musculoskeletal Interagency Coordinating Committee (long name, zero results), would be cut. Also, larger institutions like the Food and Drug Administration would be deemed unnecessary. This institution creates a false sense of security with various approved items, as seen by the numerous recalls in commercials. People must begin rejecting the principle that knowledge comes directly from the government and rather use more intelligent methods of research. The safety of food and medicine is a concern for most people and therefore can be handled by either the state or communal governments.

The federal government should be used primarily as an arbitrator of arguments between different states which includes environmental concerns. Certain institutions such as the Energy Department serve some purposes, but also need to be limited. In the case of the energy department certain environmental testing must occur to see if communities are within their limits, but its research should not be funded. If the system based on communal accountability for resources is adopted, then the local governments which are most innovative will be rewarded. Renewable resources such as wind, solar, and hydroelectric if harnessed correctly have the ability to allow a society to be more productive under environmental stipulations. Of course, water use will be monitored by higher levels of government because all communities use lakes and rivers. In addition to this more potentially volatile energy sources such as nuclear will be monitored by the state or federal authorities in accordance with the degree of the threat posed by the system. Jurisdiction in these matters is a topic that can be discussed in new amendment agreements. Although departments such as this would serve a purpose, the scientific research that is conducted would be through local or private methods.

A breakdown of federalism has occurred, but the separation of powers between the different branches of the national government have also been attacked. Executive orders have been a large part of this. In all my research I have found no clauses in the Constitution that permit the executive branch to also directly legislate. This is an extreme usurpation of power and shows the principle that power often falls into the hands of the few. People need to guard against this tendency because it can lead to unchecked power. While a president can make political promises, without the internal checks on the system there is no enforcement of these. The word of politicians is often tainted and basing a system on good intentions does not lead to stability and peace. There was no executive-legislative position in the Constitution for a specific reason and America has stumbled into a precarious situation.

Another usurper of power is the Supreme Court. When they were presented with the case of gay marriage, they forced all states to legalize it. There are a couple different important observations to review. First, large government does not need to be involved in marriage. If two people commit themselves to one another for presumably purely religious or social reasons, the government does not need to take part in the ceremony.

Second, social issues such as personal relations and drug use should be handled at a local level. The federal government also did not have any jurisdiction in this matter. The right to marriage is not constitutional and any action taken by the Supreme Court in this area would be an offense against legislative power. Under the present application of marriage, support for gay marriage should be focused at a state level. While the states also are too large of an institution to handle the issue, it is better than the national government that spans almost four million square miles. Communal governments ideally would hold onto the determination and application of religion and other social issues. Without the stability of Congressional power and the time for consideration they allow, the United States will likely be plagued with indecision and disconcerted policy making.

Good principle is most likely to survive in a system where legislative power is only exercised by the intended branch of government. The legislators' retardation of policies allows for caution and a forum for discussion. Executive orders as legislation are not consistent due to the fact that the next president can undo these policies without consideration. Whatever the case may be, republican forms of government provide more organization in this respect than monarchies. Rousseau once wrote, "One consequence of this lack of coherence is the instability of royal government, which, being sometimes directed according to one plan and sometimes according to another, depending on the personality of the king who rules, or of those who rule for him, cannot long have a fixed objective or a consistent policy; this unsettledness makes the state drift from principle to principle, and from one project to another, a defect not found in those forms of government where the prince is always the same." In this extremely long sentence, Rousseau makes a number of good points. The most important point being that the general population is usually very consistent. People will always provide for their needs when given the power, and therefore policy is concerted. However, partisanship has taken over where reason was once king, and now knowledge is subjugated as a vassal under the pretense of conquering the "greater evil".

There are many other powers of the federal government that need to be put into question, this time historical, geological, and landmark sites. There are ways to constitutionally establish these sites but it seems that this document is no longer of importance for many politicians. Establishing these places and national forests as territories, the United States could exercise authority over them. Instead, power is taken directly and this "ancient" text is ignored. It is important for the federal government to hold power over these sites because those who have no personal connection to a state will be less likely to give in to regional economic or business interests. A person from Maine is not going to consider the importance of a land developer in California when it is compared to the conservation of science and history.

Large governments serve another purpose in this respect as well. If set up correctly, popular nations can provide stability from war which leads often to the destruction of historic sites. In places like the Middle East where nations rarely exceed the level of a more stretched local government, terror groups have been able to destroy historic sites that they deem pagan.

Archeology and other branches of science can be supported in this way, but also through the work of The United States Patent and Trademark Office. Only these two tools are necessary for this objective on a federal level.

One way to stimulate a focus on the Constitution is to reintroduce it into the political scene. During the 2016 presidential race, little to no reference was made by either major party candidates or their affiliates to the governing document of the nation. The only largely publicized occurrence was the Khizr Khan controversy that occurred at Democratic National Convention. During this episode, one of the speakers for Hillary Clinton asked Donald Trump if he had ever read the Constitution. Trump came back with a highly controversial rebuttal, but the question remained.

Another method for instigating a reversion to sound principles is through small but symbolic actions of amending. Certain programs such as the Park Service or Federal Aviation Authority have existed for years without specific constitutional support. Both the states and the houses of Congress would support amendments concerning the funding of these administrations, but the practice of apathy continues. The amending of the Constitution, for this reason, would allow for a discussion to develop and a new course based partially on old principles would be established. Symbolism is an important start that can leave to substantive change. Although this can be the case, the Constitution is often considered second to personal desire for a potential reform.

A different item that is considered in a similar method is the national debt. Many government reformers comment on its increasing severity, but when something of "greater importance" comes up; it is forgotten. There are a string of arguments that this group of people uses to legitimize their thought process. However, all of these methods are based on emotion and not rational consideration. First, it may be said in regards to federal cancer research that the government needs to take action even if it further entrenches the problem of debt because the goal is righteous enough. While the goal is good, one must first ask of the plans legitimacy. It should not be expected that the United States be the sole or primary donor to these causes. Why do the countries and businesses from which we borrow not contribute the necessary funds?

In addition to this, one must ask the question of whether or not the stability that has been rendered by the federal government should be sacrificed. The ideals of liberty have saved countless lives and have provided a platform for scientific exploration, and overwhelming debt threatens this idealism in the North American region. In addition to this, there is not, and should not be a consensus when discussing scientific advancement. Many believe that a more simplistic society will better parallel the natural evolutionary system.

Another argument used by this group includes a very enticing principle. Instead of collectively stating the cost of a sector by principle, many individually place a price on packages. It must be remembered that in government every ten million dollars counts. The federal government can not and should not provide the funding for all of the citizens' individual causes. The cuts may be tough, but they are necessary to ensure a continuation of the excellence expected by American politics.

While there are many individual causes that contribute to debt, the two party system definitely has a negative effect. Many of the fiscally recommendable policies of the Libertarian Party are lost in a corrupt institution. A Republican can hardly be elected without a staunch stance in favor of military expansion or a continuation of the current funding. 2016 presidential candidate Rand Paul on the Republican side provides an example of how common sense is often ignored. Debaters harshly attacked both his constitutional support of the Fifth Amendment and his budget cuts.

On the other side, a large portion of Democratic support has been gathered by their largely superficial social reforms. As mentioned earlier these do not actually solve any deep problems, but options are severely limited. These two groups continue to argue while debt is increased. Inept leaders have been produced by the parties and it is time for change. The system which provided a degree of discussion has proven that it is incapable of handling a budget. Over involvement militarily in world affairs and bankrupt social programs have been chosen over the public good and this binopoly must be broken down. The perspective that the federal government should not be held to the different standard than ordinary citizens is beneficial. To counteract the tendency towards an ever increase to the national debt, certain reforms should be enacted. Once the problem is dealt with, an emergency clause should be created which makes it more difficult to add items to the budget. Only then can popular desires be restrained to the point where they do not self-destruct into the end of the republic. As mentioned earlier, the general will must be correctly represented but plans of protection for the system must also be put in place.

Social security makes up a significant portion of the budget but also provides a service that many have grown dependent on. While ideally local institutions would be responsible for the care of elderly and handicapped, this change will occur relatively slowly. Many would consider this to be dangerous but the opposite is true. At a smaller level, people are more tightly connected, and therefore would be more aware of the needed safeguards. In addition to this, the administration of aid would be more effective and abuses would be sufficiently dealt with. This principle can also be applied to other social programs such as Medicare, Medicaid, and all forms of "welfare". The overstretched system of the federal government is fraught with misuse and abuse. If this large government is to control such a social service, there should be more restrictions. Local examples which I have gathered from fellow residents and neighbors show the need for these. People often are given more than is needed and extravagant purchases are not rare. Restrictions beyond a ban on purchasing alcohol and tobacco products are few. Candy and other unhealthy items are still permitted for purchase.

In addition to this, programs that are largely adopted due to the needs of children are not based on their nutritional needs. People should not be encouraged to continue in this system and rather should have a motivation to find a job. Certain people, who worked at local fast food joints, calculated and limited their hours so that they would receive the maximum amount. Also, people would manipulate programs based on family needs. Although these people were not able to provide for their existing children, many increased the size of their family for the sole purpose of increasing benefits. Large televisions and other extravagant purchases would often be placed before safer neighborhoods or better food. These abuses are appalling, but other cuts prove to be arguably more important.

While social benefits are tirelessly defended by those who identify as liberals, the military is untouchable in the "conservative" camps. The term conservative can mean "marked by moderation," but this is barely reflective of most right wingers in America. Social programs are sought to be limited by many in this group, but common sense spending in regards to defense is attacked. It is actually not always defense which costs so much, but the trillions of dollars spent on foreign wars. As mentioned earlier, the United States should adopt a policy of general nonintervention militarily, but negotiate using economic prowess to support popular movements. China, which is second in military spending, only used a little over two hundred billion in this sector. In contrast, the United States spent almost six hundred billion. While this is an important function of the federal government, a limit must be placed. Anyone who proposes a decrease in both domestic and foreign spending is immediately demonized by both groups.

Another area in which many Republicans have become irrational is the federal drug war. It is estimated that close to a trillion dollars has been spent on this expenditure from both the federal and state levels. In addition to this raids have become overly common and mistakes do occur. Nonviolent offenders are sometimes given harsher sentences than murderers, and the militarization of police has severely increased the power of the government. It seems that the same flawed principles of the prohibition are being applied in much of the same method. While this bit of history seems to be remembered, it is also being replicated. It can be understood by modern culture why the prohibition brought around characters like Al Capone, but not why the drug war brings death through turf wars. If the selling of now illegal drugs was placed in the hands of law abiding citizens, the drug lords would soon disappear for lack of necessity. The government on this issue would no longer be using violence against non-violent criminals, but rather would be the defenders of business owners. In America some only advocate the legalization of marijuana, but I believe that this decision would still leave an important question unanswered. While this drug is arguably far less addictive, people still should be allowed to make decisions about their own body. Ideally the local governments would be in charge of drug legalization or restrictions. A larger government such as the state or regional must be responsible however for potential child abuse. These principles and the question of choice over one's body also comes into play with abortion.

The subject of personal choice becomes even more complicated when discussing the subject of abortion. Scientific discussion is waged persistently and, as usual, everyone automatically runs to the federal government. It seems prudent in this situation to hand the power of deciding the question of life to the state governments.

While all of these problems are important to solve, there is still a lot of ground to cover. Most of the large sections of the budget have already been covered, but many smaller figures also contribute. The interest on the debt makes up over five percent of the federal budget and if these other problems were dealt with this too would go down. In addition to this education and science as mentioned earlier should not be federal objectives and these would also serve to cut the budget. The most important point to make is that if the United States had continued to be guided by the principle of limited functions, much of this debt would have never occurred. Still, this nation must wake to the harsh reality of the mounting debt instead of continually hitting the snooze button. The problem isn't going to go away on its own.

Partisan politics also contributes to the crisis by creating a debate about relatively unimportant things. Republicans incessantly speak about tax breaks and this discussion seems to be completely separate from the national debt. While tax cuts may boost the economy, betting the security of the nation on it is not wise. On the other side Democrats like Bernie Sanders plans to increase the federal education monopoly and continue down the road to a federal-run health care system. All of these, as mentioned earlier, are direct social problems and would be best suited for communal government or maybe the states. I do agree with his plan to crack down on those who evade taxes, but how much money will this really bring in? Trials and investigations cost money. Even if it did bring in money, then why would we spend it? Does the United States Government have the attention of a five year old? Every time the United States gets paid, their first reaction is to run to the store and see what they can buy. When funds become available, the government should use them for something important like the debt, instead of trying to garner political support through "noble causes." This belief may not be very popular in Washington today, but the American republic is worth saving and it must be prioritized over the present tendency towards immaturity and irresponsible spending.

Concerning the tax code, people have much debate. While both sides argue about the details, reform needs to occur. First, a system must be maintained that the average citizen can easily understand. It is preposterous that there exists businesses with the sole purpose of filing taxes. Understanding of common citizens is also important in regards to the system of government which they live under. How can people be expected to participate in a system that they can not comprehend? Whatever the case may be it can now be seen that a reversion to the past is critical in certain areas. A truly conservative approach to the debt and constitutional principles would serve to embetter the nation. As seen by the previous examples, the Republican Party is far from conservative in its support of extreme amounts of military spending and partial disregard of the debt. Learning from the our history and returning to many of the original principles that founded this country will serve as a stable foundation to launch the United States into the future.

Chapter 6: On to the Future

While conservatism can provide a good foundation, it does not conform to the changing world around. The environment and political reform that are needed cannot be provided by this camp. Therefore, it becomes necessary to advance onward partially through the concepts of liberalism. As mentioned earlier, the terms liberal and conservative both are ridiculous to describe oneself as. Change is sometimes bad and sometimes good, so discernment should override political affiliations. It can now be seen that politics has become social and friendship is often based on one's beliefs. This can become detrimental, however, when no one is there to challenge what is considered conventional by the group. Therefore, for true discussion to occur, a wide range of ideas must be represented. Principles should be applied, while the need for new reforms is not ignored. Massimo Pigliucci once said, "The clamour to revise neo-darwinism is becoming so loud that hopefully most practicing evolutionary biologists will begin to pay attention. It has been said that science often makes progress not because people change their minds, but because the old ones die off and the new generation is more open to novel ideas."

This is obviously discussing scientific progress, but the principles can be applied to politics. The new generation is going to be the main instigators of meaningful reform. Through this act of rebellion, the basis of all government can be questioned, but should not be discarded. Earlier it was stated that the dynamic of the older and younger generations bodes well for politics. The passions and desires of each group counterbalance and provide a good stage for discussion. However, even the conservative tendencies of the older generation and the liberal minds of the new can recognize logic. This is why both young and old will come in support of the following reforms. The basis of good principles will attract the experienced citizen, while the prospect of a better tomorrow will gather those still brimming with the exuberance of youth. With these two different groups of supporters, true change will overtake America, and problems that have been hiding in the shadows will be brought into the light of discussion. Now let that discussion begin.

There are many people today that are labeled as conspiracy theorists, and, as mentioned earlier, being dismissive in discussion is not helpful. If the questions posed by these groups are not addressed, then their numbers are bound to grow. Certain groups of potential revolutionaries, who might support the following reforms, no longer feel like they are represented in the political world. In many ways, they are not, but the entire voting system is not corrupt. It is seen through partisan manipulation of votes by using the delegate system and assigning "superdelegates" that there is still a long way to go, but one should keep fighting for meaningful change. One of the many arguments used by those who have given up is that "if voting mattered, it would be illegal." For a complete explanation of this falsity, one must dissect the argument. First of all, those in power hold very little direct control over the election cycle. While they can endorse candidates and gather popular support, if one was to introduce substantive issues to the campaign and provide meaningful solutions, then party affiliations would be severed by many.

In addition to this, it has been seen today that the established politician can not ensure the position to the endorsed person until enough support has already been gathered from the citizenry. However, reform will serve to create a less corrupt election where the opinions of the general population will be more influential.

Also, the election cannot be rigged without involvement of every major media outlet. It is very unlikely that Republican and Democrat sources would choose this one issue to work together on. In addition to this, there are enough independent sources as to render this a null point. Frequent polling provides a powerful check. If the poll is extremely distorted in relation to the end results then suspicion can be raised. Proof that there is a group that controls both politicians, economic superpowers, and all media outlets is nonexistent and most of the arguments for its existence are pure speculation. One of the most used examples is that of the Federal Reserve. While this private institution needs to be audited and brought under popular power, if people would demand that it become a political issue, then this would be accomplished. While one's vote is often lost in the political machine, the system can not reject overwhelming support for reform. Now the destruction of the two party system will become the political priority.

While political reform and checks on power are important there is another thing to remember. Rosseau in The Social Contract says, "This is why a celebrated author has made virtue the cardinal principle of a republic; for all the conditions that I have named cannot prevail without virtue." As mentioned earlier the same theme is expressed in To Kill a Mockingbird when Jem Finch attempts to discredit the jury system that has become a staple in American politics. His argument stemmed from the guilty verdict brought by a group of white jurors to sentence a black man named Tom Robinson to prison for rape. It is seen before this that the argument of the prosecutor was completely false and that Robinson should have been freed. Atticus Finch being a lawyer defended the justice system. One point that is brought up is that no system can function without good people.

Rousseau again addresses the same question with the example of dueling. This practice remained common in even the early stages of American politics as seen through the death of Alexander Hamilton by Thomas Jefferson's vice president Aaron Burr. However, it had many of its roots in Europe and was considered honorable by the general population. One famous English writer named Samuel Johnson once said, "A man may shoot the man who invades his character, as he may shoot him who attempts to break into his house." Rousseau viewed this practice as cowardly, however, but he admitted that it must persist because of popular opinion of the time. This principle does not apply to institutions which are not mutually consented for on all sides like the evil example of slavery. Problems are bound to occur when people are not virtuous, but now systems will be discussed that guard against the rise of evil people to power.

The first step in introducing a system that guards against the rise of evil and power hungry people is creating a political scene where people's only viable options are not both evil. The negative effects of name recognition and money in politics will be addressed later, but the problems of the party system must be discussed first. To end this system, a large majority must admit that there is a problem that needs to be addressed. One problem is the unfairness that the parties create internally. As mentioned earlier superdelegates and the primary system has been attacked by many.

The next problem plagues both the primaries and the general election. The problem was illustrated earlier with the example of marijuana legalization, but a more recognizable situation will be listed this time. Although the theory is now largely discredited, many voters believed for a time that Ross Perot had taken the election from George H.W. Bush and given it to Bill Clinton. Perot was a third party candidate rumored to have divided the Republican side in the 1992 election cycle. This is no longer thought of as true by some, but the possibility of a similar occurrence should be discussed. The system described obviously is flawed because a candidate would be chosen based not on character or policy, but rather on the lack of opposition. This is why in the general election, third-party candidates are often scoffed at. Although more options are desirable, noble people must not participate in a fruitless battle. Direct tactics in this circumstance will be no more useful than the natives' arrows against European firepower. Instead, in this fight for increased liberty, guerilla tactics like those used by Francis Marion in the American Revolution must be adopted.

At the present moment, like certain units of the Continental Army, Americans are trying to reform politics by using the tactics of their enemies. Similar to the many battle commanders, certain modern reformers do not have the correct strategy. Instead of hoping to gain access into an already overly rigid system through direct combat, the election process must be changed. As mentioned earlier, the two generally accepted ends of the American political spectrum serve as restrictive agents. It is almost impossible to coordinate the rise of a third party without the demise of one side. While it is evil, the party system will only be brought to a peaceful end, if one rises from among its ranks. If a congressional or presidential candidate is going to rise to a position where they are able to reform, it will most likely be not through a third party. Instead, the general population must gather behind those who accept the reform regardless of party. Now that the question of application has been addressed, the policy and other issues of the current party system can be further described.

One of the most simple ways to prove the absurdity of the current and historic political party system of the United States is to point out a single fact. The two political parties that rule the federal government are also those who have the greatest influence over the state governments. The history of this truth can be seen through a passage from The Oxford History of the American People which states: "As the urban movement gathered volume, new municipalities with elected mayors and bicameral city councils were established. Political partisanship extended down from the federal to the state and municipal governments: a good democrat would no more think of voting for a Whig governor or a Whig sheriff than for a Whig congressman or President. Federal, state and local politics were so closely articulated that the misconduct of a state treasurer might turn a presidential election, and the attitude of a President on the tariff or public lands might embarrass his party's candidates for municipal office."

The effect of the mindset from this era obviously still have a deep effect on politics. Today, politics is viewed in only black and white and not different shades or colors. If one announces that they believe in a limited federal government, power of the communal government must also be lax. The inverse is also true. This, of course, is an overly simplistic view of politics. Government is not a one plus one equals two equation, but is filled with many variables. The powers and goals of the different levels do not allow for a coverall party to exist. Why should the powerful members of a party at a national level be able to influence decisions made by local governments in regard to social issues such as drug use and education? Different issues and different levels necessitate different parties. Those politicians who wish to maintain strong party holds are described perfectly in the tenth publication of the Federalist Papers written by James Madison when he states: "persons of other descriptions whose fortunes have been interesting to the human passions, have, in turn, divided mankind into parties, inflamed them with mutual animosity, and rendered them much more disposed to vex and oppress each other than to co-operate for their common good." Those people and institutions which serve only to divide should be excluded from the political process through popular demands.

Another problem that plagues the current political process is its tendency to vote upon name recognition. Like money, the celebrity status of certain citizens or families can result in an unfair election cycle. The poor and the commoners are almost never elevated to a position of power even though the presidential salary was designed specifically for their convenience. Rousseau stated, "There are three types of aristocracy, natural, elective, and hereditary. The first is suited only to primitive peoples; the third is the worst of all governments; the second is the best, and this aristocracy in the true sense of the word." While these three types are stated distinctively, there is quite a bit of overlap. Like the new African countries where people tend to fall into the control of a single leader, America tends to revert back to a tendency from colonial times. Individuals are partially judged based on their lineage and not their character or proposed policies.

While a knowledge of subconscious thought provides a bulwark against the continuation of this pattern, a system that will be detailed later will take care of both this problem and that of money in politics. Those who come from a privileged position are less likely to hold respect for the government and for those who elected them. The problems faced by the country will be viewed from the perspective of the king's son in The Whipping Boy, written by Sid Fleischman. Whenever the prince would misbehave, instead of directly punishing him, the king would have a boy named Jeremy whipped. The pain of seeing Jeremy suffer was meant to deter bad, but it actually encouraged it. The prince purposely misbehaved just to see the results.

This example is also proof of why politicians should never be allowed to be above the laws they have created. The effect of the law should pass on elected officials as well, because they will then be more careful with their actions. Whatever the case may be, many examples of officials born from more privileged or pretentious perspectives are not hard to find. Millionaires and billionaires such as Donald Trump and Ross Perot are given a greater political opportunity because of their finances, while the members of the Bush, Clinton, and Kennedy clans are overly elected.

With these latter examples, another point is made apparent. American politics and the voter base is not composed wholly of intellectuals, and has been infiltrated by ignorance in some respects. It is absurd to think of such irrational decision making, but it does occur. When Former President Barack Obama was up for election, some people voted for him for the sole purpose of making history by electing the first black president. While his election was a very important symbolic victory, policy should always be the primary concern. Policy of course was the main issue for most of his supporters, but the problem can still be addressed. This same sort of thing has happened with the run of Hillary Clinton, but there are even more historical examples. John F. Kennedy is believed by some to be elevated into the political scene partially due to his physical attractiveness. While no law can effectually scan subconscious thoughts and require reason, it is important to remain aware of one's mind. These are all Democratic examples, but the same can be said of Republicans. Some liberals would even reverse it and tell conservatives to disregard any possible racial misconceptions. Whatever the case may be, protections against ignorance need to be established.

Dealing with the threat of political parties becomes increasingly challenging when history is considered. One cannot ban the existence of these parties through a government because that would be an offense on the First Amendment. Those who choose to peacefully assemble should never be contested. However, these groups have become destructive and something must be done. If one was to manipulate the time of the general election, then the parties could be severely interrupted. This though could result in disorganization and the rule of chance would play to big of a role. Using the 2016 presidential race as an example, if the aforementioned were enacted then no nominees would be officially chosen. Assuming that no emergency party meetings occurred, all of the party candidates would be up for election. This would prove advantageous to the Democrats because the Republicans would be far more divided. Similarly if the two main parties were abolished, the already created political side with the least number of competitors would be successful. Due to necessity, new parties would quickly replace the old ones. This of course proves to be quite the problem.

A way must be found to effectively decrease the influence of parties by taking away the necessity that formed them originally, while also adhering to the principles of the First Amendment. To solve this problem a succession of reforms are required. First, an example must be taken from the current jury system already functioning in the United States. Many writers and political philosophers have twisted the famous quote about how "power corrupts" and have deepened the amount of knowledge from it. Science fiction writer Frank Herbert once said, "All governments suffer a recurring problem: power attracts pathological personalities. It is not that power corrupts, but that is magnetic to the corruptible."

While this may seem like a negative quote, its underlying implications are quite positive. Under the former perspective of power being the cause of corruption, people were left to depend on separation of powers and other checks to guard against tyranny. While these are important safeguards, systems should be set up to attract politicians with good intentions. Another good insight comes from the famous writer J.R.R. Tolkien who said, "The most improper job of any man is bossing other men. Not one in a million is fit for it, and least of all those who seek the opportunity." Elected officials, if correctly checked, are not bosses but rather public servants. Although this is true, as mentioned earlier, the pretentious attitude of certain officials needs to be checked. In addition to this, corrupt people should be filtered out of the system. The plans for this will be discussed now.

Elections have long been a topic of conversation among even great minds like Rousseau and Montesquieu. The latter once wrote, "Election by lot is natural to democracy. Drawing lots is a method of election that wounds no one and gives every citizen a reasonable hope of serving his country." Seeing the discussion, it becomes obvious that by democracy, he does not mean the purely communal system in which every citizen votes on particular issues. For a large popular government such as the United States, discussion must be more in depth. The detriments of a pure application of the lot principle can be clearly seen especially in regard to the position of president. This job usually requires both a certain degree of experience in government and high intelligence. Under lot, no filter would guard against dangerous radicals. Also, the previously mentioned concept of stability which comes from the same voting base would no longer be in effect. The direction of the country would be completely disconcerted with no consistent direction.

However there are concepts of lot that also provide for governmental benefits. First of all, people of wealth and privileged birth would not be elected based on unimportant reasons. Another benefit is that those who are corrupt or who are easily corrupted will not have a chance to fill every position through their guile. A fusion of the two systems should be considered the best solution. Through a mode like the jury selection process, a group of contenders should be chosen. After this, the limited group will be narrowed down until only one is elected. While deceitful people will be found in the preliminaries, when put up against the honest and hardworking majority, they are bound to lose. In addition to this, those of power or other notable positions will be not able to use their influence to garner support, thereby further ensuring their victory. The advantages of both lot and common elections are gained through such a system.

One who is obsessive over details might have a few questions. What happens if the preliminary group is wholly composed of those who do not know how to handle the position to which they were appointed? What if this occurs to the presidential office which is largely unchecked internally? What happens if the more common people bound to come to power can not handle themselves properly? These are all legitimate concerns and all will be subsequently addressed. First it must be admitted that there are many advantages. The divisiveness of class warfare would suffer a major defeat, while the feeling of elective privilege would dissipate. With the general people now working in high positions, Webster's "government, made for the people, made by the people and answerable to the people" would be even more true.

One must not also forget that this new system would be followed by a new surge in political activity. Parents and the general adult population would serve to educate the younger generation with increased vigor due to the fact that those who they teach have a legitimate chance of becoming a political leader of some sort. In addition to this, research on potential political leaders would increase due to the fact that the general population could no longer depend on name recognition or one-line-feel-good quotes to make the decision for them.

In addition to this, if this reform was instituted internationally, the general people in the government would serve a very important purpose. Policies would not be adopted that hurt civilians and classified information would not be held by only an elitist class. While there would remain punishment for espionage and traitorous acts, if the government has become increasingly corrupt then people such as Edward Snowden will hopefully step forward. Concerns can be brought against how he released information, but the citizenry needed to know about surveillance and other secret policies. As mentioned earlier, on an international scale, transparency in government must be gradual and simultaneous among all parties.

Answering the questions listed above will now become the primary objective. The first question does not pose a serious threat to the system. First of all, the preliminary group of potential politicians would be quite large, numbering somewhere above one thousand.

This may prove to be safe enough, but other precautions will be taken as well. A clause can be instated where a new group will be gathered every time nobody in the group scores above a certain approval rating. A system resembling this will also be important to other aspects of the proposed government.

While much of this conversation has answered all three questions, the second can not be considered completed yet. The executive branch needs extended checks on its power as seen through the abuse of modern U.S. presidents and the principle discovered by Rousseau that power often trickles to the branch with the lowest number of members. Although the French Revolution proved to be a dismal failure and nothing more than a short vacation from tyranny, it did provide an applicable concept for modern reform. Near the end, it implemented a constitution that created three different executive positions with Napoleon Bonaparte filling one. This was not successful and Napoleon proved to be a tyrant, which provided both a suggestion for the modern reformer and the historic freedom fighter.

First those who engage in physical combat for independence or internal liberty must learn from past failures. During a complete overthrow of a government, one should not depend on a single figure such as Simon Bolivar who later became a dictator, but rather take an example from the largely successful American Revolution. While comparisons are made between Bolivar and George Washington in character and fighting charisma, there was an important difference. Washington neither desired absolute power, nor would he have ever been able to achieve such a goal easily. Unlike many disorganized rebellions, the colonial forces were led primarily by the Continental Congress. Even though they were not as decisive as a sole executive guide, once independence was acquired they guarded against usurpation and a reversion back to unlawful dictatorships.

The lesson that can learned by modern reformers is even more applicable. The French Consulate, or three executive administrators, although implemented at a bad time, had a good basis. Existing today, there are two important checks on executive power. Congress has the power to both override vetoes and impeach the president. The latter should become more common through the specifying of situations in which impeachment is appropriate. The most important clause that could be added in this respect is concerning punishment for failure to complete on campaign promises.

Both of the checks are external however and internal checks can not be found. The problems and advantages of an executive department with three administrators must now be discussed. First, this system would allow for increased fortification when dealing with separation of powers between the branches. No president could make a decision without the vote of at least one of his colleagues. Therefore, if one power hungry person makes it through the previously stated reforms, then the two rational members can guard against his desires. Also, in this system, the legislatures would be more willing to impeach rowdy members when there are backups left to rule. Those replacements would be directly elected by the people as opposed to nominated vice-presidential picks which would add to the list of benefits. In the case of an emergency, a succession of officials elected through the reformed election process mentioned earlier will be available to fill vacancies. Speaker of the house will not be up for the position due to the fact that no enticement should lead Congressmen to impeach presidents for personal political gain. Now that the benefits have been listed, so should the negatives.

The sole negative that can be brought against such a system is that it would hinder administrative abilities specifically related to the military. These concerns can be negated however through more measures of reform. An emergency clause should be instated specifically for cases of conflict. During such an occasion the House of Representatives would be responsible for nominating one member of the proposed consulate. It is extremely important that such a decision be made by the lower house for one important reason. All decisions dealing with war need to be from the directly elected popular officials instead of the Senate, which under the proposed reforms would be elected by state legislatures. The bicameral system that used to be extremely intricate has lost some of its most important features. While it formerly provided a balance of federalism coupled with a compromise between different sized states, it now only accomplishes the latter. Under the proposed consulate, the people, who are generally averted to war, would remain relatively apathetic until the need arises. No special interests besides safety and security would be garnered in a group so large and socially conscious. In addition to this declarations of war which have already become useless under the modern system would also be deemed useless. Presidents would no longer have the power to begin wars without due process under the guileful name of "police action" or "armed conflict". These and other reforms would prove to be as important substantially as they would be symbolically. This symbolism will be detailed later.

The above reforms would not only be the best government, but also the most American. This statement despite its initial ethnocentric tone, is far from derogatory. America and the United States specifically have been known recently as a place with a conglomeration of different cultures. Saying that the government will be the most American only means that the best aspects from different places around the world will be considered and applied.

First, the communal system of the Native Americans, Middle Eastern nomads, and African tribes will be implemented to provide for the happiness of citizens and a diversity of choices. Also, ancient Greecien political thought that had also been reflected in Roman society will show through. Systems from the Roman Republic will be reformed to provide for increased security. Great political thinkers from western Europe and influential social reformers from Asia will be also be glorified. In the end, it does not matter who contributed or where it came from, but rather if the principles are implemented. As mentioned earlier, political discoveries, like scientific ones, should not be rejected based on racist and anti-ethnic sentiments. Now that this reform to politics has been discussed, the necessity of others will be emphasized.

While the system mentioned above serves to filter out those who have a propensity for tyranny, under this, parties could still recover and regroup. The preliminary group could be forced to join one of the two groups to gain recognition and become a real contender. Parties could then block out true reformers and continue limiting options. However, even if parties did not form, the reform above would not solve certain problems to the election cycle. If the preliminary group was composed of a majority of liberals or left-leaning candidates, then this would split the vote more and help the conservatives. The reverse is also true. To solve this problem a lesson must be taken from the country of Mongolia. As mentioned earlier, this government is corrupt and critically needs reforms, but they do provide an important lesson. In this country, instead of only allowing citizens to vote for one candidate, they are chosen based on approval ratings. One might ask how this could be a good system if it has not worked for Mongolia, but the key is correct application. Under the Mongolian government, party officials and politicians are the ones choosing the people's options which severely hinders change and cements socialist power in the country. Under the lot election, the government would have no great control over the will of the people. First, concerns with this system will be discussed and then advantages.

It might be considered that such a system does not agree with the general will, but this is the farthest from the truth. As mentioned before with the example of marijuana, in the current system, the vote can be easily split unfairly. Imagine that there are three major candidates contending for a single office, and the popular concern is focused solely on the issue of marijuana. The three candidates each hold a different stance; one wanting complete legalization, one wanting a decrease in punishment, and one wanting a continuation of the drug war. Under the current system the first two candidates both oppose the measures of the third, but the third can win even without a majority. The split between the first two groups disallows any reform from taking place. One could look at this proposed system from a perspective that creates distortions, but it is sound policy. Some would say that giving people "unlimited votes" would mean that those who vote for more candidates would have greater influence. This is far from the truth. Saying "no" is just as powerful of a decision and this lines up with both the general will and good application. Parties would no longer be able to hold onto power because hypothetical third party candidates could be supported without a disbalance in the system. Even if parties were to emerge they would be benign. No power would be held by them and they would amount to nothing more than a grouping of ideologies. However whenever the party fell out of line with the will of its members, it could be quickly and safely destroyed. This reform may be considered the most important. A system based on approval ratings would more accurately represent the feelings of Americans.

In addition to this, it would couple nicely with the previously mentioned reform of creating a new preliminary group every time no one reached a certain percentage.

Many people after all of these reforms have taken place, would still feel extremely dissatisfied at the state of politics. One major contributor to this would be the influence of wealth in politics. The lot system would allow for a decrease in this factor, but it does not address the issue directly. Candidates could still be elevated by the wealthy due to their support of policies, which may or may not be to the benefit of the general population. To institute campaign finance reform, a couple of common myths need to be dispelled. The first of these is the belief that nothing needs to change. The Republican side is filled partially by those who are not concerned whatsoever with the power of the rich. Many believe that the current role of wealth in politics helps to filter decisions through those who are more successful and therefore protect the country's wealth.

While job creation of businesses is important to the economy, if the majority of people do not believe that the current economic leaders are managing natural resources properly, then reform should be possible. A whole slate of candidates who have been bought off by the rich only fuels the belief that the system is rigged. Certain people are now saying that if one wants to make a difference in the political word, gathering enough wealth to a buy a candidate would be more effective then voting. If the business owners truly are benefitting society, then the general population will choose to uphold this position without coercion or trickery.

It must be remembered that it is society that holds and should hold control of the majority of resources. This does not have to come in the form of government property but rather through popular control of the political process. Rousseau's insight can be applied to money based politics: "Does it follow from this that the general will is annihilated or corrupted? No, that is always unchanging, incorruptible, and pure, but it is subordinated to other wills which prevail over it. Each man, in detaching his interest from the common interest, sees clearly that he cannot separate it entirely, but his share of the public good seems to him to be nothing compared to the exclusive good he seeks to make his own. Where his private good is not concerned, he wills the general good in his own interest as eagerly as anyone else." As mentioned earlier, such a large demographic does not allow the private will to have as strong of a hold. However, the general will can be tainted by the effects of money and recognition in politics and this should be accounted for. The subordination of the general will can be stopped through intelligent reform and sound policy.

Another misconception about this proposed reform is that it is unnatural or that it does not accurately represent the origins of the general will. First of all, none of the definitions of unnatural apply in this situation. When discussing the representation of the general will in society, it must be remembered that members often have to draw arbitrary lines and create mechanisms to protect this simplistic principle. While the principles should always be definitive, discussion is necessary in the areas of protection and application. Second, the general will is popular in nature and when a large portion of the citizenry feel that the current administration of principle is incorrect, then reform needs to occur.

When dealing with the specificity of these reforms, I would suggest adding both a maximum on campaign spending and a maximum on the amount that individual members of society can donate. These two reforms work together but complete different objectives. The former makes sure that rich people are not given an unfair advantage when competing against those of more common backgrounds. The latter provides a guarantee that a politician cannot rise to power through the donation of singular corporation without popular donations. Some people may believe that these two suggestions are completely unnecessary. Hopefully, in most cases, they will be, but additional safeguards, if they bring no harm, can prove to be very useful.

A different person might conclude that they do not do enough and that wealth could still prove to be influential in certain cases. While other reforms should be proposed from the conversations that stem from this section, I believe that this provides, at the very least, a good start. First of all, the number of power hungry people who make it through the system will be severely decreased. In addition to this, increased checks within the system will allow for the more popular candidates to either override their decisions or expel them from office. While this provides quite a list of goals, there are still more reforms to be created

This time, it is important for reforms to be created by other members of the general population. A discussion must begin in which useless aspects of society are discarded and political conversation and discussion take center stage. Other areas also deserve debate and science will continually be pursued, but through an increased focus in politics, society will learn to function better. It seems that the greatest challenge of human existence is not discovering the truth, but learning to live peaceably while this is being accomplished. The human race has come quite far in its systematic approach to gather information and knowledge. The principles of free speech and expression have been discovered which allows for the abolition of superstition and hindrances to advancements. Processes of observation and argument have also been adopted.

On this path it often seems that there is no common direction. There are people who even object to the generally accepted objectives of peace and knowledge. This is where it is important that the position of one's fellow human is considered. They too have been placed on this earth and must encounter many of the same questions and challenges. While force is a powerful tool to control tyrants, human goodness shines in most people. Working together for the common good of both people and their environment will prove to be quite the task, and hopefully, we are up for the challenge.

With the previously delivered information, the United States will be set out on the right path. However, there is still an important discussion that must be commenced. The liberal march to new reforms has been seen to be helpful and so has the conservative, but the most important section is still to come. Although the principle of federalism has been partially detailed under things of past importance, it will be used once again. It is seen now that it is not just the United States' federal government, but also the system of lower governments as well. Different levels should have different responsibilities and each level with its proposed powers and advantages. This includes the tribal or communal level and government on an international scale.

Section 3: The Ideal Society

It is sometimes important to create a more realistic starting point, but the idealist situation can also be conversed upon. After the first steps have been taken, it is important to have a roadmap as well. Both the instigation and continuation of the plan is important. This idealistic social structure will take care of a number of problems. Some of the most important and controversial issues including education reform, racial tensions, and the wage gap will be included. These issues when addressed by modern political commentators and politicians are only at a superficial level. Deep seated problems can not be reconciled with benefits or money. The righteous anger and systematic oppression will not be solved without innovation. As stated earlier, simple, large-scale land distribution would never be possible on a national level. In addition to this, complete demonization of business is also not healthy. The education system often suffers from recurring problems but it seems that politicians only want to throw more money into a broken system. They "nobly" attempt to fill the hole in the dike, but there wads of cash don't do the trick. It is seen that the unity throughout the system does not accomplish anything. Its only effect is to stifle competition. All of these problems and failed attempts at the solution will be discussed in relation to different levels of government. No time to waste, the revolution must begin soon.

Chapter 7: The Tribal Level

Arguably one of the most simple but true lesson comes from ninth chapter of The Social Contract: "When therefore one asks what in absolute terms is the best government, one is asking a question which is unanswerable because it is indeterminate; or alternatively one might say that there are as many good answers as there are possible combinations in the absolute and relative positions of people." As mentioned earlier government is not a one plus one equation but rather is filled with many variables. However, this does not mean that every form of government is good. The title of the chapter in The Social Contract, "The Signs of a Good Government," is very appropriate in this case. Good government while not singular, does have a few defining characteristics. These characteristics should all be extremely generalized, contrasting the belief that schooling and healthcare are rights. While these two specific items can be part of a larger goal, they are not required. A government should provide for the happiness of its citizens within environmental guidelines.

It is here that a distinction must be made. While larger government institutions must choose one direction, at the local level there should be extreme diversity between different communities. Dealing with social issues at a local level will allow for more choices in government and help to avoid confrontation as much as possible. While happiness is the ultimate goal, history has shown many different paths to it. Usually, happiness is accompanied by a certain degree of personal freedom. If this is not involved people begin to feel controlled and will resent the government. It may be said that the best system then would be anarchic. If people are all of an outstanding character, then this would be the case. However at the higher levels anarchy will not be an option because one cannot forget social obligations like environmental protection and the definition of life. Force in government must protect natural resources that are used by every community and deal with conflicts between them. Whatever the path to a successful society will be, it is important to discuss both the causes, advantages, and potential disadvantages to such a system.

There has been an unfair affront on the idea of a homologous society in recent years. While this has been the belief of racists, one must not reject a good ideology because it has been abused by different groups. In fact, the racists once again took the wrong approach. They let their emotions get in the way of sound policy. For a homologous group to be formed, minorities do not need to be deported, but rather more thoroughly integrated. It is natural for a nation to have separate cultures, but a community should not. It has been seen that birds of a feather flock together and this is an important political concept as well. Genetics and the cultural aspects of tradition, religion, and language must merge to form a united culture.

However, there are counter examples that seem to prove this wrong. The "hippie community" seems to have always coexisted well with those from a variety of backgrounds. This is an anomaly though and government must be based on a more stable branch. Even in the case of the hippies, it seems that complete integration occurred for a time due to the disregard of race. As the Spaniards and Native Americans merged to create many aspects of the Latin American culture, so modern people should not continue separately. Instead, they must form into separate communities and ensure the happiness of all members. First, a list of social issues which would be dealt with by these communities will be discussed.

One of the differences that have shaped the unending contrast of the United States is the dynamic between the city and rural communities. There has long been resentment between these groups and it needs to be addressed. In the country resentment is often present when the large cities crush their vote and institute what they consider horrible agricultural programs. While it is important that the environment is protected in relation to the sometimes negative effects of agriculture, there is already an internal check. Farmers are naturally not going to allow other farmers to take advantage of natural resources that everyone uses.

It is seen also, that cities can have a negative effect on water quality and other environmental factors. The consolidation of people can lead to various problems that I have experienced first hand. Living downstream from the capital of Iowa, the local Red Rock Lake has been infamous for its contamination and frightening algae levels.

While this is extremely small scale, there are global examples. The Ganges River in India, the largest democratic government in terms of population, provides the needed proof. In the Hindu religion, this river represents the goddess, Ganga. Bathing in the river is supposed to quicken the process of Moksha, which is the goal of every Hindu. The river is meant to represent religious purity, but physically it is quite the opposite. Rapid population growth in India has produced both increased agricultural and industrial pollution. The government does not seem to have a strict enough policy concerning environmental regulation. In addition to this, dead carcasses of both animals and humans are thrown into the river as a religious rite. Pollution is the cause of many problems, but there is a bigger problem that affects not only India, but many countries around the world.

Cities have provided important centers for thousands of years but now they are growing at an alarming rate. On much of the American east coast, large cities are merging together to form gigantic metropolitan areas. In many of these areas, shopping malls and restaurants become the main attraction, which only further increases the negative impact on the environment. It seems that under the largely capitalistic system of the United States all of the citizen's basic needs have been provided for. Now instead of trying to create a stable and steady economy, businesses began to make novelty items. This is not necessarily bad, but the government needs to continue to protect the environment. It seems that they are now largely concerned with job creation. Many politicians brag about the number of jobs which have been created, but the increase in people must also be factored.

People always search for political leaders that promise a growing economy, but stability is more important. The economy of the 1920s is desired in modernity and if this is accomplished then the economy of the 1930s will be soon to follow. Those governments and businesses on a large level do not provide stability. Instead, it is the local authorities that have the closest connection to the general will, and therefore the people's most important interests in mind. The large government of the 1920s was able to provide for far more then what was necessary, but a decade later essential like food and water were sometimes nonexistent. Under the local governments, this unstable system can be adopted, but the effects will not be widespread and individual control over one's personal situation will be increased. This example of potential collapse also provides an example of the necessity for a certain degree of immigration control on the local level. If one system fails due to the mismanagement of officials, then other societies should not be punished for their incompetence. One must remember that the general stability of local and popular government should not lead to any misconceptions about its problems.

Indian independence and democratic government has provided for stability, but problems can stem from that. Their generally peaceful attitudes and great leaders like Gandhi provided an even more stable situation.

There are a number of attitudes towards war that are important to consider. Edna St. Vincent Millay's poetry serves as a battle cry for pacifists all around the world. In the Conscientious Objector she writes, "Though he flick my shoulders with his whip, I will not tell him which way the fox ran. With his hoof on my breast, I will not tell him where the black boy hides in the swamp. I shall die, but that is all that I shall do for Death; I am not on his pay-roll." This poem discussed involvement in The Great War. Plans have already been detailed to avoid large scale wars like this, but pure pacifism is an interesting concept. It is true that if everyone practiced such a belief that the world would be a better place. However, this is not a strong enough to base a system upon.

Many within this system believe that the government naturally leads to violence or that force is unnatural. First, the violence in popular government corresponds to the violence of those that compose it. The very first of the human population died in conflicts over jealousy and more primitive matters. Therefore it is not war that can be considered unnatural, but rather the complete absence of it.

While it was previously stated that the government should provide for natural needs, it should also guard against negative natural tendencies. Nature cannot be solely focused upon. The forces of intellect can be used in favor of human happiness. In addition to this, the philosophical war against force needs to be addressed. Force was existent in a primitive form from almost the beginnings of mankind. It was then based primarily on physical strength or cunning, but it was still an important concept. The force of modern government serves an entirely different purpose. In contrast, this force equalizes all citizens and bases decision with a greater weight on intelligence. The general will, when localized, provides a quantity of choices so that the individual will can also be more fully expressed.

Other groups of people object to any sort of violence on a religious basis. While no one should be forced to fight, their arguments must be addressed. If the situation reverts itself back to the more simplistic original state, then these objectors will either be forced to participate or die. Also, if governments who do not respect the general will come to power, these people will be targets of their policies as well. It should be the job of every citizen to protect these peaceful people from those who would harm them. Even if they do not agree with the policy of war, if the cause is just, then it will benefit them.

There are many different groups that fall under the category of peaceful who have been subjugated. In the Chinese region of Tibet, there is a militaristic independence movement, but it has proved to be insufficient. The Buddhists of the region are known for their generally peaceful behavior and they have now been taken advantage of. The civilized world must form an alliance based on ideals and not borders to overthrow the occupation. Other groups within China such as the practitioners of Falun Gong have been also persecuted for their beliefs, which are generally very peaceful.

One of the largest religious groups in America has taken a different approach to peaceful religion. Christians who follow the teachings of Jesus are often criticized for supposed hypocrisy when discussing violence and warfare. Verses from Christian literary text reference "turning the other cheek" and "loving thy neighbor" and these can often be misconstrued. While a pacifist perspective can be taken, better interpretations can be found. First off, turning the other cheek does not refer to complete nonviolence, but rather an aversion to violence. While subjugation can be fought against, conflict should not be needlessly escalated. As mentioned earlier verbal conflicts should not become physical. Along these same lines, one should not base their decisions on a prideful reaction to a disrespectful act, but rather only use force when completely necessary. In addition to this, if one truly loved their neighbor, then the system that allows for their fellow citizen's subjugation would be protested, even if this means a sacrifice of life.

While this rabbit trail may have been taken as a wandering from the true thesis of this book, it was completely necessary. One cannot debate about politics without also dealing with the importance of cultural aspects such as religion. While politics and religion should have a separation, those who practice religion are intertwined with the former. Misconceptions about the interpretation of religious texts deemed important by society can lead to an end to independence and freedom. A reformer must use all tools available to rally people to the cause of the general good.

Another important perspective dealing with war is that it is completely good and necessary. Some believe that in society, the force of war provides a needed complement to the situation of peace. Many who are a part of this group believe, like me, that population moderation and environmental protection are intertwined and that these two concepts can work together nicely. However, believing that war is the mechanism to achieve the goal of a better society is absurd.

First, the use of war as such a mechanism in modern society would have a negative impact on the environment that they are trying to protect. War between a large group of people today would spell national disaster, not the natural order. The severe magnitude of modern weaponry could cripple not only the biosphere but also important abiotic features. The urge to bring back a more simplistic time is very enticing, but the problems of today should not be traded for the problems of ancient man. Rather, civilization must face the new problems with increased vigor. Natural needs were previously highlighted and these are important, but human intellect can accomplish many objectives as well. When these two forces cooperate, then good government can be found.

The same philosophical fight that was waged against the common enemy of war can also be waged against overpopulation and environmental destruction. Human intellect can be used as a tool and so can the inner goodness in the majority. While most do have an inclination towards kindness and cooperation, situations with such high tensions and emotions can bring out a worse side. This is another reason why the process that has defined America for centuries is a good example in many respects. Due process and time for consideration have allowed rational thought to dominate the political world. One might notice a possible hypocrisy in these last words. My praise of cooperation and good feeling towards fellow citizens is coupled with a harsh demonizing of emotions in general. It is here that a distinction must be made. While emotion can allow for social advancement, a political process should not depend on something so flimsy. Rather, the unchanging and rigid exoskeleton of principle and reason will define the future of politics in America and around the world.

The idea of war and pollution come from one concept that needs to be controlled by the general public: the fight for natural resources. War is often tied to this fight as seen through simple examples like land skirmishes in the West, and more complex examples like European colonization and the war between China and expansionist Japan during World War II. Pollution is driven by the fight for resources as well. The few cultural aspects that are uniform across America include a desire for wealth. This is driven sometimes by beneficial motivations like aid of society or the survival of oneself or one's family, but it is also often controlled by greed and want of power, control, and social status. Education in America has aided in the never ending pursuit of wealth. Instead of learning about the importance of popular advancement, children are taught about pure individualism. While the individual is important, this can only be true if people skills and cooperation are learned.

Contentment is a very important concept in certain ways. While a society must often complain to bring about change, one should have an end goal in mind. Today people who have all their needs met still aimlessly attempt to move "forward" with their only guide being the word "more". This ties in with the fight for resources because this forward march seems to be guided at least partially by it. Resources under communal control serve to better all in the community, while they don't under pure individual control. The capitalistic system of today has allowed very positive advances, but these must be checked by the general population's goal of maintaining both the environment and the opportunity of all. Those at the top must always be checked by the community that played a role in their rise. Therefore when the advocates of capitalism and communism begin to clash, pull up a chair and take a discerning look. Neither system is completely evil, and the system in the United States is foundationally solid. While it does need reform, the basis of it is still stable. While the rural versus urban argument has been addressed, now the larger question of race will enter the ring.

In 1963 many marched on Washington D.C. and Martin Luther King Jr. made an inspiring speech from the Lincoln Memorial. This was an important symbolic move, even though Abraham Lincoln's record concerning freedom was not pure or untainted. During his speech King passionately said, "I have a dream that my four little children will one day live in a nation where they will not be judged by the color of their skin, but by the content of their character." While many important reforms were instituted, some went too far, as mentioned earlier, and some did not go far enough. The reforms that went too far and began to encroach on the rights of all citizens were mentioned earlier, so now the future possibilities will be focused upon.

It is quite impossible that an entire nation will conform to the idealistic dream of King, but a system that rejects institutionalized racism is possible. Birds of a feather flock together and this can be applied not only to the physical, but also to the ideological. While the over consolidation of people can be seen as a negative in regard to the environment, it is sometimes important to quarantine a group of ideologically sick people to negate their effect on society. However, this will not be accomplished through force of government or coercion, but rather through the natural tendency of people. Racism and its followers, when spread throughout society, serve to instill fear into the general population. This fear can be seen through the accusations of supposed racism on both sides of modern politics. When something is not consolidated, it becomes more difficult to deal with. Whatever the case may be, the system based primarily on local government would serve to help everyone in society.

This system of separation needs to be brought about by people that generally like to be left alone and want to afford the same privilege to other people. Although injustices which deal with the oppression of freedom, life, environment, and the well-being of the civilians can be dealt with by higher bodies of government. When dealing with the ideologies concerning race, this system is perfect. As mentioned earlier, consolidating racist ideology will serve to reduce fear and increase the well-being of all who are involved. The second group of people that will separate are those who wish to preserve their former culture. These groups will form into communities and will remain distinct.

The other group that will make up most of the population will be those who decide to fully integrate and form a new culture. While maintaining principle, this group will disregard race, background, and the more pointless aspects of tradition. The problem with integration is not the differences between people but the fact that the minds of people allow misconceptions to obstruct unity. In addition to this, the term culture has been overly glorified in modern society. It used to be parallel with the present knowledge and environment of a people. Modernity has however transformed it into a pointless aspect of society comprised only of food and music.

People need to be able to conform to conditions without previous connections to out of date practices. It will now be seen that communal governments provide not only a way to separate groups that would otherwise hate or be wary of one another, but also provides a more level playing field.

When the Europeans colonized the American continents, they did so through force. The natives and then Africans were forced into slavery. Even after the concept of force had been bridled, the practice of slavery continued for some time. Popular forces then led to the end of this institution. It can be seen through this that force can be both positive and negative, but that society is still advancing forward. Problems came of course through the actions of the European colonizers and many of these have not been dealt with sufficiently by modern society.

While the system of government in America was revolutionary, the land system has not been. The land was conquered and owned by the Europeans during the colonial period. After this, the American revolution occurred and a stable system of government was introduced. The majority of land never changed hands and under the more stable government, this became increasingly difficult. Therefore, the majority of land, natural resources, and wealth was and still is controlled by the descendants of the original subjugators and the immigrants who most easily could assimilate into the society that they created. Uninformed attempts have been made by recent politicians to solve this problem, but these have only served to increase the size of the federal government and partially destroy the importance of meritocracy.

As mentioned earlier socialist policies such as free education and welfare programs are not a bad idea when implemented on a communal level. Even communism teaches several important lessons, but it has suffered from a recurring and ironic error. The governments of both the Soviet Union and the "People's Republic of China" need to learn a lesson in etymology. When breaking down the word communism, one often recognizes the similarity to common or community. It is important to note that if something is common across a region as great as the two countries listed above, then a great deal of subjugation is involved. In addition to this, the community was lost under these systems. While regional governments sometimes exist under these nations, they hardly hold any real power.

For communism to exist peacefully without the use of extensive force, then its communal beginnings must never be forgotten. Rousseau provides helpful insights in this area when he writes, "...the further public contributions are from their source, the more burdensome they are. This burden should not be measured by the quantity of the contributions exacted, but by the distance they have to go to return to the hands from which they come; when the circulation is rapid and well established, it does not matter whether much or little is paid; the people will always be rich and finances will flourish. Correspondingly, however little the people gives, when that little does not return to it, it soon exhausts itself in continuous payments; the state is never rich and the people is always penurious."

As can be seen through this illustration, it is necessary that the people see their money at work. At a federal level, administration of social systems will always be clumsy and disorganized. In addition to this, misuse will be rampant. The attempt is sometimes noble but it is like trying to scrape paint with a backhoe. It will not only be ineffective, but in many cases damaging. Instead of enacting worthless reforms that only entrap and enslave, a true plan of reform must be adopted. As Voltaire said, "It is difficult to free fools from the chains they revere." Although this can be the case, in certain circumstances the force of information alone will prove to be strong enough to break these. Due to these facts, a real reform must be implemented.

What will be done about the need for real reform and what reforms should be adopted? Well, as mentioned earlier a society based communal rights will be established. This would, therefore, allow any group that is able to gather enough followers to gain access to land and the beginning stages of wealth. With the direct access to natural resources in the hands of individual communities, it seems that the issue of the wage gap would also be at least partially reconciled. No business would be able to control a river unless if it benefitted the immediate community and was not being a severe detriment to the environment. Cities would still be important trade centers for the communities, but they would no longer signal the destruction of nature through large conurbation movements.

For one to gain extreme wealth under such a system, one would have to aid multiple communities which would prove a tricky task. The local people would be more likely to handle the task of extracting natural resources and assembling parts to make a living. It is important to remember that each community would need to be self-sufficient. Essentials such as food could come through the trade of important materials with other countries or through more direct means. Whatever the case may be, the local government would not only have to please the people which they rule, but also stay within environmental and moral restrictions. The former set by several different larger institutions and the latter set by the states. While these are some of the issues that will be dealt with through the tribal government, there are still more.

It can be seen that the local authorities can handle the conflicts caused by race, wealth, and between urban and rural areas, but it can also handle many more issues. One issue that it can handle is that of religion and its cultural effects. Dealing with this aspect of society can prove to be tricky due to the strong emotions felt by all involved. Although outbursts of rage can be common, there are rational people who can deal with this subject calmly. However, this does not describe the general attitude of most who are involved in the discussion. Christianity is the dominate religion in America and this competes with Islam, while atheism is growing as a dominate force. Although the Book of Ecclesiastes says that "everything is meaningless," most who practice Christianity do not use this nonchalant attitude when dealing with opposition. Islam, while also a monotheistic religion, does not cooperate well with Christianity. This conflict is further magnified by the opposition of atheists to all religion.

The beliefs of people when dealing with religion are actually far more complicated than this, seeing that there are hundreds of groups, but this representation serves the purpose. On all sides, there are people who try to misrepresent good government and politics by conforming it to their beliefs. Passionate groups, such as many of the sects within anarchy, believe that religion is evil and forms a control on society. The latter is true, but that can be said about all beliefs, not just in regard to religion. As an example, if one has just watched Jaws, it is possible that they might feel an immediate aversion to swimming. They may even feel unsafe in a hotel pool or a lake. An onlooker might consider this person strange, but this horror film fanatic is not affecting anyone. Even if this belief spread, one can not stop its spread. Especially when discussing with anarchists, would the force being used to end religion be less than that which it exerts on the people. It can now be seen that the above belief is illogical due to the fact that it would require an excessive amount of control.

Other nonanarchist atheists may still believe that religion has negative impacts on advancement. Here it may be appropriate to explain a generally accepted social truth. While most understand the idea that the pursuit of happiness is beneficial, some question the importance of advancements in science and other areas of learning. Their beliefs would be defended under this system, but this natural tendency of humans must be explained. The pursuit of knowledge is not a result of blindness, but rather an attempt to escape it. Since the introduction of extreme intellect to the once animalist world, humans have always searched for meaning. We learned how to gather food and survive, but we would not be contented. We then moved on to the growing of crops and raising of livestock. Learning how to capture instead of chase food was important for the basis of modern society. While human ambition should be checked to avoid a destruction of happy existence, knowledge is key. Even more primitive humans can be seen through archaeology and paleontology to have participated in the questioning of existence. As more information is gathered by scientists, philosophers will attempt to fill gaps and lead the pursuit of knowledge forward.

Now that the reasons for advancement have been discussed, the concerns of atheists in regard to this can be addressed. Those belonging to Christianity and other religious groups have participated in several fallacies when talking about atheism and some of these need to be addressed. The most important of the logical inconsistencies is in concern to the motivations of the atheist group. While evil intention can describe individuals, it should not be used by onlookers to overly generalize a group. This question seems to be asked frequently: If atheists believe that there is no point to our existence, why do they argue so vehemently for their cause? Out of numerous personal motivations, one might seek to gain social status or acceptance. On a higher level, atheistic thinkers might solely be participating in the human pursuit of knowledge.

Atheists are not only tormented by constant misconceptions, they also are sometimes inhibited by those who disagree. The argument of the religious who disagree will be given after this, but every important perspective should be viewed. In many ways, it is believed by atheists that religion is an inhibitor to advancement. They believe that the creation of a new culture, as mentioned earlier, should be based on direct observation and the conclusions gathered from these. Also, many resent religion because it has spent a significant portion of time reconciling old beliefs with new science. In addition to this, many can be led to believe that the passion often accompanying religion is a primary cause of war and conflict. This group should be allowed to fully focus on their objectives without distractions, while also not dragging others behind them. While society and beliefs are important, the beliefs of free expression and speech are pivotal. Voltaire sums up a helpful attitude towards other people when he said, "Think for yourselves and let others enjoy the privilege to do so too."

Those who identify as religious compose a large majority in the United States. While a relatively small group, there is much controversy surrounding the Islamic community. It is inappropriate to engage in theological discussion about the "correct interpretation" of religious text in this situation, so political application will be the main focus. Many Muslims feel like they are not represented fairly by both the media and politics. Terror attacks from Middle Eastern countries enforce a negative stereotype of the whole group. Under communal rule, Muslims would be allowed to form together and not deal with such harsh scrutiny from these sources. However, this may pose some safety concerns in the minds of conservative Christians. What if they use communities as bases for terrorist activities? What if more radical Muslim groups try to enforce aspects of Sharia Law which are incompatible with good government? These questions must all be answered to calm any of the usual fears which accompany the beginning of a revolution.

First, the cultural safeguards of communal government would serve to relieve certain elements of resentment which are often left to fester. Cleaning the wounds of past offenses will allow for healing to begin. This concept can be applied to many different areas of human interaction including religion and race. In addition to this, the state and federal governments will serve to check any dangerous activities, no matter what source they come from. Items found in Sharia Law like death penalty for criticizers of Allah would never find a home in a society that favors free expression and exchange of the ideas. As with most cases, however, diversity in the group can be clearly seen so generalizations that accompany policy making should be avoided in personal interactions.

Those of most every religion have certain concerns pertaining to a belief in atheism. One now widely held belief among the religious is that atheism has led to mass murder, specifically in the case of the Holocaust from Nazi Germany. Bodie Hodge from the Answers in Genesis team contributed to "A Pocket Guide to Atheism" by writing in his section the following: "Germany had been buying into Darwin's model of evolution and saw themselves as the superior 'race,' destined to dominate the world and their actions were consequences of their worldview. This view set the stage for Hitler and the Nazi party and paved the road to World War II. He continued, "World War II dwarfed World War I in the total number of people who died. Racist evolutionary attitudes exploded in Germany against people groups such as Jews, Poles, and many others. Darwin's teaching on evolution and humanism heavily influenced Adolf Hitler and the Nazis."

First, from the text of this quote, the attack of humanism should be addressed. Although the definition has changed throughout time, it is generally accepted as an emphasis on human importance and their ability to create logical conclusions. It also includes a general disregard for superstition, but most religious people would not define their practice as such. If one is religious, a belief in humanism is not contradictory. Most major religions today believe that their god created humans with a special purpose. Using the intellect within oneself to observe and gather information should not be demonized. In fact, the team at Answers in Genesis largely use humanistic arguments when defending the Bible. Their goal is to take physical evidence and interpret it in a way that allows for a continuation of their other beliefs. While human power is obviously limited, it can be seen that the pioneers of science have not run into the cage wall as of yet.

In addition to the importance of humanism, this section attacks the belief in evolution. While this theory does not prove atheism, it provides a philosophical path to that conclusion. The merit of Darwin's work will not be discussed in this book, but false bases for attacks will be destroyed. Now from both a scientific and political perspective, racism has been negated. Hitler's interpretation of the theory was extremely incorrect. Diversity provides more genetic variation and therefore better offspring. Despite this fact, it is important to discuss race openly. Any concerns people have with the generally accepted account shouldn't be awkward or heated fights, but rather a peaceful exchange of information and interpretation. Why do people always escalate arguments to unnecessary levels? The answer is not righteous anger, but rather it is pride and the need for social acceptance. When one places their intelligence equal to their self-identity, whenever someone attempts to contradict a point, it is seen as an offense.

Whatever the case may be, the policies of racism also have no political background. The history of violence because of race can now be thought of as absurd. Races such as Slavs, Germanics, and Anglos were more easily intermixed for the sole similarity of skin color. The African and Asian populations were not rejected based on intellect or civility, but solely through unimportant differences that were perceived to be irreconcilable. It can now be clearly seen that many of the perceived differences concerning race in America come from a cultural source. Different entrances into the country and the long history of each provide a different background from which different conclusions can be reached. Whatever the case may be, there are still some illogical attacks that need to be addressed.

Even if Hitler's perspective was correct and evolution proved instead of negated racism, knowledge would still need to be pursued. One cannot convert to a religious attitude for the sole reason that it is necessary for peace. This proposed conclusion should never be accepted. Voltaire once said, "If there were no God, it would have been necessary to invent him." This is no longer believed to be true. Atheists have contributed many things to society becoming scientists, philosophers, and common laborers. Their unique stance on a variety of issues have provided deep discussions and have been an important aspect of skepticism in America. They do not want to be constantly demonized, but rather engaged. Now that the baseless concerns of the religious have been addressed, more defendable beliefs will be listed in regard to the necessity of communal governments.

It is often necessary to separate discussions about personal beliefs and politics. It is not the job of political theories to argue for the merit of a single belief, but rather take the positions that are generally accepted and plan a system that includes all of these factors. While atheists often view the religious as an inhibitor, the feeling is reciprocated. People from various religions believe that their god is punishing America for its sins. The culture of the United States does not line up with certain religious restrictions or laws, and many believe that the correct path is to return to these principles. If people believe this, then forming into separate and distinct communities should protect them from the current culture. It seems that both the problems of the theistic and atheistic are found in the same place. Another problem that religious people face is more specific to the Christianity. Many in this group believe that while composing a majority of societies members, they are not represented correctly in the school system or by the government. Federal funds, collected primarily from them, are going to an education system that does not align with their beliefs. While at this large of a level there needs to be separation of church and state, why should this institution monetarily support any ideological cause. Both Christians and atheists feel as if they are being held back by the other so why is nothing done about it. It is now obvious that reform is necessary.

Religious people have now banded together and created a movement known as intelligent design. Those who support this group's attempt to gain a hold in the public schools claim that it does not have any basis in superstition and that it comes from scientific principles. They believe that life could not exist without the work of a being with an intelligent and creative mind like humans. Claiming also that the relatively new field of abiotic evolution does not provide strong enough proof, many become even more dedicated. Evolutionists, on the other hand, believe that the theory has not been given a sufficient amount of time and that significant advances have already been made. These issues need to be solved. People who claim that the government should force the general population to fund something that is against their common beliefs do not have a good hold on politics. Advancements in science from a particular direction should not be forced upon a people because they are not hurting anyone through their ignorance.

What is extremely pertinent to everyday interactions is not how we came to be, but rather the present reality. The study of the past can never be purely scientific and speculations are common. As mentioned earlier, philosophy can help to fill in information gaps, but many times people interpret evidence very differently. These different perspectives necessitate a unified move towards separation. The irony is apparent, but the concept is concrete. These two groups must admit the obvious differences and advance forward in the different directions. As science moves forward and information is increased, maybe one side will be proven correct unmistakably and ideological unification will once again be a possibility. This time it will not be based on control, but rather common respect for the truth.

Religion and race are two of the biggest issues facing America today but there are more. The controversy over homosexuality and transgenderism are now at the forefront of politics This issue as mentioned earlier is closely tied to the social institution of state marriages. Many conservative Christians and people from other religious movements claim that marriage is not only social, but also a religious institution. Under different sacred texts from several large groups, a ban on such activities is apparently in place. Therefore it is said by members that holy marriage is under attack.

On this side also there are those who believe that these practices are unnatural. Many questions are asked. How are these practices in accordance with the evolutionary model? Can the Y gene in men really be split so that one is born with the body of a male, but the persona of a female or vice versa? Christians as mentioned earlier also sometimes believe that people as a whole will be punished for the actions of the supposedly sinful society. This provides another piece of evidence for the importance of communal government. Social issues will be handled locally, and therefore will affect the least number of people and provide for great diversity in thought. If one believes that marriage is religious then a paper from a state department should not be considered of great importance. The connection between deity and marriage should be hypothetically stronger than the latter with the government. When the Roman Emperor Claudius banned marriage during the time of St. Valentine, was the religious implications of mating lost for Christians? Whatever the case may be, the perspective of the homosexuals and transgenders will now be given.

The LGBTQ community often holds a very different set of ideals. While some hold to a different translation or interpretation of certain religious texts, many are agnostic or atheistic. In response to the natural argument, some may point out the animal examples of bonobos and bottlenose dolphins. In society they are often plagued by people's misconceptions and prejudice. Homosexual partners want to gain the equal rights to marry and the benefits that accompany this. While some of their opposition claims that they are misusing the principles of the Civil Rights movement like government officials believed Daniel Shays misused the concepts of the American Revolution to gain support, the formerly countercultural movement has some serious concerns.

On a state and federal level, legislation against this movement is extremely inappropriate. This should be considered a serious offense on personal liberty. However, it is seen that both groups based on their often different perspectives should not be forced to coexist. While open minded people would be able to accomplish this, law cannot force the social advancement of a people, but rather can only outlaw physical and not psychological or emotional oppression. However, the shooting at an Orlando nightclub against those celebrating gay pride shows another issue that needs to be handled by tribal governments.

While restrictions on dangerous explosives and forms of advanced weaponry will be placed on federal and state levels, if communities still have concern, then other reforms can be enacted. Most communities will abide solely by the state and federal regulations, but the few exceptions should be allowed to institute greater reform. The ideas of experimental government will also be in play. Many believe that it is cruel or twisted to "experiment with people's lives." However, who is the arbitrator going to be in such a situation? The country is split and what is worse than death is unwarranted control. Only through a tribal system will the most effective means for cutting gun deaths be found.

Do guns serve a purpose in society or are they useless instruments of destruction? No man can say for certain without a large degree of speculation. Conservatives claim that more gun laws cause increased violence using large cities like Chicago, New Orleans, and Miami as examples. Liberals counter saying that the drug war, social inequality, and tensions are a more leading cause. Criminal access to guns is also discussed. If a gun ban were placed, would criminals still have access through the black market or domestic creation? Would other methods of death increase like beatings and strangling? It seems that none of these questions can be definitively answered. Any piece of evidence that surfaces is subject to conflicting accounts and a variety of internal factors. Therefore, at least in part, gun access and firepower should be controlled at a more local level. This would, in turn, necessitate a possible control of immigration on a local level. While this issue is often very heated, there are worse ones yet.

Gender roles within a society further complicate the situation within the nation, and therefore proves the need for tribal government. While it is obvious to see that women can function in many traditional male fields of work, the topic still breeds controversy. In politics, it is seen that the majority of Americans want equal political rights for women, but the question of involvement in society is still fought between two very stubborn groups. It is important to begin with the perspective that subjugation is not being discussed. Women and men alike would be allowed to freely disband from a community without any complicated loopholes. Now that this is taken care of the perspective of more traditional aspects of society will be given first.

This group often claims to have the forces of nature on its side. It is seen from a biological standpoint that men are generally stronger physically. In more primitive days this meant that men were given leadership positions based on the former importance of this principle. It is said that this has become an important part of the male genome and taking this away compromises masculinity. While the difference between the genes of races has been shown to be very minimal, gender is a whole separate case. Some on the side of male leadership in society point to the Y chromosome which gives men different sexual organs. They believe that this also causes psychological and characteristic traits that are very distinct. Most on this side do not believe that one sex should be considered as less, but rather that they should compliment each other. Some point to the fact that different roles have been archaic in civil society. Women who allowed for the continuation of life were then not expected to also provide for the family's physical needs. Certain people in both the feminist and transgender movements say that many sexual characteristics are social, rather than natural. This is contested by a significant portion of society, but both sides need to be viewed.

Whatever one's belief may be, it is important to always remain rational and use natural emotions as evidence and not methods of arguing. Research on either side should not be railed against for not aligning with one's views, but rather for not aligning with fact. This concept applies to almost every side of any argument, but now the feminist perspective must be given.

People from this group often believe that masculine dominance is not a natural need like sex or food, but a negative tendency that needs to be corrected. Like the weaker weaponry of Native Americans against European invaders, feminists believe that women were largely subjugated throughout history when strength and not intelligence was the main concern. When confronted with the argument that society functions properly with male leadership, many from this group point to Native American tribes that constructed functioning matriarchies. Some believe that stereotypical female compassion would serve to avoid conflict and negotiate peace, if they were raised to higher positions.

The wage gap, although contested by the opposite side, is another major point that is brought up often in conversation. Feminists claim that it is the result of inequality like the situation of minority populations, while their opponents say that women choose to earn less by tending to enter lower paying careers like education or childcare. One might argue that women tend to be more mentally attached to their children, but most of this is pure speculation. While some fathers in the animal kingdom pose a threat to their children, some form an important protective force. Human intellect can negate negative animalistic tendencies, but one must determine if they truly have a negative impact.

Some federal politicians claim that they are going to fight for equal pay, but what plan of execution do they have in place. One cannot enter the mind and examine the intentions of employers. It is seen that federal involvement has not helped the situation of all people, but hurt it. By attempting to form one ideologically homologous group from the United States, these politicians hinder diversity and choice. This should not be a question of subjugation as mentioned earlier, but sometimes it is. No options are available. If a woman wants to live her life in a more traditional role or as a leader in a particular society, this should be a personal choice. The goal of society is not always uniformity and complete equality, but rather correct organization and function. Now it can be seen that something definitely needs to be done.

It can now be seen that the tribal level should have control of many important cultural aspects of society and should also be the protector of its members' happiness. Rousseau writes, "Upright and simple men are difficult to deceive precisely because of their simplicity; stratagems and clever arguments do not prevail upon them; they are not indeed subtle enough to be dupes. When we see among the happiest people in the world bands of peasants regulating the affairs of state under an oak tree, and always acting wisely, can we help feeling a certain contempt for the refinements of other nations, which employ so much skill and mystery to make themselves at once illustrious and wretched?"

Unlike many different thinkers from the Age of Enlightenment, Rousseau did not solely look to the future, but wished to save the benefits of the past. Originally from Switzerland, he saw the canton system there to be simply brilliant. In many different works, he emphasized the importance of common citizens understanding the government. Simplicity was the solution in many cases. The great American philosopher Henry D. Thoreau's words were originally meant for individuals and society, but they can be applied to government: "I do believe in simplicity. It is astonishing as well as sad, how many trivial affairs even the wisest thinks he must attend to in a day; how singular an affair he thinks he must omit. When the mathematician would solve a difficult problem, he first frees the equation of all incumbrances, and reduces it to its simplest terms. So simplify the problem of life, distinguish the necessary and the real. Probe the earth to see where your main roots run." One cannot forget their beginnings in government or nature. Whatever the case may be, simplicity, diversity, and happiness are three important reasons to support tribal government. Now the powers that preserve these will be discussed.

In addition to control of the cultural aspects mentioned earlier, certain powers must be given to this level of government. First, power to protect its resources must be afforded. While the power of people to leave at any time is necessary, the question of wealth still poses a problem. Plans at local levels will vary throughout the world, but they hold the control. If one extracts all of an important resource from a region, they can not leave and bring this with them to another society without retribution. This is necessary so that every society can protect itself from those who seek only personal wealth and glorification. Another right of the local governments includes some control over immigration. Those societies that wish to increase immigration restrictions will be limited due to the want of freeing travel, but they will still exist. As mentioned earlier both those people who congregate to avoid complete integration and those societies which choose to place even stricter gun control policy on its citizens will need this right. Although policies will vary on gun rights, the tribal system will reduce it through an increased connection to people. Another power that needs to be held by the local government is the control over the economy. As mentioned earlier through the control of wealth exiting the community, people and resources are all components of society. Over the years, many different arguments from several groups have proven the need for this.

It is said by some that a socialist movement is making its ways across America. I would be happy, but it is accompanied by a movement towards large government power and limited choices. The constitution and individual choice are going to be mocked, while people implement "one size fits all" reforms that will be utter failures. Pointing to the Scandinavian countries, that have a fraction of the people and less division economically when dealing with ideologies, is not a stable argument. Rather these reforms need to be enacted at a local level. It should not matter whether a traditional or industrial economy is implemented or whether it is capitalist or communist. However, the wealth will be forced to work for every citizen through the psychological testing of higher governments.

Whatever economic system is implemented, freedom will be preserved. It will be the people who ultimately decide what government they will live under. The capitalists and communists both bring up good ideas. The emphasis on competition and choice is not only applicable to different local governments, but also within separate societies. If a capitalistic system is implemented, the most efficient methods of extracting resources and building wealth will be implemented. This will allow the general citizenry to experience extreme luxury. However, the resources must always stay in the hands of the general population of the locality and if they are not pleased with the system in place, then reform becomes necessary. A socialist or communist system that is based upon communal government can survive because, as mentioned earlier, people will see the effect of their work and money. Also, the argument between traditionalists and industrialists also needs to be addressed.

If a traditionalist society can maintain happiness without modern luxuries, then this should not be discouraged. Applying Thoreau's ideas about simplification and self-denial on a literal level could serve to increase happiness through an active role in nature. However, those who prefer more complex lifestyles should be able to choose this if they are within the environmental requirements. With all of these controversial and explosive issues now defused, the larger institutions of government should become the main focus.

Chapter 8: The Other Levels of Government

Before different levels are described specifically, general rules should be discussed that apply to every institution of government larger than tribal. After the election of President James Polk, Ralph Waldo Emerson wrote, "The real life and strength of the American people, find themselves paralyzed and defeated everywhere by hordes of ignorant and deceivable natives and the armies of foreign voters who fill Pennsylvania, New York, and New Orleans." He continued, "The creators of wealth and conscientious, rational and responsible persons,... find themselves degraded into observers, and violently turned out of all share in the actions and counsels of the nation." This proves several important concepts.

First, it necessitates a need for controlled immigration. If a large portion of people come from an entirely different section of the world, some sort of assimilation must occur. By this I am not referring to language or religion, but rather ideology. A people must learn and appreciate an established system before they seek to destroy it. The next point that is important to discuss involves the checks and balances of a system. On a smaller communal level, few checks are needed. For this level, I would suggest a single ruler or small group of rulers who is directly elected and checked by the people. Tyranny is not to be feared because popular uprisings against a local ruler would not be addressed by the higher levels. A system would be ideally set up so that if a ruler's approval rating dropped below a certain mark, he would be, in most circumstances, peacefully ousted. However, on larger levels of government, many checks on power need to be present. Now this will become the main topic of discussion.

It has been previously stated that the larger the government, the more checks that are necessary. The inverse statement is also true. However, certain people don't know why or how this should be the case. The former question will be addressed initially. The answer is that one must protect intelligent societies from the dangers of ignorance. One cannot fully anticipate wildfire, but certain factors should lead one to prepare for such a situation. Ignorance is a tricky topic to deal with politically due to the fact that there is no fair method of finding an unbiased arbitrator. Under the proposed system, intelligent people will bond cohesively and the ignorant will do the same. Those who are ignorant by choice will be forced to live under a government of their own creation.

When unintelligent people choose to not follow the words of the wise, they will personally pay the price. However, when these people are thereafter represented in higher governments, they pose a threat to more intellectual communities. Rousseau once wrote, "The people is much less often mistaken in such choices than is a prince, and a man of real merit is almost as rare in a royal ministry as a fool at the head of a republican government." While this proves true in many circumstances, there are important exceptions. In most cases, the intelligent from a democratic society provide important debate points that are then used by the general population. However, when people are willfully ignorant, this system no longer functions correctly. How are ignorant people expected to choose wise leaders? A system that balances safety and functionality will now be discussed.

As mentioned earlier there are going to be four levels of government: tribal, state, federal, and global. Following the current pattern of order by increasing size, the state will be the first focus while the global is last.

The state government does not hold great power, but rather serves to unite the power of the tribes in the case of a federal usurpation. All money for the federal government will be collected by the individual states on the same day, so if it once again "becomes necessary for one people to dissolve the political bands which have connected them with another" then this will be possible. Open communication will be had between the different states as to make this possible.

A balance must be maintained through the state and federal dynamic. A state must hold a minimum amount of tribes as to distinguish it from its members and check abuses dealing with children and life. In addition to this, the number of tribes in one state must be limited as to distinguish it from the federal government and keep one group from alone being able to overthrow this institution. A number of states within a single federation must be kept above a minimum to accomplish the same objective, while the number must also not be so great as to render the states useless.

Whatever the case may be, the state must set up a government based upon these principles and others. In all likelihood, the communities that will be decided upon will look no different than the landscape of modern America. Under the supervision of both the state and federal governments, lines will be drawn on several bases. If one would consider this work to be extremely subjective than they would be correct interpreters of the situation. There are several principles that guide this work, but almost infinite decisions are possible.

The bases will primarily focus on the number of resources. Those areas with little resources will become larger communities with a smaller number. Likewise, areas with large amounts of resources will be filled by smaller communities with a larger number. This will all maintain a good balance. One might point to historical examples and formulate questions. What happens if a greater number of resources is discovered in a particular area? Would these people then be forced to give up sections of land? While some may say that this is a good plan that can be enacted, it is not required. If people are not knowledgeable about such resources when the communities are created, then all groups are equally as likely to win this lottery.

If communities were divided upon this principle, then communities would not be safe. Under this system the Dakota natives still might be forced to move off their land if the situation of discovering gold in the Black Hills was hypothetically repeated. It is important to maintain the sanctity of communities.

Secondarily, present lines that have already been drawn due to culture and religion may be considered. One does not want to repeat the mistake in the Middle East where the former European colonizers did not take this into account. This will not be the primary concern however. The border creation talked about in this situation would be at a communal level so those who are dissatisfied can either learn to coexist or move to form a separate community. Borders will not be redrawn unless a community decides to divide. The fusion of two communities will also be allowed but only under limited circumstances. It is important to note that while the borders of the communities will be relatively unchanging, the states may change relatively frequently.

The borders of the states, and that of the new nations for that matter, are not necessarily going to be identical to the present situation. It may be thought that in the area of North America, around four nations will reside. Those which mainly compose area around the Arctic Circle will of course be larger due to the size of the tribal territories that they are composed of, but this is a good rough estimate. The states will be similar to the size of Colorado under normal circumstances, but again this will fluctuate based on the climate and resources of the land.

The true power of the states will come almost wholly from the tribes. Once the system is in place, the states can choose what communities replace those expelled by the federal government, but if one community decides to secede, then the borders of states must be redrawn. No community can be without state organization so if a middle state decides to split then the plans of action are relatively open. If a different established state has not reached its maximum members then a section of the former state can join its ranks. Another option is to split the state and if the nation has not reached its maximum for a number of states, then each can form a new union if the number of communities in each is above the minimum.

If this system seems too complex, it may only be a matter of perspective. The same people who would have problems with this sense of simplicity, would, if their beliefs are consistent, also think that the present government is simplistic. While there are different definitions when discussing this word, one must admit that simplicity does not work unless if it is also logical. The system today does seem outwardly ordinary. The inward mechanisms are complex, but elections are simple enough. There are only two viable options. The decision is pretty cut and dry. However, the process by which these two candidates are elevated is extremely complex and not based on the principles which should govern simplicity. Money, beguilement, and attacks are all at play. It is not through pure popular methods that these two candidates are chosen but rather poorly drawn districts that are created by the established political parties in government and bribery. Options are the result of a system based on principle and this is what this idealistic society would bring to the table. There would not be one or two, but a plethora of options. People would be forced to get involved and understand government instead of checking the box that says vote "all Republican" or "all Democrat" on the ballot. People would once again be able to change the government without the need for physical violence or unstable upheavals. Now that this problem has been addressed, the power of the proposed state governments will be highlighted.

Two issues that should not be handled by an unchecked government are child abuse and the definition of life. While there are many options for potential state governments, decisions like this should not be made without the consensus of a larger group. The state government could not institute decisions that instruct but only those that restrain. As an example, a state government would not deal with the healthcare issue of whether society will provide birth control products, but they can ban actions like the beating of children. Now that this has been more fully explained both sides of the issue must be allowed to form their argument.

In the federally focused system of today, there is bound to be unnecessary controversy. This was stirred when videos were released that allegedly showed an account of Planned Parenthood officials selling fetal tissue to the highest bidder. The truthfulness of this can be questioned, but abortion must be given an answer. This issue needs to largely be looked at from the perspective of Atticus Finch in To Kill A Mockingbird. A system is never going to function if everybody within it is corrupt. Each group must not seek control over the other group, but rather look for an opportunity to deal with the problems facing their community or region. While this issue has been ideologically elevated to the level of state government, there is still much room for difference of opinion.

Many within the United States hold a number of different opinions when dealing with this controversial issue. One side believes that the fetus is obviously a small human and the right to life trumps any want of choice. Under the present system, they not only live in a culture that opposes them, but they are forced to participate in something that they consider murder.

This is important to note, but there is a completely different side to the argument. Potential scientific advances using the pluripotent embryonic stem cells are interesting topics of conversation and these can be used to save the lives of those who are already in the world. However, their desire to survive a disease should not be used as an excuse if a fetus is to be considered a human. These two sides argue back and forth with much passion. One's religious beliefs are also bound to play a role in one's stance on the issue. While the separation of church and state is important to avoid the establishment of a single religion, one's entire perspective of existence is obviously going to have some effect. Those who are adamantly religious tend to be more definitive in their decisions. Most either choose to be for or against the practice based on their definition of human life. Those who identify as atheist or agnostic may take a more arbitrary stance however. Believing largely in the chance creation of existence, it may be said that society is the true judge of what is defined as human life.

Whatever one's stance may be, it can be seen that society is and should be the judge of the final decision whether it lines up with a general sense or morality or not. On such a subject, the decision is not always clearly right or wrong. The discussion will continue in the hopes of finding a resolution to the ideological fighting.

The definition of child abuse must also be handled by the state which will give due time for consideration. Physical punishment for children can be seen from several different perspectives. Many people look back on the punishments that they received and were not permanently scarred. Rather it can be seen by some that it provided discipline and a correction of bad behavior. However, opinions vary widely when dealing with this issue.

On a communal level, while adults can easily escape any potential oppression due to the small size of the territory, children are often stuck because of the inherent dependence which comes with that age range. Therefore instead of having local authorities deal with the issue, the state will become involved. There are several different stances on this issue that are important to discuss. Again, some in the religious category have a tradition that upholds their beliefs. Proverbs which is a book with significance to both the Jews and Christians says, "Whoever spares the rod hates their children, but the one who loves their children is careful to discipline them." While freedom of religion is key, if a practice is deemed inhumane by the rest of society then the belief can continue but the action has to stop.

Discipline is of great importance to some, but others believe that the practice of negative reinforcement teaches children that power comes from those with greater physical strength. As mentioned earlier, force is not necessarily a bad concept, but it needs to be held by the general population. Whatever one's belief may be concerning this, the system detailed above both allows for variations, but also a consideration of such an important matter.

Now, the general principles that guide this level of government can be seen. In addition to this, the social laws that can be created by such a government have also been discussed. However, the constitutions from state to state might differ and an example must be given as a basis for creation. The state government, unlike the tribal level, should have more checks on its power. The three main branches of government: executive, legislative, and judicial should be separate bodies. The legislature should be bicameral, representing both the people and the different tribes. Laws will be passed through both of these houses to be instituted. It can be seen now that the happiness that accompanies tribal rule, can be combined with the organization and cooperation of modernity. Unification for diversity is a key concept in this regard. Whatever the case may be, it can be seen that the simplicity of the tribe has continued to a certain degree with higher levels. Although more checks have been set, the options of such a system have been maintained. Now it becomes necessary to shine a light on the federal government.

The state governments prove to be an effective check on federal power. While now more popular in nature, the states act similar to the nobles in the medieval system of Europe. As seen through the example of the French Revolution before it turned for the worse, some nobles joined the third estate to form the National Assembly. Their land and power served as a firm foundation for those participating in the rebellion. However, there should be checks within today's system that also afford rights to the federal power. While this power will be checked internally through state participation, and externally through the threat of force, the government will still be functional. It now becomes necessary to list these in the following paragraphs.

Environmental concerns and misuse of natural resources both need to be addressed by this level of government. While a minimum amount of members in a given community was previously mentioned, a maximum number was never given. This may seem odd given that overpopulation in parts of India, Bangladesh, and China has wreaked havoc. However, an invisible line would be drawn under the new idealistic system. As mentioned earlier, the federal government would place environmental restrictions on the tribal level. While the state government can make restrictions in this area as well to decrease federal involvement, they will not hold the majority of power. The federal restrictions would be the same across the board. Those who wish to build industrial or highly populated civilizations follow rules just as strict as those for agriculturally based societies. This is important because population would not be encouraged to perpetually grow. If an urban community wishes to grow in population then innovative solutions to environmental problems will be necessitated.

Indirect force by the federal government is key in this situation. Population would be an issue handled by the local authorities and fear of large depopulation programs would have no basis. In addition to this, federal subsidies for wind, solar and hydroelectric would not exist, but indirectly they would be encouraged. Programs such as hydroelectric plants and larger roads may have to be handled by the larger form of the state governments, but power will remain firmly in the hands of the people. If restrictions set by the federal government were not followed and the subsequent warnings were disregarded, then expulsion becomes a possibility.

This will be extremely rare and if the former residents successfully petition the state in which they live to allow them to form a new government, then land will not exchange hands. However, if these people continue to participate in damaging practices then they can be removed. Many people might fear for the existence of their lands which have been in the family for generations. However, local residents will have a strong influence in the decisions of the smallest form of government and if their cause is not tied to solely personal gain, the friends and family that compose the community will sympathize with the cause of these people. Expulsion due to environmental protection should hardly ever happen. The level of the federal government was chosen for this task because of its size. Local desires for economic success will not taint one's love of nature or tendency to use natural resources wisely. People in the state of Washington are far more likely to vote against the destruction of California redwood trees then local contractors who can gain wealth and luxury from such a venture. However, this example brings up another problem.

What can be said about those natural sites that pose a great importance to those outside of a potential community? The federal government should be able to mark off lands for archeological and historical purposes. Natural sites of beauty and national forests will also be allowed. Sites such as these should not be put in the hands of local people who may compromise their love of these places for their love of money. In addition to this, when sites are important for science and the gathering of knowledge, they must also be handled by this institution. Important sites in the Middle East have been destroyed because no stable and large government was available for their protection. Information concerning ancient civilizations that still has pertinence today may have been destroyed because there were no checks on fanaticism. Large governments best protect these sites due to their isolation from issues with local economies and society. Any destruction of these sites would be considered a felony because information is the key to unlocking the metaphorical dungeon of the human experience. We are here and our purpose has been discussed by many, but information and knowledge must guide the discussion forward. Whatever the case may be, this level of government will have other responsibilities concerning the human pursuit of knowledge.

The idea of patents and trademarks have been historic, and they will change only slightly when discussing this idealistic society. Although community governments are allowed to make claims in their constitution concerning their right to all ideas produced within their borders, if individuals choose to move from that area then they are no longer bound by this. Therefore individual innovation will be encouraged. Science and clean energy which will be encouraged by communal population opportunities will also be aided through the individual rewards of intelligence and excellence. While science should be helped in these ways, the current administration has gone far above what is recommended. As seen throughout society, most people hold a natural inclination towards advancement. Science and information serve to answer some of their deepest questions about life and existence. National not-for-profit organizations and communal research will serve to continue scientific enlightenment. In addition to this large universities will survive and prove meaningful. However, as mentioned earlier, the education system will not be strictly controlled by the federal or state powers. One may desire an explanation.

Different groups are going to interpret the information and facts differently. Therefore it is necessary to replace the rigidity of a state monopolized program with more local schooling. When politicians claim that everyone has the right to an education, they do not know what they are talking about. They obviously have very little connection with both principle and reality.

First off, why would people support large government control over an area where they have repeatedly failed. One may say that government would not control the system, but only fund it. This, however, would not prove true for long. The power of the purse is very critical in this situation. As seen through federal funding of high schools, once they have the ability to take away funds on which the schools have become dependent; federal policies will be established. It is a kind of "enact or retract" policy that forces greater control from large governments.

People in many states have now pushed their governments to begin funding (controlling) prekindergarten classes. Why must large government have so much power and influence in early childhood development? It may be said that this is an accurate representation of the general will and that one should not protest its effect. However, most social issues should be handled at a very low level. While everyone is never going to be happy with a policy, localizing as much as possible causes more choice and freedom for people. In addition to this discussion and good arguments almost always serve to change the minds of a popular group.

Another person might question why government involvement has or would cause a monopoly. Some may point to the existence of private education and claim that competition exists. Although this is true to a certain extent, too great of educational control is exercised by the federal government. From an economic standpoint, the government has given its own option a high advantage over its competition. It can extract money from the general public and make its option free. While it allows for the existence of private schools, this policy puts them at a severe disadvantage.

Due to this and a general lack of independent spirit, many private schools have received funding from the government and given away much of their autonomy. The federal and state governments have also limited the degree of competition that is allowed. Private institutions are allowed to exist, but minimum amounts of hours and a subject list are enforced by the government.

Those who may have progressed to higher levels at a quicker pace are stuck in a sort of three-legged race with hundreds of students. If a student has decided his life path and wants to be a part of more focused studies then this must be done during free time. After hours of being locked up in a building and homework on top of this, most teens are going to need some mental relaxation.

The education system that is enforced upon the children of today takes those who are excited about learning and turns them against it. The attainment of knowledge is now seen as a chore and not a goal. Does one really think that the great minds from the Age of Enlightenment and ancient Greece were created from conformed education and not individual brilliance? Whatever the case may be, it can be seen that local education provides the best option. Not only will intellectuals naturally bond forming groups that will no longer be held back academically, but different options will breed true competition and educational innovation.

Another absurdity of state or federal education is its lack of cultural individuality. While this can refer to religion and language, this refers largely to the economic and governmental setup. If a culture seeks to find happiness in the "simplify" ideology of Thoreau, who should stop them? Do these people who will most likely be dependent on herbal medicine really need to learn about the general health procedures of modernity? Of course, those within these tribes will be allowed to choose their own path once they reach the age of reason, which is to be determined by the states, but most will choose to follow the culture that they were born into. Are the educational aims of agricultural and industrial communities really going to be the same? Why do we force conformity to feign unity? Answer these for yourself and then follow your conscience.

More important powers that would be placed in the hands of the federal government would be that of defending the country and negotiating treaties. These two obviously fit together, but certain people might believe that in an ideal society war should be banned altogether. While this will not happen, important reforms will be implemented that either end or severely diminish violence on such a large scale. Whatever the case may be, people are always going to use death of their enemies as a way to address irreconcilable problems. Negative human tendencies can be controlled, but not annihilated. It is important that individual power to reform government through the primitive concept of force is not completely destroyed. When the government no longer plays by the rules, nonviolent etiquette will be tossed out the window. Sides will be drawn, but this situation will almost always be avoided.

Under the idealistic system, federal governments will be few. A rough estimate would place the number under fifty compared with almost two hundred today. Each would be relatively equal in the amount of resources and therefore people, so no country could gain dominance over another. A strict balance of powers would then be in place. Something even far greater than what was created by the Congress of Vienna after the fall of Napoleon. This system coupled with global governance would almost ensure a peaceful and free worldwide society.

However, some may disagree and say that there is no need for this power in federal hands. But, as the states check the federal, so the national must check the international. The power to wage war also protects individual citizens and communities. If one like Edward Snowden is successful in escaping a country, then he will not be punished unless his crime is internationally recognized. The strong power of both Russia and the United States and the animosity between the two groups allow such a man to survive even after committing such a deed. While the case of Snowden might be seen by some as inappropriate under the current system, it would not be under the ideological system placed before you now. Transparency would be attained through international negotiation and this would continue to persist in part through informants. One physical weakness but ideological strength of popular government is its connection to the general population. Not only do the common people elect officials, but they also are elected when the system is pure. Reforms to elevate commoners to positions of power have already been discussed so this will be ignored now. However, these commoners in government would be able to not only whistleblow on subjects of international transparency, but also on those concerning potential voter fraud and other types of internal corruption. While this covers most important areas of the proposed federal government, there is still one aspect up for discussion.

So far only one potential reason for federal expulsion of a tribal group has been discussed. However, in addition to expulsion on grounds of environmental harm, there should be other types of accountability. It was mentioned earlier that the main goal of tribal governments was to create happiness. What better level of government than federal to ensure this? While expulsion on these grounds will be rare, it is necessary that there is a system in place that allows for change and the discard of deficient or decrepit governments. There are a number of reasons why the state government would not be a fair judge in this respect.

First of all when this system is implemented, one of the original states would have the power to expel all of their minority members without consideration. It may be said that discrimination by the state is still possible when this level of government chooses who is to fill vacancies. However there is a system that when implemented could eliminate this risk. All applications for potential tribes would go through a department of the federal government. When information about this is spread to the state officials, things like race, religion, and ethnicity can be left out of the report. Those who compose reports on a federal level about a potentially new tribe or the expulsion of an old one will also be separate from those who make the final decision to avoid discrimination as well. It can now be seen that the federal government would be a better arbitrator in this circumstance.

One power that has become increasingly controversial is that of roads and infrastructure in general. Some supporters of federal control in this area tend to over complicate this issue, while their opposition artificially simplifies the situation. In the latter group, many point to the example colonial British America and the postcolonial United States. While the establishment of postal roads was detailed in the current Constitution, private companies controlled shares of this market for quite some time. Those who oppose the creation of private roads may say that it would be too costly or inefficient monetarily. This, however, is the wrong point to focus on. Competition within this system may actually drive the price down. In addition to this, payment methods could be found that are more advanced than the modern toll booth. It can be seen that under the present system that even where toll booths are not present, citizens still pay through gas taxes and other means.

Even though the monetary question has been answered, the environment and logistics have not been addressed. Who would control how much land is taken for such projects? If it becomes the individual communities or states then, as mentioned earlier, there may not be enough concern. Roads handled by communities would often not be maintained and indirect. Individual groups would protest these within their territorial limits so construction would be delayed frequently. States, while they would handle the situation better, would still be plagued with many of these problems to a slighter degree. Who would control access to major cities presently? Communities would monitor access individually to a certain extent idealistically, but under the system today, private companies would feud over rights to lands. Individual landowners can not be forced by these companies to sell in parallel lines. States would create controversy by allowing access for some groups but not others. Monopolies in this way would still be created. However, unlike through government direction, people would not have as much control. Competition is a very good concept to establish, but popular control is necessary for different areas.

No purely capitalist or communist government are to be desired. While definitive lines are desired, a different form is taken in this circumstance. The definitive line does not come through a complete support of a singular economic system, but through a vigorous defense of popular influence. Capitalism can descend into manorial states and feudal societies when not subject to control by the citizenry. However, communism completely disregards the importance of individual innovation and reward systems. A more mixed system should be implemented on a local level and it can now be seen that some of the most seemingly complex issues in the world today can be solved through a simple process of consideration.

While the federal government would be fair in all of the powers delegated above, there should be general trends for which the common citizenry should look. As innovation increases and the methods for governing tribes improve, requirements by the federal government should either stay consistent or become more stringent. One appeal of having the federal government holding this power is the gradual betterment of society. Without the accountability created by higher government, the lightly checked local government could be overrun by tyrants who rule only for personal gain. If the local government is more heavily checked then it begins to lose much of ancient luster and appealing simplicity.

Now the federal system that holds these powers will for a time be the focus. Most of the aspects of an ideal federal government have already been discussed in "Needed Realistic Revolutions" and when combined with the additional powers listed above it should be functional, freedom loving, and stable. Those who are blessed enough to experience the coming of such reforms will obviously have other suggestions. Some may favor the incorporation of the tribal governments, while others may deem this unnecessary. If an effective means of accomplishing this without losing functionality, like through an attempted tricameral legislature, can be found then I would support such a move. However, I believe that the people's connection to their tribal liberties is bound to lead them towards policies favoring the system that has allowed this. Enforced education concerning this system will not be necessary due to the fact that the intellectuals in the large majority of communities will continue to carry the torch of freedom. Any change to the system will be vigorously debated among this group as to avoid baseless changes. In addition to this, the change to the executive, which has already been discussed, would create three main presidential positions. Now that the role of the federal governments in an idealistic world, globalization will become the new topic.

It may seem that the Olympics are a point of unity, but it is quite the opposite. It rather shows the utter disorganization of the global governments. While these games serve as an important stage to spread to ideals of freedom and popular government, the Olympic torch is far from the torch of liberty. Instead of uniting under the useless banner of sports, why don't people gather around a more important cause? Should we attempt to unite based purely on existence or good ideology? Usurpers of power like Vladimir Putin sit and watch the games when they should be sitting in prison. Many athletes from the China are asked to represent a country that does not represent them. Is this unity? Countries like North Korea are not countries but only large plantations. Wealth is harvested by forced labor. North Korea's main internal objective is not prosperity for the general population, but personal gain and power. Like the edicts that outlawed the slaves from learning to read in the South before the Civil War, this "nation" attempts to quiet the voices of popular dissent. Through propaganda and limited speech their narrative has become forced.

I berate these countries and ask: if the government and social programs that are instituted currently were good, why are they limiting criticism? One who has a strong argument needs no high position. What is held by strength could be kept by intellect, if it is truly sound. This is not a fight between communism and capitalism, but rather the forces of tyranny versus popular government. If people have nothing to gain through the implemented form of government, then it should be dismantled.

This is not the only way that the Olympics show disunity. Smaller nations like Tuvalu and Equatorial Guinea, that under the idealistic system would only create several tribes, are pitted against much larger nations such as the United States and China. The country of Ukraine is asked to compete against Russia, who continued to occupy some of their territory in Crimea. The Olympics is not a show of unity, but rather a mirror of a harsh reality. Those countries that are large and strong can take advantage of the smaller ones. There is no balance of powers anymore. The balance is only at the higher level and if Russia takes territory the US and other powers either don't care or don't care enough for war. While it is true that such wars should not happen, neither should territory stealing. A real system of balancing powers needs to be instituted. In an idealistic system, no nation would be large enough to gain an advantage over the other. Territory would not be stolen because a hypothetical Ukraine would be just as large as its neighbors.

Russia claims that those in Crimea are ethnically Russian and want to join the larger nation. While these arguments can be contested, even if this was true, the Russian government would not serve to represent them correctly. As mentioned earlier they are presently being ruled by a tyrant who disregarded sound constitutional policy. Instead of seeking representation from an overly inflated government, the principle of federalism must be applied to tribes who will actually have what is best for the people in mind. Whatever the case may be, this plan will take maybe centuries to execute. The global government will play a critical role in this plan.

As shown earlier, a certain degree of animosity must be kept between the separate nations to help in transparency. Therefore global government will not hold any power, but rather will be a coalition of nations negotiating on several different issues. With large governments, balance and peace are the main objectives as opposed to the happiness and well-being of individual citizens. It can now be seen that population control should come through human ingenuity and innovation instead of environmentally and economically destructive wars. Cooperation for peace is consistent with human tendencies and this should be encouraged. Whatever the case may be, the responsibilities of this international coalition will now be discussed.

The first topic for negotiation should obviously be the disarmament of all nations. All nuclears and formulas for them should be completely destroyed. It is not appropriate that any individual or group holds the power to immediately throw the world into a war that could threaten existence. This process of disarmament will most likely come through a gradual and simultaneous system. These principles will not be fully applied for many years, but it is important to discuss what it will resemble when they come to fruition. Total disarmament of the government should never occur because it must be able to defend itself from baseless rebellions that are not supported by most of society. However, the strength of a federal government should never be more than that of a majority of its members. This principle of disarmament works nicely with the next topic of discussion.

Transparency is an issue that has been brought to the forefront of politics in recent years. During a debate in the 2016 primary race for the Republican presidential nomination, Congressman Rand Paul fiercely debated New Jersey Governor Chris Christie over the Fifth Amendment. While certain political commentators believed that Christie won the argument, his victory was not due to rationality, but rather a purely political call to emotion. When Paul tried to talk about reality rationally, Christie pandered to baseless fear from those who were uninformed about the

Constitution. Rand Paul began the conversation by saying that the Fifth Amendment needs to apply to cyber property. Instead of countering with a logical argument Christie brought up the 9/11 tragedy. He evoked an illogical emotion in the crowd that may have given him the political victory.

There are a couple things to learn from this encounter. First, it shows the necessity of constitutional principles and due process. If constitutional restrictions were lifted directly after the massacre, innocent Muslims may have been imprisoned. While it is important to balance safety and privacy in modern culture, collectively the world should advance together to increased transparency. This will couple nicely with the ideals of disarmament. If regular inspections are not objected to by the federal governments, then the nuclear threat and large wars can be more easily avoided. As one everybody should move closer to both of these goals and make sure that decisions are not made based on emotion but information. Now that all of the idealistic levels have been discussed, a safe path to the plan's completion must become the new focus

When discussing both realistic and idealistic changes, the plan of execution is one of the most important points. While the explanation of principles and political concepts accomplishes something, without an outline of proposed actions many of the ideas will lack the necessary momentum to gain fruition. Successes must be celebrated after every completion and a benchmark must be maintained. Order is essential and this is what will be the focus for this section of the book.

The first section of reforms that are to be enacted come from chapters five and six of this book. It does not matter in what order the conservative or liberal policies in these chapters are attained. While one might claim that the roots must be established before the tree grows, they are looking at it from the wrong perspective. "Roots" does not necessarily mean past reforms. These do provide a stable foundation in many cases, but so can conventionally liberal policies. Voting reform will allow the general will to become more firmly established and purely represented. There can be nothing more stable than this. When the public feels as if their government is not representing them, then problems are bound to arise. Voter turnout has been diminished through insufficient checks on this system and this must change. People must begin to feel like their vote matters. Lack of finance reform and unfair political district drawing have both plagued the system. The party system that has limited options and left those on both sides dissatisfied. Great steps must be taken to restore faith in the system. More extreme and liberal policies such as the three presidential positions in the executive will come after simpler changes have been digested. Simple reforms like those listed above must precede the more complex and ideological plans.

Throughout the time that these reforms are taking place, an international confederation can still function. The disarmament and transparency measures are both of importance. Large and powerful countries such as the United States, Russia, and China can begin negotiations that hopefully will include North Korea and Middle Eastern threats as well. However, these processes that increase safety will only be truly implemented once the idealistic reforms have come to pass

Many may reject to the more idealistic reforms because they would include a destruction of modern countries. Deep nationalist ties would be severed and some people for a time might lose parts of their identity. Whatever the case may be this end to nationalism would be followed by something even greater. People would no longer tied most strongly to their national government but rather to their tribe.

Some of the writers of the Federalist Papers hinted at the fact that they believed the general population would be more connected and loyal to the state governments because of their proximity. However, the opposite has proved to be true. People for a time identified with their states accomplishments before the destruction of this system occurred. After this process was broken, the federal government assumed some of the states' rights and responsibilities. This collapse had one main instigator: division. People in a state are far from ideologically and economically homologous. The cities vote for extremely different policies then the rural communities do. Often the cities are allowed to make the decision on an important social issue for the entire state. Values are obviously going to be different between these two types of communities.

This is a very simple case of adapting to one's environment. Those in the cities live around a greater diversity of people and therefore become more tolerant when it comes to beliefs and customs. In contrast, country folk are more spread out and therefore can socially express their opinions without fear of retribution. Both the tolerance of the cities and the open conversation in the country is good, but not when they are forced under the same government. A dividing line must be set.

So as seen thus far, people are far less likely to bond to their states because the same wedges exist at this level as do on a federal level. Farmers would be more likely to bond with other farmers on a federal level than stockbrokers on a state level. Those in the New York countryside differ from those in "the Big Apple". This problem is taken care of on a communal level however because the country and the city would both be able to choose different paths socially. Whatever the case may be, there are still several problems that complicate the application of idealism. If this ideal system is to be implemented on a global level then problems begin to arise. The most important being the volatility of the Middle East.

In The Social Contract, Rousseau states, "Freedom is not a fruit of every climate, and it is not therefore within the capacity of every people. The more one reflects on this doctrine of Montesquieu, the more one is conscious of its truth. And the more often it is challenged, the more opportunities are given to establish it with new evidence. In every government in the world, the public person consumes but does not produce anything. Whence does it obtain the substance it consumes? From the labour of its members. It is the surplus of private production which furnishes public subsistence. From this it follows that the civil state can subsist only if men's work yields more than they themselves need." This brings up a number of good points.

First, it highlights a potential reform that would only work if adopted on an international scale. If the federal governments across the board were allowed to control an important market to raise the money that they need, then this would not only provide a means for the government to raise the necessary funds, but also it would allow for a method of protest that could be used by the common citizenry. If the large institution began to usurp power than through self-denial, one could stand in defiance. However, this plan would be hard to implement due to the fact that the different tribes value commodities differently and therefore it would be challenging to find an appropriate market.

It may be said of all governments that a surplus is needed for subsistence, and it can now be seen that the Middle East has one. Popular government could function off of the extreme oil profits, but rather everything is controlled by a dictator in many circumstances. As seen through the hundreds of examples of rebellion throughout the world in the first section, freedom is fought for on an international scale. It is not limited to Europeans march to freedom from monarchy, but also through the Native American fighting spirit. They fought and died for liberty even when the odds were much more bleak. Middle Eastern countries have begun reforming and popular dissent is rising in authoritarian communist countries in Asia. It can now be seen, that this message of principle does not solely spread through word of mouth, but it has been passed down from generation to generation through the instincts of nature. While this may be the case, the Middle East still does pose some important questions.

Should the whole world wait for reform while one region holds them back? One cannot expect to force a people to accept freedom and the group is likely not to cherish it if they were not part of its creation. In addition to this, the system should not be implemented internationally before being tested on a smaller level. It might be said that the U.S. could implement the idealistic policies before the rest of the world, however, this is not the case. As mentioned earlier federal governments would be sizably smaller than the United States and these with the exception of islands, all lands would be connected. In addition to this dividing this country into pieces before any reform in other countries would disrupt the current balance of powers. While this has recently shown to be ineffective in many regards, it still serves a purpose.

Under ideal circumstances, the three main countries of North America: Canada, the U.S, and Mexico would join in the cause together and begin implementation. The Caribbean islands and nations tangent to already participating members could also join. To start out with, pioneering and adventurous states would begin the system within their borders. Notes will be taken of the example and aspects can be tweaked accordingly. After a large majority have consented, then the system will advance closer to full completion. States must obviously be redrawn to fit the parameters of amounted resource and the government will be implemented. It is a good idea to begin with this large of a territory because then the alliance formed between these newly emerging nations would be equal or greater in power than the current situation on the continent. The bond of freedom between these new nations would be much stronger than before and this would create a stable situation. However, these reforms may take decades or even centuries. Whatever the case may be, the first step must be taken.

The initiation of such a movement must prove to be meaningful and symbolic. It must prove that the whole nation is backing the ideals and principles that have been presented. It can not be backed by a single state or region but by the whole country. The political region of the United States will once again be the "city on a hill" that John Winthrop described and the American Revolution proved. As we were a testing ground for large republican government, so will be the case with these reforms. It is sad that such an initiative act must come through the party system. Third parties are doomed to fail under the present system and it is this that will be first addressed. A commoner must be found among the ranks of civilization to initiate such a revolution. While it must be remembered to remain loyal to principles and not people, if I remain steadfast in this cause; then I would gladly accept such a responsibility. Therefore in 2036 AD, once the required age is reached, this symbolic move will take place. A party will be chosen opposite of the incumbent, whoever that may be, and a running mate will be selected based on popular vote under the system based on approval ratings. And now, a quote from the future.

Conclusion

"Hello, Americans. As I stand before you here tonight, this great nation stands at a crossroads. The validity of the founding principles does not stand at question, but rather the direction to which they should be taken. The torch of liberty has shown through the darkness and highlighted a route but now action must be taken. It has been seen time and time again that politicians far too often pit different groups against each other. Instead of advancing forward together, many choose to take sides. Many in the news choose to focus on the differences, arguing in a constant battle; black versus white, conservatives versus liberals, rich versus poor, and young versus old. It can be seen that these groups may always exist, so instead of choosing favorites, politicians should praise the principle of cooperation always emphasizing the role each plays.

Race should not be a line of division and political opinions should not be based on the time of a concepts creation, but rather the founding principles of the doctrine. Wealth need not be demonized, but extreme power must be controlled. Age should not be a point of controversy, but rather this dynamic should be praised. The contrast of these two age groups check one another and provide a good discussion on all topics.

One might wish upon a particular movement the absence of opposition, but reality shows that unquestioned systems rarely function correctly. A government must be created that balances the natural needs of society while also controlling negative tendencies. Anarchical systems must be rejected and social obligation must be enforced. Healthy limits should not be seen as hindrances to freedom and protection of human rights. Economics should not trump the environment and large institutions should not control smaller ones.

Tribal government must not be seen as a rejection of civilization, but rather a proposed arrangement of people. While this is important, the roots of society must support its existence. Today the party system and monetarily controlled politics provide rocky soil that does not allow for the American liberty tree to flourish. The fruit of this tree has been infected through corruption and want of political gain. To solve deep problems, radical solutions are necessary. Not plans that give large governments more power, but rather a system that allows for communities to provide for their own people. The problems of minorities will not be forgotten under such a situation and the superficiality of the current administrative actions will be shown. One will not be asked to pick between the lesser of two evils, but rather will be given abundant options. Those on either side of the conventional political spectrum will no longer feel as if they have been cheated. One should be able to choose candidates of quality without fear of causing an upheaval of balance. Coerced unity will be rejected as a political ideology and unity despite differences will become commonplace.

A system will be accepted that allows for options and no longer forcibly binds any individual or group. The intelligent will be allowed to explore without those that they may consider ignorant. The work of those who have gone before and surrendered life, liberty and happiness will not be forgotten. Although many names have been forgotten, the effect of these warriors is still profound. They did not fight for us and yet indirectly they did. One day the liberty which they may have desired for their immediate family and community will spread throughout the world. The collective actions of all freedom fighters from every era of history may now bond to form one collective result. I beckon and America must answer the call. Go with me on a journey back to the past and on to the future. The lives of those mentioned provide an ample foundation for creation. This revolution is inevitable and it will be remembered for generations to come. Of all those large revolutions in history, this may be the last. While changes will still be made long after our deaths, this will be a revolution to end revolutions. The final advancement of society towards collective freedom and individual choice. With this, I announce my bid in race for the office of the president of the United States of America. Now that the path has been chosen, may we all follow the light of liberty into the darkness."

www.ingramcontent.com/pod-product-compliance
Lightning Source LLC
Chambersburg PA
CBHW062051270326
41931CB00013B/3033